ID0984493

THE TEACHING OF GEORGE ELIOT

William Myers

The Teaching of George Eliot

1984

BARNES & NOBLE BOOKS

TOTOWA, NEW JERSEY

First published in the USA 1984 by
BARNES & NOBLE BOOKS
81 Adams Drive
Totowa, New Jersey, 07512

Copyright © Leicester University Press 1984

Designed by Douglas Martin
Set in Linotron Janson by Alan Sutton Publishing Ltd, Gloucester
Printed and bound in Great Britain by The Pitman Press, Bath

Library of Congress Cataloging in Publication Data

Myers, W. F. T.
The teaching of George Eliot.
1.   Eliot, George, 1819–1880–Criticism and interpretation. I.   Title.
PR4688.M93   1984   823'.8   83–26615
ISBN 0-389-20450-1

CONTENTS

In memory of my father

WILLIAM GEORGE MYERS

1900–1963

Preface

I HAVE been working on the material of this book for some years, and many of the opinions expressed in it have appeared elsewhere. In particular parts of Chapter 9 are reproduced, with permission, from the second number of *Prose Studies* so ably edited at the time by my colleagues Philip Dodd and the late Ian Hilson, to whose tact and patience I am much indebted. I owe a special debt also to Isabel Rivers, whose forthright judgments and skilful editorial advice have influenced the way others as well as myself have come to regard this book. Philip Collins and J.S. Cunningham read through the penultimate version and their criticisms have been invaluable. Finally, underlying all my work on George Eliot has been the advice and encouragement which I received many years ago from my postgraduate supervisor, the late I.R. Browning, Fellow of Pembroke College, Oxford. I am glad at last to be able to put that particular indebtedness on public record.

Introduction

Contexts, Intellectual and Critical

GEORGE ELIOT thought of herself as a teacher. So did her contemporaries. John Morley's review of Cross's *Life and Letters* takes
particular note of the famous letter to Frederic Harrison in which
she writes of 'the severe effort of trying to make certain ideas
thoroughly incarnate, as if they had revealed themselves to me first
in the flesh and not in the spirit'.[1] It goes on to discuss George Eliot's
interest in contemporary philosophy, especially the ideas of heredity, evolution and psychology in the works of Auguste Comte and
Herbert Spencer, and adds that just as the novels were in effect
imaginative applications of

> this great influx of new ideas, so they fitted in with the moods
> those ideas called up . . . Other artists had drawn their pictures
> with a strong ethical background, but she gave a finer colour and
> a more spacious air to her ethics by showing the individual
> passions and emotions of her characters, their adventures and
> their fortunes, as evolving themselves from a long series of
> antecedent causes, and bound up with many widely operating
> forces and distant events. Here, too, we find ourselves in the full
> stream of evolution, heredity, survival, and fixed inexorable law.[2]

A year earlier, in 1884, a fuller analysis of this teaching had
appeared in a useful anonymous essay entitled 'George Eliot moralist and thinker':

> More than one critic has already pointed out . . . the close
> relation of her teaching to that of Comte, Darwin, Lewes, and
> Spencer . . . But . . . we maintain that when passed through the
> alembic of her mind, these doctrines attain a consistency and a
> unity hardly to be found in the works of any of the writers named
> above.[3]

The author goes on to outline 'the leading generalizations of
biological science' on which George Eliot based this philosophy.
These are, that human beings are as subject to scientific law as all
other forms of life; that life can be defined in terms of relationship

between organism and environment, evolution being the history of successive adaptations of organic structure and function to complicated external conditions; and that both animal and human consciousness correlate directly with outward manifestations of life, and like them are subject to law. Personality is thus the specific pattern of consciousness and behaviour which results from the interactions of a sensitive organism and its environment.[4] He adds:

> To the genius of George Eliot we mainly owe the application of this law to the higher phases of human life, where for each individual the forces of the environment largely consist of the moral and social influences of his fellow-men.[5]

The essay continues with a description, based on examples from the novels and poems, of certain ideas – especially Comte's – which the writer finds in George Eliot's works. He pays particular attention to the Positivist conception of religion as the means by which man evolves into full harmony with the world around him, including his fellow-men. This is achieved by the gradual evolution of minds in which the innate impulses of egoism are organically subordinated to those of altruism, a process necessarily painful because it requires a total readjustment of man's originally intensely self-centred cerebral structure. In this moral evolution of the race as a whole, conscience is the anticipation, more or less complete, of that final organic harmony between consciousness and the world around it towards which the human race is progressing.

Unfortunately the scale and level of generalization on which claims of this sort were made and indeed have to be made about George Eliot's writing tend to be self-defeating. However, if we take as a representative sample of her mature prose the opening paragraph of the fragment of her unfinished last novel, and allow our conceptions of 'evolution, heredity, survival, and fixed inexorable law' to colour our sense of it, the importance of coming to a closer understanding of George Eliot's conceptions in this field becomes apparent. The paragraph reads:

> This story will take you if you please into Central England and into what have been called the good old times. It is a telescope you may look through, a telephone you may put your ear to: but there is no compulsion. If you only care about the present fashions in dress & talk in politics and religion pass on without offence as you would pass the man with the telescope in the Place de la Concorde, not mounting to look through his lenses and then abusing him because he does not show you something less distant

and more to your taste than aspects of the heavenly bodies. Allow
those who like it to interest themselves in the sad or joyous
fortunes of people who saw the beginning of the Times newspaper, trembled or felt defiant at the name of Buonoparte, defended
bull baiting, were excited by the writing of Cobbett and submit-
ted to some invisible power which ordained that their back waist
buttons should be nine inches higher than those of their Fathers.
These people did not manage the land well; they knew little about
subsoils and top dressings, allowed trees and hedgerows to take
title of their acres & in all ways helped the weather to make bad
harvests. But their farming was picturesque & it suited the
preservation of game. A large population of hares partridges &
pheasants had short but let us hope merry lives between the times
when they were made war on by the superior race who inter-
vened between them and the unscrupulous foxes that would have
killed & eaten them without ulterior views. And as many foxes
were allowed to remain & enjoy their known pleasure in being
hunted were handsomely provided with covers. It was a bosky
beautiful landscape that was to be seen almost everywhere in our
rich Central plain, when a little rise of ground gave the horseman
a possibility of seeing over a stretch of tree-studied hedgerows
enclosing here & there the long roofs of a homestead & merging in
woods which gave a wide-spread hint of the landowner's mansion
hidden away with its park & pools & resounding rookery far
away from the vulgar gaze.[6]

It would be easy, and perhaps it would once have been fashionable,
to dismiss the references here to the telephone, the telescope, the
Place de la Concorde and the writings of Cobbett as random
intellectual word-play, but to the mind attuned to the evolutionary
speculation of the period the passage is dense with implicit connexions which give it the profoundest unity. France was the birthplace
not only of revolutionary politics and the myth of Bonapartism, but
also, and far more importantly, of a revolutionary theory of history –
Positivism – which united technological developments like the
telephone, improved knowledge of subsoil and top dressings, the
ecological and evolutionary balance of hunter and hunted, the
psychology of bull-baiting, astronomy and the development of
public opinion on topics as diverse as Cobbett and fashion into a
single, comprehensive and elaborately articulated theory of human
development. George Eliot implicitly invites the reader not only to
imagine a particular place in Central England in the broader context
of a barely remembered historical past, with its particular social

and class structures, its curious fashions and its faded prejudices, from the point of view of his own no less ironically perceived modernity, but also to locate himself if he will – there is no compulsion – within a quite specific if vastly extensive intellectual landscape.

That landscape is the subject of this book, which takes seriously the view of George Eliot's contemporaries that her writing was not simply influenced in a relatively haphazard way by her philosophical and scientific reading but was deliberately and consistently an attempt to synthesize in fiction an elaborate and coherent theoretical analysis of the human situation. This analysis was primarily an empiricist one, grounded in the notion of law. It assumed that there were laws governing human life not only at the biological level but at the psychological and sociological levels as well, laws which could be observed and codified. It attempted to define the relations between man and society at large in terms of the psychology of the individual, and it represented human life as being in a state of continuous evolutionary flux. Human evolution was analysed in terms of the development of the individual mind, especially in its relations with the mental life of the community which was its medium.

We can get a fuller, if still only approximate, sense of these conceptions if we turn to the work of writers known to have directly influenced George Eliot's thinking – Spencer, Bain (a friend of Lewes's, a fellow Positivist, and the leading Associationist psychologist of the day), Comte and Feuerbach. Spencer was the first English writer to combine the study of evolution with that of the mind. In particular the concept of 'correspondence', developed in his book *The Principles of Psychology*, is central to any discussion of the thought of George Eliot and that of her circle. The degree of life in any organism, Spencer suggests, depends on its active correspondence with the complexities of its environment. The single cell exhibits simple reactions, limited in both space and duration; the mammal responds to relatively large areas of space, lives longer, and reacts to the subtlest minutiae of sight, sound, smell and touch; man's intelligence extends this sensitive correspondence with the physical environment still further in space, time, detail and 'generality' – correspondence with generalities being the ability to discern attributes; the progress of philosophy and science is thus a part of the very evolutionary processes they reveal.[7] Intelligence, moreover, adds the social character of human life to the environmental factors with which men learn to correspond, and their ability to do so evolves in the same way as do all their other abilities.

An important aspect of Spencer's evolutionary theory is his attempt to replace the mechanical, economic and social optimism of some of his contemporaries with a concept of progress based on these ideas about mental development. Another is his rejection of the traditional mechanical analysis of mental phenomena which characterized classical Associationist psychology. Spencer refused to think of ideas and feelings, of Memory, Understanding and Will, as separate entities acting on each other as if they were parts of a machine. He believed that just as the organs of the body show a mutual dependence in their complex actions and reactions, so there must be a continuity, a mutual dependence and an ever-advancing consensus in the operations of the mind; and as the demarcations between physical functions are imperceptible, so the classifications of Instinct, Reason, Perception, Conception, Memory and Imagination can only be regarded as roughly convenient groupings.[8]

Animal life is initially instinctive; but it slowly learns to improvise new reactions and add them to its repertoire, that is to remember. Intelligence is the same phenomenon as memory under a different aspect, since the organism can only use its memories by making comparative judgments between them. Thus instinct, memory and intelligence are simply different aspects of the one indivisible fact of man's mental life. And as man's store of inherited and acquired reflexes increases, as the range of his memory grows wider and his intelligence becomes increasingly searching and complex, his feelings too become subtler, richer, more detailed and more expansive.[9]

Spencer was not alone in this movement away from mechanistic Associationism. Herbart and Beneke in Germany, and John Stuart Mill and Alexander Bain in England, were also beginning to see man's mental life in more organic terms. In his introduction to his father's *Analysis of the Phenomena of the Human Mind*, J. S. Mill, quoting Dr Thomas Brown, suggests that ideas are associated in a way more analogous to the chemical union of elements than to mechanical bonding.[10] This new approach to classical Associationist concepts was carried as far as it could be by Bain, whose studies of mental phenomena were as concentrated and detailed as Spencer's were extensive and generalized. The two had this in common, that neither thought of mind and body as in any way distinct from each other; for both, man is a single complex fact of organic nature, susceptible to objective analysis as a body and subjective analysis as a mind.

Bain's position can be summed up briefly. He sees no value in making any distinction between Feeling, Emotion and Consciousness: they 'express one and the same fact or attribute of mind.'[11] He admits that the laws governing the Intellect are distinct from those of Consciousness, the Intellect being capable of a distinct group of activities (disciplined rational thought) which are manifestly different from other mental operations. Nevertheless, the Intellect is inconceivable without the activity of the senses, i.e. of Consciousness, which belongs to the body as a whole. In the same way, the Will consists exclusively of the control which the brain exercises over the muscles and which develops out of the natural and spontaneous energy of the body. Will is an acquired power. In babies and young animals muscular movement is random – simply a relief of excited energy. Gradually the pleasures and pains of movement create appetites and aversions, the senses feed the intellect with the stuff of knowledge, and the child begins to control its life by controlling its movements.[12] Here we come to the heart of Bain's approach. The will is nothing more or less than subtle dispositions of energy through the neuro-muscular system at the prompting of the emotions; but the emotions themselves are manifestations of bodily activity. 'What we take as [physical] signs of the emotion are a part of its own essential workings, in whose absence it would be something entirely different.'[13] Moreover, the power that rationality has over the mind depends on the emotions inextricably associated with ideas as they are conceived by the Intellect. Thus in Bain's view it is impossible to describe the three attributes of mind, Emotion, Volition and Intellect, as working independently of each other: 'It is always to be remembered, that although scientific method requires us to take the different aspects of the mind apart, yet in the mind itself they are always working together; Emotion, Intellect, and Volition, concur in almost every manifestation'.[14] Equally it is impossible to describe any state of mind, even the most tranquil, without giving some account of what is happening in the body. Intellect, Emotion and Will, Mind and Body, form – to use Spencer's word – a consensus.

In *The Senses and the Intellect* and *The Emotions and the Will*, which together form a single work, Bain attempted a systematic and accurate account of a large number of mind-body states. But his interest to the student of George Eliot lies as much in the general character of his work as in its detail. Both were sensitive to the emotional significance of bodily reactions and to the Will as a complex combination of energy, appetite and muscular response. Certainly Bain's ideas can be regarded as giving specific significance to George Eliot's wish 'to make certain ideas thoroughly incarnate, as if they had revealed themselves to [her] first in the flesh and not in the spirit.'

If we combine Bain's analysis of mind and body with Spencer's account of evolving correspondence between organism and environment, an imaginatively ample view of human development emerges. It remains to relate such a view to the facts of history, and here Comte becomes important. With Comte the Development Theory assumes a moral, in fact an overtly religious, significance. Comte's doctrines all relate to his belief that man has a profound inner need to relate the world meaningfully to his own life. The only way primitive man can do this is to imagine everything is like himself, alive, sensitive and conscious. He therefore lives in a universe of fetishes; he can approach the inanimate world as a living consciousness – persuade it, punish it, coerce it. Gradually, however, he comes to realize that stones and trees, and even animals, do not after all have human reactions, and so he posits a series of gods, each controlling different aspects of the universe. These too finally give way to a single, omnipotent, but still conscious and approachable God. However, as the notion of will and consciousness governing the universe is removed further and further from the actual physical world itself, man can observe and analyse events taking place in the absence of direct intervention by the deity. He can posit the existence of metaphysical 'forces' to replace the gods he formerly imagined were in direct control of things. Madness, for example, is first supernatural possession, then a disturbance of the principles and energies activating the mind. Finally, however, in more and more fields of enquiry, beginning with the simplest and working up to the most complex, man learns to study and codify sequences. He grasps the notion of law as the most effective method of predicting and so controlling future events, and thus passes from a Metaphysical or Negative (i.e. anti-theological) view of the Universe to a Scientific or Positive one. He can then finally discard all thought of a supernatural order co-existing with the visible one.

The development of a Positive theory of the universe, which Comte traces in considerable historical detail, is, he suggests, matched by a corresponding moral development. He discerns four innate tendencies in human life – emotion and reason, selfishness and sympathy. Primitive man is organically emotional and selfish; his reason and fellow-feeling are active but weak. Progress consists in the steady strengthening of reason as a source of doctrine and of sympathy as the basis for action. Thus the doctrinal development of religious conceptions is matched by a moral development of religious sympathies, though these two tendencies proceed with a certain independence of each other, and it is possible, for instance, for a man's moral development to be in advance of his doctrine. Ultimately, however, man's intellectual appreciation of the universe will be wholly positivist and his moral reactions to it wholly selfless. At this point, moreover, because of the grand predominance of their selfless instincts, all men will also enjoy complete harmony with each other, and the human race as a whole will be in a completely harmonious relation with the physical universe.[15]

Before going further into the details of Comte's religious theories, this is a convenient stage at which to consider Ludwig Feuerbach's *The Essence of Christianity*, which George Eliot admired and translated. The idea of mental evolution is as much part of Feuerbach's system as of Comte's, 'the progressive development of religion' being for him 'identical with the progressive development of human culture.'[16] Thus the religion of primitive man is as limited as his social organization and the scope of his ideas in general: 'The "savage", whose consciousness does not extend beyond his own country, whose entire being is a growth of its soil, takes his country with him into the other world.'[17] Feuerbach's basic premise is that though God does not exist his predicates do – in man. In religion man gives objective reality to his highest conception of himself, and worships it: 'in religion, consciousness of the object [God] and self-consciousness coincide.'[18] But though man worships man in worshipping God, he does not worship his own individual nature, but the limitless potentialities of the race as he discovers them in others, in the 'Thou' with which he recognizes his fellow-men.[19]

It is not difficult to see how these ideas can be integrated with the body of evolutionary and psychological theory which we have been considering. It is clear, for example, that Comte's theories concerning the origins of religious conceptions tend to support the basic theses of Feuerbach. If savages discover life and consciousness and a will in the inanimate world, they are doing nothing other than Feuerbach says all men contemplating their god ever do – seeing in the object of their worship an image of themselves. Again, Feuerbach's concept of the Thou as the element in religion which unites men to each other through the god they worship is exactly paralleled in Comte's doctrine of evolving altruism. And just as Comte defines the intellectual progress of man in terms of the nearness of his reasoning in religious matters to the Positivist norm, so Feuerbach measures moral and emotional progress by the character and personality of the divinity men worship.

It remains to consider Comte's analysis of the moral content of religion. He had a strong tendency to categorize. Men are rational, active and practical in his system, women emotional, passive and moral; society falls naturally into three classes, the active class (soldiers and later industrialists), the speculative class (priests, philosophers and scientists) and the affective or moral class (the workers). There are three stages of religious development – the Spontaneous, the Inspired and the Revealed (Fetishism, Polytheism and Monotheism): in the first feeling predominates, in the second imagination and in the third reason. In each of these instances the passive and emotional categories have the greatest moral potential, since the altruistic faculties develop in the emotions. The emotions have freest play in the primitive mind. Therefore the richness of man's moral life depends on his ability to maintain contact with the primitive experiences of fetishism, shorn of its egoistical characteristics: in fetishism we discover the sources of spontaneous affection and sympathy.

In planning a 'religion' based on these conclusions, Comte advocated a return to a modified form of fetishism. Without abandoning its rational conception of the universe, the religious mind would endow the physical world as far as possible with imagined feelings and sensitivities, so that it could continually stimulate the sympathetic emotions as well as the intellect. The harmonious correspondence with the inanimate world which Comte envisaged for Positivist man involved his feelings as well as his intellect. This aspect of Comte's thought is, of course, notorious. Nevertheless, the central idea behind his new fetishism is very important, especially if it is linked to certain ideas of Bain's. If man's moral sensibilities are closely related to his primitive life, because the emotions have greater range in the primitive mind, and if the emotions themselves are inextricably involved in the reactions and sensations of the body, then simple, primordial experiences of mind and body have immense moral importance. The combination of such an approach with an extensive vision of the whole range of evolving life could certainly have a considerable effect on the imagination of a novelist like George Eliot.

It has to be acknowledged, however, that the relevance of this considerable body of speculation to a sensitive reading of her novels is not as obvious to some of her readers as it seemed to Harrison and Morley, and never has been. In Henry James's review of Cross's *Life*, for example, we get a notably non-didactic novelist's view of the matter. Specifically, James complains about 'the absence of free aesthetic life' in her nature; the artistic mind, he argues,

> existed in her with limitations remarkable in a writer whose
> imagination was so rich. We feel in her, always, that she proceeds
> from the abstract to the concrete; that her figures and situations

. . . are deeply studied and elaborately justified, but . . . are not
seen in the irresponsible plastic way. The world was, first and
foremost, for George Eliot, the moral, the intellectual world; the
personal spectacle came after; and lovingly, humanly, as she
regarded it, we constantly feel that she cares for the things she
finds in it only so far as they are types. The philosophical door is
always open, on her stage, and we are aware that the somewhat
cooling draught of ethical purpose draws across it.[20]

He goes on to suggest that this ethical purpose 'constitutes half the
beauty of her work', that her 'preoccupation with the universe
helped to make her characters strike you as belonging to it' and that
'it raised the roof, widened the area of her aesthetic structure'; but
the note of unease persists, and was to be heard in the work of
James's successors when interest in George Eliot's achievement
revived following the publication of F.R. Leavis's celebrated essays
in *Scrutiny*.[21] For a long time thereafter critics were distrustful of her
'preoccupation with the universe', and if her 'teaching' received any
attention, it was not for its philosophical insight, coherence or
originality, but for its intuitive organicism or wise worldliness that it
was praised.[22] Her positive and forthright convictions were seen as
embarrassing encumbrances, or as being so qualified and compromised by the subtle organization of her texts as to be peripheral, the
qualification and the compromise having acquired the centrality
which some of her best-informed contemporaries discovered in her
doctrines and her principles. In general, however, attention focussed
on rhetorical strategies, and the tension between idealism and
realism in her work. This common pursuit was especially fruitful
and forms the background against which my own work has
developed.[23] In particular I must mention the essay which should act
as a guide and warning to any critic interested in elucidating George
Eliot's world-view: W. J. Harvey's 'Idea and image in the novels of
George Eliot'.[24] In this book I have not tried to locate George Eliot's
sources with the specificity Harvey rightly criticized. However, in
the case of a mind such as hers I cannot accept his judgment that 'we
need to operate on the level of the general commonplace rather than
on the level of the specific example',[25] nor that it is enough to point
out instances where another writer's 'cast of mind would find a
sympathetic response in George Eliot.'[26] This may apply to her
British contemporaries (Bain, Bray, Spencer and Huxley), but the
action of European thinkers, particularly Feuerbach and Comte, on
her work is demonstrably less diffused. Nevertheless, I have tried to
give detailed substantiation to a number of points raised in Harvey's

essay, and in general to respect if not to match the multivalent tact which he rightly called for in this field, and himself so readily achieved.

I am indebted, of course, to the less prominent and more distinctly scholarly work which runs parallel with this critical tradition and which has attempted to elucidate George Eliot's intellectual perspectives. Work in this area has taken three forms: general accounts of George Eliot's thought,[27] particular studies of aspects of her reading and their effect on individual texts,[28] and broader discussions of her place in nineteenth-century intellectual and literary humanism.[29] The first section of this book inevitably recapitulates many conclusions to be found in the work of writers in the first of these groups, notably Basil Willey and Bernard Paris. However, in addition, I have attempted to demonstrate the broader logic of George Eliot's position, its dialogue with itself, in a way that has not been done before. I have also given prominence for the first time to George Eliot's fascination with animistic fantasy, its intricate and intimate action within the human body, and its pervasive presence in human culture. Finally, I have emphasized her interest in history and the historical typicality of such characters as Tom Tulliver, Felix Holt and Gwendolen Harleth in a new way. All this has depended on acknowledging Comte as a persistent and major presence in her work, something that has been consistently questioned by major scholars, notably G. S. Haight.[30] The apparent crudity of Comte's later writing makes this questioning very understandable. Approached sympathetically, however, even his Religion of Humanity is demonstrably a more serious intellectual construct than it at first appears, and fused with Associationist psychology (as in important respects it is in the novels) it offers a particularly interesting view of history as an evolutionary process which can be accurately described in the vocabulary of the psychological, biological and social sciences.

New interest in the close detail of George Eliot's thought, as indicated by the publication of the second group of studies mentioned above, has in the main developed relatively recently, and for two reasons: the appearance in print of some of the notebooks and of the catalogues of her library and Lewes's,[31] and the new respect that is being given to the latter[32] after years of unjustified disparagement. This has helped to modify the 'anti-didactic' or 'anti-ideological' assumptions of mainstream George Eliot criticism, though the trap of detailed attribution of sources pointed out by Harvey has not always been avoided. Another negative effect has been to concentrate attention disproportionately on George Eliot's later works because these coincide with Lewes's work on *Problems of Life and Mind*. But the latter was not new ground for Lewes: it was the summation of years of study, thought and writing. In any case the broad lines of his psychological speculations were anticipated to a significant degree in the work of Bain, whose writings George Eliot undoubtedly knew, and whom I cite throughout this book as a contemporary whose opinions and assumptions she was likely to sympathize with and respect as being consistent with her own world-view. That world-view, however, is generally neglected in the more particular studies of sources and influences to which I have been referring. It needs also to be understood as a body of thought which defines rather than resolves the problems to which the novels are addressed. Nor is it enough, in my judgment, to treat it with the generalized brevity characteristic of the third group of studies to which I have referred, those broader discussions of George Eliot's work which attempt to place her achievement in the intellectual history of the period generally. Feuerbach's religious system, for example, provides more than an overall theory of the phenomenology of religion; it also facilitates highly specific readings of particular religious doctrines and practices. Positivism and Associationism can be no less illuminating in particular instances.

The function of the first part of this book, therefore, is to fill the gap between the kind of broad but succinct summary of George Eliot's position offered in U. C. Knoepflmacher's earlier studies in this field, or Laurence Lerner's excellent book *The Truthtellers*, and the close analysis of recent studies, notably by George Levine. In the second part I take up the challenge of Calvin Bedient's important book, *Architects of the Self* (1972). Though wrong-headed on some points, notably the Teresan element in *Middlemarch*, Bedient subjects George Eliot's world-view to a trenchant and specifically Nietzschean analysis. This I amplify by providing detailed documentation of his very broadly based attack, and extend by introducing Marx and Freud into the discussion as well as Nietzsche. Bedient's weakness, however, is that, like James, Leavis and many other critics, he treats George Eliot as 'a case'.[33] It is a legitimate approach in its way, but the present book is written in the belief that a more basic job has to be done first: the explication, critical analysis and, if possible, the defence of her conscious intentions as an aesthetic teacher. I am concerned, in short, with the novels as George Eliot understood them. I believe that she saw most but not all of what is there, and that she intended what she saw. I also believe – and this is the view which is most fully developed in the third part of this book – that she was herself aware of major weaknesses in her position, both intellectual and psychological, and that her overt, conscious and describable strategies in connexion with those weaknesses take us to the heart of her teaching, that is to her own intensely personal, deliberately developed and highly individual contribution to a body of empiricist humanist opinion which she shared with Lewes and many of her contemporaries, and which still has an important presence in our own culture.

This is a very unfashionable project, yet I would not want it to be thought of as necessarily challenging either New Criticism or Post-structuralism. The following argument of Jacques Derrida's, for example, seems to me to be fundamentally sound:

> The 'subject' of writing does not exist if we mean by that some sovereign solitude of the author. The subject of writing is a *system* of relations between strata . . . Within that scene, on that stage, the punctual simplicity of the classical subject is not to be found. In order to describe the structure, it is not enough to recall that one always writes for someone; and the oppositions sender-receiver, code-message, etc., remain extremely coarse instruments. We would search the 'public' in vain for the first reader: i.e., the first author of a work. And the 'sociology of literature is blind to the war and the ruses perpetrated by the author who reads and by the first reader who dictates, for at stake here is the origin of the work itself. The *sociality* of writing as *drama* requires an entirely different discipline.[34]

I hope I have not indulged in anything so crude as 'the sociology of literature' in this book, and I believe I could offer a theoretical defence of its procedures. Such a defence would be based on a conception of writing precisely as drama, in which 'performance' is understood to be inseparable from 'meaning'. In George Eliot's case, I suggest that this drama manifests itself, for her and for us, on two levels, on the immediately intuitive or experiential level, the level of the feeling and the felt personality, and on the level of cognitive activity, the level of criticism. To quote from a work of phenomenological analysis quite as pressingly contemporary as Derrida's:

> the complexity of the experience of man is dominated by its intrinsic simplicity. The complexity itself of this experience simply shows that the whole experience, and consequently the cognition of man, is composed of both the experience that everyone has concerning himself and the experience of other men . . . All this tends to compose a whole in cognition rather to cause complexity. Thus this conviction of the intrinsic simplicity of the

experience of man may be considered as an optimistic aspect of the cognitive aims that confront us.[35]

Reading, I believe, is one of the situations in which it is possible 'to compose a whole in cognition' out of the simultaneous experience of oneself and others (one's fellow-readers as well as the author whose 'presence' modern criticism finds so elusive). It is an optimistic aspect of this book, in other words, that it is based on a conviction that both the critic and the common reader can know even as they are known.

Part One: Convictions

1 Morality and religion

THE scientific conception that men are subject to law, to which the author of 'George Eliot moralist and thinker' gives such emphasis, did not, George Eliot believed, dissolve morality in a deterministic flux, but on the contrary was its true basis. This idea had been lengthily developed by her friend Charles Bray in *The Philosophy of Necessity*, and was much reiterated in her own early journalism, where she frequently attacks the Christian doctrines of forgiveness and eternal rewards and punishments. The rigour of scientific determinism, given the moral twist then popular with writers such as Bray, Buckle and Greg, thus effectively replaced the sternness of George Eliot's adolescent Calvinism. The idea is well summarized in a passage from W.R. Greg's *The Creed of Christendom*, which George Eliot quoted in a review in 1851:

> Again – you have broken the seventh commandment. You grieve – you repent . . . but 'you know God is merciful – you feel that he will forgive you.' You are comforted. But no – there is no forgiveness of sins – the injured party may forgive you – your accomplice or victim may forgive you, according to the meaning of human language; but *the deed is done*, and all the powers of Nature, were they to conspire in your behalf, could not make it undone; the consequences to the body – the consequences to the soul – though no man may perceive them, *are there*, – are written in the annals of the past, and must reverberate through all time.[1]

The same idea reappears in another review written 15 years later: 'the gradual reduction of all phenomena within the sphere of established law, which carries as a consequence the rejection of the miraculous' is, George Eliot asserts, a 'supremely important fact', and 'has its determining current in the development of physical science', that is, in the 'great conception of universal regular sequence, without partiality and without caprice . . . which is the most potent force at work in the modification of our faith and the practical form given to our sentiments.'[2] The modification of sentiment she has in mind is precisely that experienced by Duke

Silva in *The Spanish Gypsy*, when he cries out in anguish:

> Pardon? Penitence?
> When they have done their utmost, still beyond
> Out of our reach stands Injury unchanged
> And changeless. (p.307)

An intense awareness of the incalculable, irreversible and unending consequences of our actions, rather than an illusory and ultimately self-centred vision of heaven and hell and an arbitrary providence miraculously intervening and redeeming us, provides the only humane and intelligent motivation in the moral life.

The novels insist repeatedly on a naturalistic morality of this kind. The moral egoism of both Lantern Yard in *Silas Marner* and Florence in *Romola* takes the form of a preoccupation with personal salvation and miracle. Miracle, Feuerbach contended, is the product of a 'theoretically narrow' monotheism which reduces nature 'to an object of arbitrariness' the plaything of a God 'who will not let his servants come to shame'.[3] Silas's catalepsy and the casting of lots in the one case, visions and the trial by fire in the other, are historically connected. George Eliot notes at length the enthusiasm for scriptural exegesis which Savonarola stimulates among sedentary artisans in Florence, thereby suggesting the imminence of that tradition of personal faith and private judgment which may have introduced new notions of personal responsibility into the religious life of Europe but which also underlies the hysteria and egoism of Lantern Yard and links it with the dangerous outpourings of the prophetess Camilla.

But emancipation from superstition does not automatically bring moral advancement. Godfrey Cass in *Silas Marner* could never share the delusions of urban dissenters; Tito Milema in *Romola* is a sophisticated agnostic; but neither is less of an egoist in consequence. Godfrey feebly worships the 'god' of 'Favourable Chance', Tito is blandly insensitive to the effects of his actions on his own nature. Both are central characters in narratives which elaborately exemplify the central lesson that once choices are made 'the consequence to the body – the consequences to the soul – though no man may perceive them, *are there*'. Any one who performs an action he feels to be immoral is at once involved in secrecy (no one must know about Molly or Baldassare) and a brood of guilty wishes, specifically the hope that the person one has injured will die. All subsequent decisions and all existing and future relationships are determined under these pressures. Godfrey, Tito, David in 'Brother Jacob', Greg's adulterers – none of them can enjoy frank, unstrained relationships with any one. This is one reason why confession plays such an important part in George Eliot's fictions from 'Mr Gilfil's Love-story' to *Daniel Deronda:* it is the only way of countering the deceitfulness and corruption of motive logically entailed in a wicked action.

Thus stated the consequential morality of the novels appears over-simple. It is indeed suspect and so are the narratives embodying it. But neither can be considered in isolation from the interesting tensions in so many of George Eliot's fictions between the varying moral awareness of primitive and sophisticated people (Dolly Winthrop and Tito Milema, for example) and between different tendencies in the same personality. Hence the 'great problem of the shifting relation between passion and duty' (Bk VI, ch. 2) which confronts Maggie Tulliver in *The Mill on the Floss.* The 'co-incidence of duty and happiness'[4] was, as we have seen, a particularly elusive ideal for Positivists. In 'the tempests which arise in the complicated system of human existence', Comte wrote, '. . . the natural co-operation of Love with Faith does not effect a complete equilibrium, but a state of continuous movement' by which human nature becomes 'more and more religious'.[5] But in the end, for Comte, feelings are primary. Hence his assertion that 'happiness . . . cannot reside either in our thoughts or our actions, but exclusively in our sympathies, and their highest recompense is their existence.'[6]

The primacy thus accorded to feeling accounts in large measure for the ambivalence of George Eliot's attitude to 'progressive' ideas in an article so apparently committed to scientific perspectives as 'The Influence of Rationalism'. A considerable part of the essay is devoted to attacking superficially optimistic ideas about progress; 'witchcraft to many of us is absurd,' it suggests, 'only on the same ground that our grandfathers' gigs are absurd',[7] and is in any case still tolerated in the form of spiritualism; and though no 'seances at a guinea a head . . . can annihilate railways, steamships, and electric telegraphs, which are demonstrating the interdependence of all human interests, and making self-interest a duct for sympathy',[8] the mere fact that moral progress is thus dependent on material change is a clear sign of its fragility and uncertainty. And if enlightened views are often merely fashionable, traditional superstition can be a sign of moral depth. George Eliot accordingly registers her respect for men like Bodin and Glanvil who continued to believe in witchcraft when their contemporaries, with a 'certain keen narrowness of nature',[9] were viewing the matter more sceptically. It is characteristic of 'large minds', she suggests, to have 'an indefinite uneasiness in an undistinguishing attack on the coercive influence of tradition', and this must continue as long as there is no 'profound research into psychological functions or into the mysteries of inheritance,' and no 'comprehensive view of man's historical development and the dependence of one age on another.'[10] A similar point is made of Savonarola and Fra Salvestro in *Romola*:

> Fra Salvestro had a peculiar liability to visions . . . Savonarola believed in the supernatural character of these visions, while Fra Salvestro himself had originally resisted such an interpretation of them . . . another proof, if one were wanted, that the relative greatness of men is not to be gauged by their tendency to disbelieve the superstitions of their age (ch. 41).

Throughout George Eliot's fiction this willingness to countenance 'superstition' recurs. The community with which the Rev. Amos Barton communicates so feebly on the level of doctrine is the community which values his wife on the level of feeling, and which earlier supported Caterina in her flight and Mr Gilfil in his lonely old age. To understand the significance of this stupid, kindly wisdom, however, and the virtues of a backward or primitive way of life, it is necessary to turn to *Silas Marner*, a novel which with skill and indirection engages with a number of important aspects of George Eliot's teaching and to which we shall therefore have need constantly to return. One of its principal concerns is the relation of intellect to feeling in man's moral development, and in this respect the placing of Mr Macey is crucial. There can be no question but that Mr Macey and his brother Solomon are highly intelligent men – but their world has only a peripheral use for intelligence and no respect for it. This is painfully evident in the Raveloe sense of humour; from Squire Cass, cheerfully insulting Kimble and then tapping 'his box, and [looking] round with a triumphant laugh' (ch. 11), to humble Ben Winthrop telling Tookey that his 'inside . . . isn't right made for music: it's no better nor a hollow stalk' (ch. 6), the successful joker is the man who delivers an emphatically worded insult. Humour, George Eliot suggested in her article on Heine in the *Westminster Review*, was compatible 'with a great deal of barbarism'; it was a relic of the savage's cruel mockery of his defeated enemy. Wit, on the other hand, she associated with 'the ratiocinative intellect'[11] – and Mr Macey has wit. His is the famous epigram, also referring to Tookey's singing, that there would 'be two 'pinions about a cracked bell, if the bell could hear itself' (ch. 6). Mr Macey's natural intellectual bent makes his pompous egoism particularly convincing. To an almost Dickensian degree he is the victim of his office of parish clerk, but his jealousy, cantankerousness and conservatism are not really Dickensian, if only because George Eliot has been careful to suggest that he has a personal history to account for his pomposity, as Mr Wopsle in *Great Expectations*, for instance, does not. Moreover, in spite of Mr Macey's absurd self-esteem and insensitive tongue, one seeks out his company on the page. The marriage of Eppie and Aaron would have been a thin affair without him. The narrowness of his vision and the triviality of his ambitions are perpetually on display, but his eloquence, pride and hunger for recognition so plainly derive from an active, under-utilized intelligence that he is never contemptible. (The contentment and balance his brother Solomon achieves making his music are especially useful in enriching our sense of the Macey family's potentialities.)

Mr Macey's importance in *Silas Marner*, however, is not simply that of a generous, perceptive and amusing characterization. As a genuinely intelligent man he authentically embodies the final ignorance in which all human beings – the reader as well as the characters in the story – are condemned to think and act. In a very strongly written passage in his *Autobiography*, Spencer was to argue that in future religion would consist of a sense of wonder at the vastness and complexity of reality, and a sense of fear that 'of all that is thus incomprehensible to us, there exists no comprehension anywhere'.[12] After reading *The Origin of Species* George Eliot felt similarly. All explanations of how 'things came to be', she wrote, produce 'a feeble impression compared with the mystery that lies under the processes'.[13] This idea clearly yet ironically underlies her account of the debate in the Rainbow Inn between the proponents of the tinder-box theory of the theft and Mr Macey, the defender of traditional pieties, and the point she establishes in the course of this debate is that there is no essential difference between their ignorance and our own:

> When the robbery was talked of at the Rainbow and elsewhere, in good company, the balance continued to waver between the rational explanation founded on the tinder-box, and the theory of an impenetrable mystery that mocked investigation. The advocates of the tinder-box-and-pedlar view considered the other side a muddle-headed and credulous set, who, because they themselves were wall-eyed, supposed everybody else to have the same blank outlook; and the adherents of the inexplicable more than hinted that their antagonists were animals inclined to crow before they had found any corn – mere skimming-dishes in point of depth – whose clear-sightedness consisted in supposing there was nothing behind a barn-door because they couldn't see through it;

> so that, though their controversy did not serve to elicit the fact
> concerning the robbery, it elicited some true opinions of collateral
> importance (ch. 10).

This is as witty a parody of the 'metaphysical' phase in the dialogue
between faith and reason as it is a fair picture of a pub debate. When
we add to it the moving account of Silas's discussions with William
Dane – 'Such coloquies have occupied many a pair of pale-faced
weavers, whose unnurtured souls have been like young winged
things, fluttering forsaken in the twilight' (ch. 1) – the range of
intellectual activity alluded to in *Silas Marner* becomes apparent, and
the essential task which George Eliot has undertaken in the novel
clarifies itself, namely, to expose the insecurity of all convictions
even while affirming the importance of having and holding on to
them.

The novel's principal source of moral wisdom, Dolly Winthrop, is
an example of this deeply responsible agnosticism. The virtue which
Dolly most earnestly recommends – what she calls trustening – has
admittedly a great deal to do merely with being 'set up and
comfortable', and her musings on the subject of Luck do not seem to
be all that far removed from Godfrey's feeble hoping against hope:
'all as we've got to do,' she tells Silas, 'is to trusten . . . to do the
right thing as fur as we know, and to trusten' (ch. 16). Silas's
response to this advice does not make matters clearer. 'That drawing
o' the lots is dark,' he says; 'but the child was sent to me: there's
dealings with us – there's dealings.' It would seem in fact that Dolly
finds great things to say by accident – in the merely mechanical
repetition of proverbial wisdom:

> 'it's like the night and the morning, and the sleeping and the
> waking, and the rain and the harvest – one goes and the other
> comes, and we know nothing how nor where. We strive and scrat
> and fend, but it's little we can do arter all – the big things come
> and go wi' no striving o' our'n – they do, that they do' (ch. 14).

Dolly is thus always convincingly of her world and therefore slightly
ridiculous: 'things come into [her] head when [she's] leeching or
poulticing' (ch. 15); her phrase, 'there's the breaking o' limbs'
suggests fractures absurdly commensurate with Virgil's tears for
things; and she and Silas settle into the mindless vacancy of his
assertion about dealings. But this very ignorance also enables her to
be, in Feuerbachian terms, an instinctive polytheist – unlike the
miracle-mongering fanatics of Lantern Yard. The fact that she
always refers to God in the plural is a technically specific sign of a

religious constitution wholly free from religious egoism. The point that Dolly has grasped, moreover, is that Luck is not a solution but the problem: the 'big puzzle' consists in the fact that justice is achieved in Silas's case only through flagrant improbabilities, yet it is precisely in the face of such moral chaos that trustening is necessary, as the essential condition of all fruitful human co-operation.

And this of course is the lesson Silas has to learn: the value of co-operating with the community of Raveloe, in spite of its many shortcomings, for Eppie's sake and with her help. The adjustments he makes to village life are in themselves trivial and are made in ignorance, but they are nonetheless convincing and important. He discovers how dependent he is on his neighbours and how he must therefore respect their needs and feelings, their customs and courtesies. His openness to suggestion, his eagerness to appropriate the forms of custom and belief, not so much because they are true but because they are neighbourly, is crucial. 'I want to do everything as can be done for the child,' he says. 'And whatever's right for it i' this country, and you think 'ull do it good, I'll act according, if you'll tell me' (ch. 14). He even takes up smoking out of 'a humble sort of acquiescence' in what the world holds to be good. This is not a minor virtue. Faced with the disastrous Luck of Godfrey's revelation, he can nonetheless achieve the truly heroic acquiescence of 'I'll say no more. Let it be as you will. Speak to the child. I'll hinder nothing' (ch. 19).

The lesson he has learnt is one Comte would have recognized, for George Eliot has effectively translated into the idiom of Raveloe the key Positivist concept of Submission. This idea lies at the heart of the moralized notion of scientific law which she so insists upon in the Greg and Lecky reviews. It is a major theme also in all her fictions from 'Janet's Repentance' onwards, reappearing in each at the same point of the action when the moral and psychological entanglements which have accumulated steadily throughout the narrative are at last resolved, and the right conditions are finally created for altruism to come decisively into play.

'Complete submission', according to Comte, is the absolute pre-condition of a morally whole life. Without it 'feelings would be ill-regulated . . . thoughts incoherent . . . action a mere source of disorder.'[14]

> Whether our obedience remain involuntary or become voluntary
> whether it be confined to the natural laws of the world or
> extended to the institutions of man's creation, it always consti-

tutes the first condition of any amelioration whatever . . . By it
our intellect is brought to reflect more perfectly the universal
economy it has subsequently to idealise, by developing the
subordination of man to the world . . . At the same time
submission always tends to make altruism prevail over egoism by
repressing personality, from which all revolt proceeds.[15]

The word 'personality' (sometimes translated 'character') has a
special sense in Comte's thought. In other respects the idea of
Submission which he develops here is identical with Bray's theory of
consequences and is not unrelated to Marx's materialism or Freud's
reality principle. It derives from the notion of process in nature, man
and history, by which the laws of matter and life ensure that seed
brings forth fruit after its own kind. Ineluctability, however, far
from imprisoning or alienating man, is a condition of progress and
growth, for determinism is humanized when man learns to act
within it instead of seeking through egoism and fantasy to separate
himself from the world and other people in an illusory and selfish
autonomy.

The ideal of Submission, however, highlights a contradiction or
tension inherent in the ethics of scientific law on which it is based
and which it enforces. To the extent that it is scientific it predicates
intellectual development; to the extent that it is social, as in *Silas
Marner*, it sanctions stability and acquiescence in the world as it is.
This tension was undoubtedly seen and welcomed by George Eliot,
and it accounts for the complexities in her representations of, for
example, traditionally-minded clergy in her early fiction, and the
supporters of the evangelical revival and Methodism. She understood both positions thoroughly, her attitudes to each being clearly
represented in two early articles on religious egoism, 'Evangelical
teaching: Dr Cumming' (1855) and 'Worldliness and Other-
Worldliness: the poet Young' (1857). At the heart of her disgust with
Cumming is his occupation of 'a metropolitan pulpit'[16] and his
patronizing remoteness from (to quote his own words) "'the peasant
on the hills . . . *amid the mountains of Braemar and Dee-side*'".[17] In her
experience authentic evangelicalism was deeply rooted in provincial
life. Related to this conviction is her strong dislike of the Anglican
establishment. She treats the nice balance of temporalities and
spiritualities suggested by Young's relations with the Duke of
Wharton, for example, with a contempt comparable with that
reserved for Lush's relations with Grandcourt in *Daniel Deronda*.
The accents of provincial and middle-class rectitude in the essays are
characteristic. In spite of her Anglican background, George Eliot

has a place in the great tradition of provincial dissent which produced John Bunyan, Herbert Spencer and William Hale White. The splendidly unpleasant rantings of Lawyer Dempster in 'Janet's Repentance' are from the world Hale White knew well, and they reveal a thorough familiarity with the ways in which traditional pieties can be brutally invoked by the crude mindlessness of small-town self-interest.

Two kinds of illumination resist this small-mindness in the early fiction: the evangelicalism of Mr Tryan which Dempster attacks, and its apparent opposite, the established order of the Anglican Church which he purports to defend. Authentic representatives of the latter are Mr Cleves in 'Amos Baron' ('a man . . . most likely sprung from the harder-working section of the middle-class' – ch. 6), Mr Gilfil in 'Mr Gilfil's Love-story', a gentlemanly and humane latitudinarian, and Dr Kenn, in *The Mill on the Floss*, a high churchman, who for all the tall candles on his altar belongs in practice to 'that natural order' of priesthood, the sympathetic middle-aged (Bk VI, ch. 9). Dr Kenn's belief that 'the Church ought to represent the feeling of the community, so that every parish should be a family knit together by Christian brotherhood under a spiritual father' (Bk V, ch. 2) is particularly interesting. It suggests that even the most traditional, 'Catholic' religious principles are susceptible to sympathetic Feuerbachian interpretation. And this is why, of course, opposition in the novels between Broad or High churchmen on the one hand, and evangelicalism and even dissent on the other is often a matter of appearance only. Mr Cleves sympathizes with Mr Barton, Dr Kenn with the erratic and far from orthodox Maggie. The reason for this tolerance is clear: all authentic religious experience is in its essence a humanism, however indirectly perceived, and this applies as much to evangelicalism and dissent as to latitudinarianism and Puseyism. All true religious perception converges on a single object, man. But this does not make religious differences trivial. There has been a tendency among critics (notably Derek and Sybil Oldfield, writing on *Scenes of Clerical Life*, and John Goode, writing on *Adam Bede*)[18] to represent the Feuerbachian dimension of George Eliot's thought simply in terms of Feuerbach's commitment to the 'divine instinct of benevolence which desires to make all happy, and excludes none.'[19] But in fact George Eliot valued religious doctrine, ceremony and discipline, not for the general contribution they made to furthering the abstract principle of altruism, but for their capacity to register in detail the specific potentialities of man, good and evil.

This seems to have been particularly true of Evangelicalism. George Eliot apparently regarded the Evangelical Revival as the means by which the doctrine of consequences, so thin and barren when stated abstractly, made its presence felt historically, with all the mental vividness and spiritual energy of religion. At the heart of the evangelical experience of conviction of sin in 'Janet's Repentance', for example, is an intuition of necessity, 'that complete sense of . . . sin and helplessness, without which [Janet] would never have renounced all other hopes, and trusted in [God's] love alone' (ch. 18). Out of this experience comes the desperate but regenerative impulse to confess by which the soul is restored to a respect for the truth, accepts responsibility without equivocation for all past actions, and approaches the future with a proper sense of caution. At the same time, confession breaks down reserve. It makes possible a direct and passionate communication of feeling between human beings. This double experience of caution and passionate openness is manifested in the developing relationship between Janet and Mr Tryan. Janet's confession arouses Mr Tryan's sympathy; but sympathy is simply 'a living again through our own past in a new form' (ch. 18); hence the confession of his own melodramatic sin. In this shared experience of mutual frankness, a love develops between them which, because of her unhappy past and his failing health, they both must approach circumspectly. In the end, faced with his imminent death, they have no alternative but for each to strive for 'entire submission, perfect resignation'. We are thus once again at the Comtean heart of George Eliot's religious thought.

It would be a mistake, therefore, to regard religion in George Eliot merely as a symbolic or imaginative expression of her morality, which only requires translation into an appropriately modern philosophical idiom to be properly understood. On the contrary, without the capacity for religious living, that is for belief, ritual and discipline, even rational, godless, altruistic man would wither as a moral being. The ability to be religious is an ability to explore man's potentialities with an energy the irreligious or unfervent mind cannot match. It is in this sense, as a work which not only illustrates the various moral and religious perspectives which I have outlined, but which also attempts to intensify and enlarge the religiousness of the reader, that *Adam Bede* should be read.

It seems sensible, when analysing religion and morality in *Adam Bede*, to start with Mr Irwine, who, though he fails at least partially as moral mentor to Arthur Donnithorne, is in other respects the ideal country parson, an intelligent, open-minded man, who has the measure, as a country gentleman, of the gap between himself and his parishioners. He knows, for example, that there is never any real likelihood of Dinah Morris's Methodism disturbing Hayslope's way of life. 'The village mind' is slow, unemotional and erratic; it 'does not easily take fire, and a little smouldering vague anxiety, that might easily die out again' (ch. 2) is all the effect Dinah's preaching will have on it. But this does not mean that Hayslope is irreligious, as the admirable study of Lisbeth Bede makes clear. Lisbeth has a very narrow intellect, and is difficult to bear with, but she can feel deeply within the narrow range of 'family affections and neighbourly duties' (ch. 5). Her condemnation of Hetty as a poor porridge-maker springs from a half-articulate sense of the importance of domestic skills in cementing family affection. She irritates Adam, but has the moral insight to insist that he, not Seth, must make Thias's coffin: 'Thee wast often angered wi' they feyther when he war alive; thee must be the better to him now he's gone . . .' (ch. 4). Her humble but honourable place in the scale of moral sensibility is firmly established, when, in her great mourning speech for her husband, her peasant mind forces out the idea of love and duty surviving death:

'. . . I wonna ha' no tay: I carena if I ne'er ate nor drink no more. When one end o' th' bridge tumbles down, where's th' use o' th' other stannin'? I may's well die, an' foller my old man. There's no knowin' but he'll want me' (ch. 10).

The religion of Hayslope, then, is by and large pre-doctrinal. The issues about which Mr Irwine has to counsel his nephew, on the other hand, are post-doctrinal, ethical rather than religious, and both carefully avoid any reference to religious teaching in their conversations together. The same is true of the Rector's conversations with Adam on similar issues after Hetty's seduction has become known. Adam himself is not in any case interested in doctrine. 'It isn't notions sets people doing the right thing,' he insists, '– it's feelings' (ch. 17). The narrative which develops out of Arthur and Adam's friendship and Arthur's betrayal of it, therefore, is carefully presented in terms which enable George Eliot to explore the morality of consequences with the minimum reference to specifically religious conceptions.

Essentially the elaborate contrast between Arthur and Adam centres on their differing attitudes towards the truth. In Arthur, a 'native impulse to give truth in return for truth' (ch. 28) is grounded in a trivially egoistical need to think well of himself, and not in a sympathetic sense of how wrong-doing irretrievably and unpredictably damages the lives of others as well as of oneself, both internally and practically. By limiting his considerations of the results of his actions to Hetty and himself, Arthur permits himself to make love to her. Thereafter his conscience itself comes into conflict with his innate impulse towards truthfulness. Duty becomes 'a question of tactics' (ch. 28), punishment a bitter confrontation with the inevitable results of his own misdeeds. Even before he learns of Hetty's pregnancy, which he had half-anticipated, he encounters processes of retribution which he had not anticipated in the shame he feels in Adam's presence, for Adam now embodies 'what Arthur most shrank from believing in – the irrevocableness of his own wrongdoing' (ch. 29).

This erosion of truthfulness in Arthur is contrasted with Adam's loyalty to the truth. His hymn in the first chapter indicates a spontaneously pleasurable attachment to conscience and work – both in their different ways contingent on plain fact. For Adam 'the sperrit o' God' is in the solid world of consistent cause and effect which Arthur finds such a trap. He feels secure in the thought that the universe remains 'faithful to its own laws' and can therefore be relied on in every circumstance to provide us with work to do and so with 'a grip hold o' things outside [our] own lot' (ch. 11). His altruistic love of work is organic. So is his susceptibility to the influence of rank which derives from a 'large fund of reverence' (ch. 16). Submission to external fact is thus as much the co-ordinating principle in Adam's manhood as it is of Dolly Winthrop's neighbourliness.

In its treatment of these issues *Adam Bede* is often impressive, notably in its fine realization of the Rector's failure to achieve a sufficiently frank and open relationship with Arthur. However, when the full consequences of the seduction are moving to their brutal conclusion, the entire theme of truthfulness and responsibility is in danger of seeming intrusive and doctrinaire. Specifically Adam's debate about ethics with Mr Irwine on the very eve of the trial, which virtually repeats the earlier one between Arthur and Mr Irwine at the end of the first book, is emotionally irrelevant at this juncture. In both conversations Mr Irwine contends that moods belong to a man as much as his intentions and that responsibility even for half-involuntary acts cannot therefore be evaded. Adam's mood before the trial is a desire to see Arthur exposed: 'it's right people should know . . . it was a fine gentleman made love to her,' he insists. '. . . You'll be doing her a hurt by sparing him' (ch. 40), an argument which Mr Irwine admits is sound, but which is conveniently forgotten. Instead attention focusses on the 'evil consequences that may lie folded in Adam's presumptuous . . . desire to punish' Arthur (ch. 41). Such a concern with Adam's moral development is both intrusive and illogical; for if 'our highest thoughts and our best deeds are all given to us' (ch. 10), why not our worst? Besides, it is emotionally and morally inappropriate to concentrate the reader's attention on possible developments in Adam's future moral life when the woman he hoped to marry is in danger of being hanged.

Later, however, the theme acquires greater appropriateness. Adam first feels something of the tragic force of consequential moral logic, when he declares in a rather wordy speech, '*it can never be undone*' (ch. 41) on the eve of the trial. With considerably greater effect the debate on this subject is resumed with the guilty Arthur at the end of the fifth book and the dignity both men achieve in Arthur's spelling out the final lesson to Adam is unexpectedly moving, especially as the presence of Hetty in their thoughts reinforces the idea of deeds which cannot be undone as no mere discussion could. Adam's wound seems sufficiently deep and permanent to give his cry, that no one pitied her enough, especial force, and Arthur's taking out her handkerchief as soon as he is alone confronts us with a painfully tangible sign of man's terrible helplessness in the face of the past.

However, the fact, already noted, that this theme is worked out without any reference to specifically religious issues cannot be ignored, especially since the Hayslope world is no less divorced from religion, at least in a doctrinal sense. This makes all the more troublesome Dinah Morris's overtly Methodist interventions in the action, especially as George Eliot clearly regards Dinah as a centrally significant figure in the novel's teaching taken as a whole. This, admittedly, has been questioned. John Goode, for example, believes that Dinah ought not to be regarded as 'George Eliot's tribute to Feuerbach, the higher nature who sublimates her love of human beings through Methodism',[20] and that her dreaming is represented as 'a limited response to reality'.[21] But as an anomalous woman preacher, uncritically dramatizing basic Protestant theology as Wesley did in 'the Scriptural way, the Methodist way, the true way',[22] Dinah delineates for George Eliot a complex and very specific form of Christianity, the individual essence of which has to be both interpreted and valued. Attention focusses not on Dinah's limitations, therefore, but on the truths latent in her dreams.

The organization of the opening chapters emphasizes these concerns. The conversation in Burge's shop takes us into a barely rememberable past when Methodism and much else were still in process of formation. The real nature of early Methodism and its ultimate destiny are consequently a mystery to the characters as they are in different ways to the novel's readers. Valentine Cunningham, for example, has shown that the attitude towards dissent in mid-Victorian fiction was consistently negative.[23] George Eliot evidently expected her readers to have the usual reservations about Dinah's religion, with even the non-conformists among them being embarrassed by its possibly subversive elements. Seth Bede's function in the first chapter is thus essentially reassuring. Socially he is harmless and he is also decently pious. For similar reasons the novel's potentially most embarrassing scene, in which the heroine preaches a sermon, is largely presented through the judicious if slightly complacent eyes of the gentleman passing by on horseback. His position, like Mr Irwine's later, is that of an educated, neutral observer, and his failure to react with alarm is meant to put us at our ease.

But these protective tactics which so largely determine the presentation of Dinah only increase the need for an explanation or interpretation of Methodism which is consistent with the author's atheism. A reply to those who objected to this anomaly (when it became publicly known) was of course readily available to George Eliot in Feuerbach's assertion that 'he alone is the true atheist to whom the predicates of the Divine Being, – for example, love, wisdom, justice, – are nothing'.[24] Dinah's speeches, after the sermon, frequently avail themselves of the possibilities afforded by this claim. She assures the love-hungry Seth, for example, that 'we've nothing to do but to obey and to trust' (ch. 3); what is to be obeyed and who is to be trusted are left unstated. The carefully uncompleted sentence, however, is at best only an expedient, Feuerbach's divine predicates require a subject in which to inhere. *Adam Bede* is written to make that subject manifest.

The carefully developed contrast between Dinah and Hetty is largely organized to facilitate this epiphany. Hetty, we are told, is one of those 'cunningly-fashioned instruments called human souls [which] have only a very limited range of music' (ch. 9); even in her direct agony, she is entirely uninfluenced 'either by religious fears or religious hopes' (ch. 37). In fact her mental life is barely above that of an intelligent animal. As Goode notes, a number of characters in *Adam Bede* are accorded this semi-human status, Lisbeth Bede and Bartle Massey's labourers among them. Assumptions about an unbroken psychological continuum between 'animal' and 'human' states were common among evolutionists like Spencer and Lewes. Lewes was to maintain, for instance, that 'the savage has by no means so great an intellectual superiority over the ape as the highly

cultured modern has over the savage'.²⁵ George Eliot's account of
Hetty, however, is in one respect unusual. Hetty is pathologically
deficient in that instinctive sympathy with the world which Positivists associated with the fetishism of primitive experience. The
orphan of feckless parents, she is coolly indifferent to the Poysers
who give her a home. Her sole interest is 'the pleasing reflection of
herself in . . . polished surfaces' (ch. 6). Towards Adam she feels
only a sense of power in his devotion, and she is strong-willed
simply out of fear of ridicule. Even the images describing her beauty
emphasize her deficiencies: she is 'kitten-like', with the 'false air of
innocence . . . of a young star-browed calf' (ch. 7). In other words,
she is virtually psychopathic. For that very reason, however, she is
of particular interest to the Feuerbachian student of religion.

What she represents becomes clear in the 15th chapter, where
she is described making a little altar of her looking-glass and
worshipping her own image. Religion, Feuerbach wrote, is 'the
solemn unveiling of a man's hidden treasures . . . the open confession of his love-secrets'.²⁶ This literally is what Hetty does. However, having nothing divine in her nature, she worships only surfaces,
appearance, possessions. She is indeed a true atheist. Dinah,
however, as a true Methodist, eschews ritual. Closing her eyes, she
is 'enclosed by the Divine Presence' by 'a Love and Sympathy
deeper and more tender than was breathed by earth and sky'.
Without knowing it, and so without egoism, she makes her own
interior resources objective and divine; she herself is the distinctively
Methodist alternative for a vanished deity.

This accounts for one of George Eliot's most distinctive rhetorical
tactics. When she describes 'a Love and Sympathy deeper and more
tender than was breathed from the earth and sky', for example, she
merges Comtist and Methodist perspectives (by an unobtrusive use
of the indefinite article and a reverential capitalization of abstrac-
tions) in a way which effectively conceals the differences between
her orthodox readers and herself. Crabb Robinson complained that
such procedures destroyed 'all comfortable notions of right and
wrong, true and false'.²⁷ However, a reply to such objections is
written into the novel itself. The love of 'woman or child, or art or
music,' George Eliot maintains, is finally indistinguishable from
religious feeling; 'autumn sunsets, or pillared vistas, or calm majestic
statues, or Beethoven symphonies' lead emotion 'beyond its object'
to a 'sense of divine mystery' (ch. 3). The conscious objects of
sublime feeling – a woman, a symphony, a god – are only different
ways of entering a level of mind where distinctions break down and
altruistic impulses are given life.

On this basis she can explain another anomaly – how a nature as rich in promise as Adam's can be attracted by one as empty and morally frivolous as Hetty's. To Arthur Hetty is an exciting temptation. To Adam she is a religious experience, and like Dinah's talent for prayer, Adam's love is more important than its object:

> There are faces which nature charges with a meaning and pathos
> not belonging to the single human soul that flutters beneath them,
> but speaking the joys and sorrows of foregone generations . . .
> just as a national language may be instinct with poetry unfelt by
> lips that use it. (ch. 26)

Hetty's beauty is thus genetically a product, not of human sexuality, but of human morality. Adam's obsession with it is thus directly comparable with being 'wrought on by exquisite music' (ch. 3). These ideas were by no means original. A number of contemporary writers sought to show connexions between the aesthetic and moral emotions;[28] reliance on the inheritability of acquired characters was if anything even more commonplace. It is by inheritance and temperament, therefore, rather than by grace and revelation, that Adam and Dinah have access to authentic religious experience.

In contrast, though no less fully in accordance with text-book principle, Arthur and Hetty are repeatedly presented in terms of triviality and lack of depth. Arthur prefers *The Beggar's Opera* and 'The Ancient Mariner' to Wordsworth's contributions to *Lyrical Ballads*. Even when he addresses Hetty tenderly, it is only 'as if she were a bright-eyed spaniel with a thorn in her foot' (ch. 13). Arthur and Hetty's function, however, is not simply to represent the moral and religious negation of all that is positively embodied in Adam and Dinah. In the development of the novel's ethical perspectives, Arthur, as we have seen, becomes a moral man, briefly and touchingly Adam's mentor. In the development of its religious perspectives Hetty becomes something no less important. The process begins with the account of her wanderings at the end of the second volume, when Hetty is for the first time described in the strong clear prose of George Eliot's best manner. The next two chapters were written 'more rapidly than the rest of the book, and . . . left without the slightest alteration on the first draught'.[29] The imagery, however, retains its tough, theoretical base: Hetty is still placed at the lowest – most atheistical – level of sensitivity. On the other hand the images are no longer condemnatory. On the road to Windsor, Hetty finds courage to speak to a sour-looking waggoner because his shivering spaniel has 'some fellowship with her' (ch. 36). This tiny, fetishistic enlargement of her emotional life is ironically yet gently combined with a deft reminder of the shallow tenderness of Arthur's talking to her as if she were herself a spaniel. Now, however, the small-animal imagery invites sympathy as well as judgment. Later when Hetty contemplates suicide by another dark pool, her gradual return to life is triggered by 'the rapid motion of some living creature – perhaps a fieldmouse' (ch. 37) – rushing through the grass. Physically and psychologically 'out of all human reach' she is hardly more than a wild, isolated living thing without species or identity. She may kiss her arms 'with the passionate love of life', but the distinctively human ability to think and feel as a member of a community is lost to her; she can see 'nothing in this wide world but the little history of her own pleasure and pains'. The tough ethical and conceptual framework within which she is judged is the same as it has always been, but she is no longer the 'little vessel without ballast tossed about on a stormy sea' (ch. 31) of earlier prettified descriptions. On her journey the account we are given of her 'narrow heart and narrow thoughts' (ch. 37) becomes impersonal and diagnostic. We accept that she really does cling to life only as the 'hunted wounded brute clings to it'; brutalization is a comprehensible effect, and thereafter an inevitable cause of her exclusion from society. Paradoxically, one consequence of this exclusion is to make it apparent in a sense for the first time that Hetty really does belong to the universe, and that she has to be accounted for if the universe is to be adequately understood.

By an adroit piece of narrative strategy, the novel delays this necessary placing of Hetty as long as possible. Thus we are denied all contact with her for the seven chapters following the account of her journey. Even at the trial she is impenetrably remote. This relentless imprisonment places her firmly at the moral centre of the novel. She, and no one else, has become the psychological and ethical mystery which the reader has to comprehend. This is why Adam has also to be taken seriously at this point in the very role in which he is generally thought to be least satisfactory, that of Hetty's lover. His practical ineffectiveness for so much of the narrative is undoubtedly irritating, yet at this point it wins respect. In this Bartle Massey plays an important part, with his provocative assertion that 'it's stuff and nonsense for the innocent to care about [Hetty] being hanged' (ch. 40). Only Adam, it seems, is sufficiently appalled by the outrage that is about to be enacted on Hetty's body. Yet his role is 't' have to sit still, and know it, and do nothing' (ch. 46). The inattention of all the other characters to the main issue, and his own helplessness in the face of their indifference, make him finally acceptable to the reader. His ineffectiveness is now functional; it is no longer dressed up as manly activity. As he tells Arthur later, 'I felt as if nobody pitied her enough – her suffering cut into me so' (ch. 48). Only our feeling after the 37th chapter, that perhaps not even George Eliot's pity for Hetty is sufficient, could transform the priggish, idealized workman of the first volume into the hero of the third.

It is not through Adam's agency, however, but Dinah's, the embodiment of a specific religious belief, that the narrative finally penetrates the mystery Hetty has come to represent. Her intervention in its closing stages, as the device of the reappearance of the horse-rider makes clear, constitutes the ultimate religious revelation towards which the entire narrative has been moving. For Feuerbach, the essence of religion was 'the immediate, involuntary, unconscious contemplation of the human nature as another, a distinct nature'.[30] Comte wanted to formalize this religious encounter with human nature, to make, for example, the 'mother, the wife, the daughter'[31] objects of systematic contemplative prayer. According to the latter principle, however, Dinah is not just the one who prays, but herself a proper object of worship. Lisbeth Bede significantly mistakes her for an angel, and Seth sings hymns to her. Iconographically she is in fact virtually divine. She remembers thinking as a small child that Wesley had come down from heaven, 'like the picture in the Bible' (ch. 2); the images of Christ and Wesley then merge – 'Jesus Christ really did come down from heaven, as I thought Mr Wesley did' – and finally she herself stands against the sunset just as Wesley describes himself as doing in Southey's *Life*.[32] The preachers have become indistinguishable from each other and from the gospel that they preach. (E.H. Corbould's painting of the scene shows Dinah in an appropriately Christ-like pose.) Later Dinah confesses that she would like to bear 'all the anguish of the children of men . . . as if I were sharing the Redeemer's cross' (ch. 30), and as if she were not a child of man herself. This goes a little further than Adam's suggestion that 'she must look as if she'd come straight from heaven, like th' angels in the desert' (ch. 30), but it matches the last glimpse we are given of her, preaching and holding a child on her knee. It may also explain George Eliot's description of her as a resuscitated corpse. She is, in effect, the Christ of the Resurrection, the embodiment of *humanity's* capacity to save, that is to incorporate into its own larger life even as lost and empty a thing as Hetty Sorrel.

Whatever reservations one may have about this evaluation of Dinah – and these I shall discuss later – there can be none, I think, about what George Eliot achieves when this narrative development is seen from Hetty's point of view. Just as the narrative in the first

book circles round Hetty's physical presence, so after her imprisonment there is a similar indirect circuitous approach to her mind. Her
appearance in court hardly lessens our sense of her remoteness. She
is no more than a 'white image' (ch. 42) totally unresponsive except
to her uncle's name. The evidence gives no clue to her inner life and
yet is tantalizingly suggestive. Formerly patronizing words and
images have become disturbingly appropriate: 'hard immovability
and obstinate silence' no longer suggest an intolerant misreading of
adolescent moodiness, but rather scrupulous and sensitive observation. Clearly the truth about her cannot be uncovered by a legal
process. The community cannot understand her because she is
outside the community.

This situation is resolved, however, when Hetty steps forward
and is clasped by Dinah. As with Caterina in 'Mr Gilfil's Love-
story', a human being to cling to has become Hetty's greatest need.
The embrace is therefore impersonal – it simply restores her to
human society by making it possible for her to confess. The chief
fact which this confession reveals is that the infanticide was a trivial
event, the action of an instinctively subnormal girl who never liked
holding her niece and was incapable of 'movements of maternal
affection' (ch. 43) towards her own baby. A major part of the
meaning of the third volume is lost if the modern reader tries to
soften Hetty's crime by interpreting it in the light of a later
psychology. Throughout her agony Hetty was dominated simply by
shame and the desire for comfort. She may have had a brief,
fetishistic sense that the world was alive and reproaching her, and a
weak if painful stirring of maternal instinct, but her interior
paralysis is the effect largely of mental emptiness. The horror of this
situation is that a barely human creature, who stares at Dinah 'like
an animal that gazes and gazes, and keeps aloof', is intelligent
enough to know that she is going to be hanged.

These two ideas, Hetty's minimal humanity and her impending
death, are equally necessary in bringing one of the novel's most
important insights into focus. In the last chapter of the second
volume, George Eliot rather portentously asks why 'Man's religion
has so much sorrow in it?' – and makes the thoroughly Feuerbachian
assumption that liturgy and religious iconography are communal
acts of self-awareness and self-evaluation. It follows from this that,
as Feuerbach put it, not only 'the suffering of love, the power of
sacrificing self for the good of others', but 'suffering as such', must
enter into religious experience.[3] Hetty is empty of more important
feeling and therefore her experience is indeed suffering as such.
Consequently her agony confronts us with the authentically reli-

gious value of the crudest, most rudimentary human feeling. As Feuerbach put it: 'It needs only that the ordinary course of things be interrupted in order to vindicate to common things an uncommon significance, *to life, as such, a religious import*'.[34] Hetty is barely human, but her impending death (a brutal interruption in the ordinary course of things if ever there was one) gives her life an extraordinary vividness, an uncommon significance. This delicate, pretty girl, who has and is nothing, thus rouses in us a tragic sense of mystery and value. Adam's feeling that 'his brain would burst at the anguish of meeting [her] eyes' (ch. 46) truly expresses the intensity of the response which her situation evokes.

Hetty's standing in the third volume is thus the reverse of her standing in the first two. With her narrow, shallow, hard interior life, she stood originally for the true atheism to which faith in God or lack of it was irrelevant. She, not a universe without a first cause, was the vacuum created by irreligion. Now, however, the relentless attention given to her inner emptiness has turned her into a religious experience in her own right. The focus of religious attention, having ceased to be God, ceases also, at the climax of the novel, to be the divine potentialities of supremely gifted individuals and becomes, not an abstract phrase like 'suffering as such', but a frightened, stupid, pretty girl who is going to be hanged for killing her baby. Hetty, not Dinah, becomes for a time the novel's *alter Christus*.

The force of this idea is so impressive that it also transforms our sense of the issues which Adam and Mr Irwine were discussing on the eve of the trial, for the doctrine of consequences acquires adequate structural and moral force only in the light of Hetty's confession. Indeed Hetty has to be reprieved in order to make room for this idea. Her death at this stage would have made consideration of broader issues very difficult; but by barely saving her life, George Eliot can more freely express her unyieldingly stern vision of the moral order in the last brilliantly staged encounter between Arthur and Adam in the wood. Thus as a matter of logical and aesthetic necessity, the two great lessons of the novel, the authentically religious value it discovers in the most primitive human experience, and the terrible notions of duty which its doctrine of consequences gravely imposes on the human spirit come finally and movingly together.

In many ways *Adam Bede* is a clumsier, more laboured work than *Scenes of Clerical Life*. Nevertheless, in the act of writing what was originally planned merely as the fourth of the *Scenes*, George Eliot apparently discovered that fiction of the kind which suited her talent was not only admirably adapted to making a fuller statement of her basic convictions than she had hitherto thought possible, but that it could also modify, develop and enrich them. *Scenes of Clerical Life* is on the one hand an attempt to understand and evaluate the religious life of the English provinces in the last 30 years of the eighteenth century and the first 35 of the nineteenth, on the other to extend the reader's moral awareness and sympathy. *Adam Bede*, however, tries to be more than informative and moral. It offers the reader an enlargement of his *religious* consciousness, comparable in its way with the reading of Thomas à Kempis which enlarges Maggie Tulliver's consciousness in *The Mill on the Floss*. With this new sense of the didactic potentiality of her fiction, George Eliot apparently felt able to broaden the range of her teaching in her subsequent novels. But teaching and learning in the major fiction always involves more than intellectual assimilation and assent, since both are experiential, all experience is potentially religious, and religion is of its nature founded in a sense of mystery and uncertainty and yet strengthened, like Dolly Winthrop's, by a capacity to accept limitation and ignorance without loss of faith in oneself or others. Thus while George Eliot's major fictions are all firmly based on precisely understood and often clearly articulated opinions, they are never – like Harriet Martineau's, for example – merely opinionated.

2 Heredity and psychology

THE Associationist psychology of which Bain and Lewes were leading proponents was the culminating achievement of an intellectual tradition dating at least from Locke's rejection of the theory of innate ideas and his insistence that the mind, originally a *tabula rasa*, becomes a storehouse of simple ideas derived from either sense or introspection which associate together according to specifiable laws of mind to form complex ideas which in turn become objects of knowledge and discourse. By the time George Eliot began writing, descriptions of those laws had become diverse and complex. Romantic emphasis on the importance of the emotions, Lamarckian notions about the inheritance of acquired characters, speculation about the mind-body relation, and analogies drawn from chemistry and biology had considerably enriched Associationist speculation. An organicist view of mind had developed which was by no means invariably characterized by the precision and common sense which Locke had believed he was introducing into the study of mental phenomena.

George Eliot herself provides numerous instances of this indiscipline. We 'think it an immense mistake,' she writes in an early essay, 'to maintain there is no sex in literature'. Rational thought, she admits, is sexless, but 'in art and literature . . . every fibre of the nature is engaged', and since the maternal emotions of women and their 'comparative physical weakness' both introduce 'a distinctively feminine condition into the wondrous chemistry of the affections', women have something 'specific to contribute' to the fine arts in general.[1] However, granted 'the small brain and vivacious temperament' of the French, as against 'the larger brain and slower temperament of the English and Germans . . . the *physique* of a woman may suffice for the substratum of a superior Gallic mind, but is too thin a soil for a superior Teutonic one'.[2] Later, reviewing an essay on Chatterton by David Masson, she accepts his suggestion that the Church of St Mary Redcliffe may have become a 'fetish' for Chatterton because his ancestors had been sextons there, and could thus have 'acquired in gradually increasing mass, a store of antique associations, to be transmitted as a fatal heritage' to the young poet.[3] As a final example one may cite her attempts to explain Hetty Sorrel in *Adam Bede*. Hetty's parents, we are told, were feckless and therefore Hetty is so too, but as we noted earlier, they also transmitted to her a beauty of face and form which was apparently a genetically inheritable manifestation of noble and pure lives lived by some of her more remote ancestors.

George Eliot's leading ideas on these matters are clear. She perceives a strong and knowable relation between mind and body. She therefore regards men and women as being differently constituted mentally, just as they are physically. She also thinks of the accumulating 'associations' of idea and feeling which are transmittable from one generation to another as a process which among other things accounts for national and racial characteristics. How these ideas influence her early fiction can be seen in the characterization of Caterina in 'Mr Gilfil's Love-story'. Caterina is Italian and therefore passionate, musical and therefore physically as well as emotionally sensitive; she is also tiny in her *physique* as well as feminine, and she is therefore small-brained; and all these factors make her liable to breakdown under the pressure of strong feeling. In general Associationist speculation seems to have been particularly useful to George Eliot whenever she wished to depict mental disorders of one kind or another.

Breakdown and disorder take many forms in her fiction, but they are invariably a sign of a character's inadequate relationship with society. Spencer's principle of correspondence, together with Lewes's repeated emphasis on 'the social medium' and Comte's definition of life as 'a continuous and close adjustment to internal spontaneity with external fatality',[4] shows why this should be so. They all suggest that species and even identity derive part of their essential nature from the environment, and that the external fatality to which man, in particular, must adjust in order literally to be a man, is the human community. This accounts for the 'inhumanity' of a cold-hearted careerest like Tito Milema in *Romola*. His Greek origins are not important. As a child-in-exile, however, he has no community to internalize; his stock of moral associations is therefore limited – hence his capacity for the special kind of corruption which his history unfolds. 'Conscience', wrote Bain, '. . . is an ideal resemblance of public authority',[5] not 'a primitive and independent faculty of the mind', but an imitation within ourselves of 'the government without us'.[6] Tito is not entirely lacking on the socially derived moral resource of shame, a 'reflex which will exist even in the absence of sympathetic impulses' (ch. 9), but the model in his case is not specific, not local enough. His moral life is traditionless; he has no personal memories 'of self-conquest and perfect faithfulness' (ch. 39), and he is indifferent 'to the ideas [and] prejudices of the men' amongst whom he moves.

Other forms of severance from the social medium, morally less drastic than Tito's, are just as susceptible to Associationist explanation. An intense intellectual life desocializes the mind of Romola's father, for example. The understanding, Feuerbach writes, contemplates an insect 'with as much enthusiasm as the image of God – man'.[7] A similar idea lies behind Comte's belief that intellectual pursuits often lead to 'hardness and pride' and 'an exaggerated sense of individuality, which effaces and perverts our conception of the universal connection of the whole human race'.[8] This in essence is the complaint Dino makes against his father. Such judgments on the scholarly mentality were virtual commonplaces in the mid-Victorian period. Bardi's intense preoccupation with his reputation, his symbolic blindness, and his collector's mania in effect constitute a text-book case of associative malformation which Bain would have had no difficulty in recognizing:

> Along with the original emotion of knowledge, there may spring up an associated or acquired emotion towards the machinery and operations of the individual mind whereby the search is maintained. This is not more wonderful than the factitious feeling towards books in general that grows up in the mind of the student, or towards money in the miser.[9]

Baldassare (the foster-father whom Tito abandons to his fate) represents a third kind of mental disintegration in *Romola*. He experiences not a distorted and distorting formation of associated ideas in the form of habitual responses like Bardi (though he too is a scholar), but a pathological disorder of the brain by which the associative processes are disrupted physically. The illness 'from which he had risen with body and mind shattered' (ch. 30) was evidently a stroke. He just manages to keep in touch with external reality, however, and is therefore not mad in a technical sense, Comte's definition of insanity being precisely a mental state in which the 'reflecting process' overpowers the 'sensations in energy'.[10] (Bain, too, writes of internal ideas obliterating present sense-experience, the 'climax of [this] state [being] actual insanity';[11] and Lewes was to get into a slightly embarrassing tangle when he analysed Dickens's mental powers in precisely these terms.)[12] By these criteria, Baldassare is technically sane but he is also very vulnerable in terms no less psychologically specific. Amnesia, disorientation in a strange city, and Tito's rejection combine to make him highly excited. Such states were said by Bain to produce 'an almost uncontrollable discharge of energy and power, as if the nerve centres were rendered incontinent and profuse by some temporary alteration in their nature . . . Every sensible impression made during this state', he suggests, 'causes a more than average effect'.[13] Suggestibility of this kind even makes it possible for an idea

> to act itself out in opposition to . . . those interests that the will should side with – the deliverance from pain and the furtherance of pleasures. This forcible possession is commonly the conse-quence of *great excitement* accompanying an idea, of its taking a more than usual hold on the mind, whereby it does not pass away with the intellectual currents, but remains and predominates over every other thought pressing for admittance.[14]

In Baldassare's case, the intellectual currents have anyway virtually dried up; he is already excited when he enters the Duomo; and Savonarola is a supremely effective preacher. The result is Baldass-are's obsession with the theme of Savonarola's sermon – retributive justice. In Bain's terms, he is 'laid hold of, through a sort of infatuation, by a feeling that in no way contributes to [his] happiness . . . [an] image of a person [he] hate[s] . . . a certain train of ideas' which goads him 'on to a pursuit'.[15] Bain describes these as normal processes of mind, though obviously dangerous ones. Baldassare's brief return to normality takes the form of his remembering Greek. As for so many of George Eliot's characters, memories – 'the fine fibres of association' (ch. 38) – are human life itself. Thus Baldass-are's mental processes become a symbol of how the past can be concealed but never effaced, and a carefully wrought, apparently scientifically defensible illustration of some grounds for that belief.

The fourth and most significant instance of the breakdown of appropriate associative processes in *Romola* is that of Savonarola himself. In his case the problem arises, not from deficiency, malformation or trauma in his mental life, but its excessive intensity, at once corporeal and spiritual. The description of his hands makes this clear: 'in their exquisite delicacy', we are told, they 'seemed transfigured from an animal organ for grasping into vehicles of sensibility too acute to need any gross contact' (ch. 62). We are certainly left in no doubt about the physical basis of his mind as he anticipates the fire 'with shuddering vibrations to the extremities of his sensitive fingers' (ch. 64). Moreover, the fact that his thoughts, feelings and choices are thus grounded in an especially sensitive and tautly nervous body apparently accounts for his tendency to see visions. The real danger in Savonarola's case, however, is his wilfulness. Bain has some interesting observations on fanaticism such as Savonarola exhibits:

> If we are strongly bent upon securing some one special end [he writes] . . . the proper course is . . . to kindle a blaze of excitement and fury which over-rides all comparisons and annihilates all counter motives. This is the proceeding of a Peter the Hermit, a Daniel O'Connell . . . As regards the work to be done, nothing can be more effectual; as regards the happiness of the agent, the immolation is often remorseless.[16]

The vivid descriptions of Savonarola's preaching are often influenced by such ideas. 'God', Feuerbach wrote, '. . . is essentially an object of the heart's necessity, not the mind's freedom'.[17] As a God-intoxicated man, Savonarola wilfully allows his mind to become a prisoner of the heart, and even if this service of the heart's necessity also commands George Eliot's respect, in the end she allows him to disappear enigmatically into defeat, imprisonment and an ignominious death.

As well as providing George Eliot with models of mental breakdown, however, Associationism also provided her with models of mental restoration. Both are strikingly in evidence in *Silas Marner*. This may seem surprising in a work which by George Eliot's own account came to her first 'as a sort of legendary tale'.[18] However, she resisted the temptation to write it in verse, and the very act of working it up in prose seems to have encouraged her to develop her material in carefully considered naturalistic terms. At one level these naturalistic perspectives are those of common sense. After Silas's first attack of catalepsy, for example, we are assured that he returns at once to perfect normality, even though a 'less truthful man than he might have been tempted into the subsequent creation of a vision in the form of resurgent memory [and] a less sane man might have believed in such a creation' (ch. 1). Again, years later, though he continues to search for his stolen gold, even after he has seen plainly enough that it has gone, we are nonetheless assured that he is not mad, since his blind hope is still 'capable of being dissipated by the external fact' (ch. 5). As we have seen, both these apparently straightforward assertions about his sanity are in fact based on technically specific text-book definitions of madness.

The same tactics are employed over the question of Silas's obsessive behaviour. His compulsive weaving, for example, is compared with the way in which solitary prisoners mark 'the moments by straight strokes of a certain length on the wall', and with the actions of 'wiser men . . . cut off from faith and love', who sink themselves in 'some erudite research, some ingenious project or some well-knit theory' (ch. 2). Similar confusions of means and ends appear in works already quoted by Bain and others to explain manias of all kinds. Men like Silas Marner and Bardo Bardi were repeatedly cited in explanation of each other's associative processes by George Eliot's contemporaries as well as by herself.

If hoarding and weaving save Silas's sanity by creating coherent networks of substitute associations for those he loses through his betrayal in Lantern Yard and the superstitious rejection of his strangeness by the people of Raveloe, his situation remains perilous. He has lost, after all, that 'sense of unity between his past and present life' (ch. 2) which George Eliot valued so highly. She thought of the past being carried into the present internally as an organic accumulation of inherited and remembered emotions and externally in the traditions of society; and the rupturing of both kinds of association, though it might not induce madness, certainly cuts the individual adrift from the human condition in its fullness. Silas's cry, 'there is no just God that governs the earth righteously' (ch. 1), makes him, in effect, a Feuerbachian atheist; to lose one's sense of godhead is to lose one's sense of humanity as well. Dehumanization is thus no mere metaphor for George Eliot. Its possibility was written into contemporary evolutionary theory. The description of Silas's life being reduced 'to the unquestioning activity of a spinning insect' (ch. 2) is certainly less metaphorical than it appears. Like Hetty, he ceases almost biologically to be human. The literal transformation of godless and therefore isolated man into a beast is taken as far as science and prose will allow it to be.

This dehumanization is primarily a matter of the feelings since incorporation into humanity is grounded in sympathy. For the Associationist, however, such feelings cannot be isolated from sensation, and consequently Silas is unmanned corporeally as well as emotionally, his lack of a sympathetic life being reinforced by the physical harshness of his existence and in particular by the absence of those sensations of warmth, softness and sweetness which Bain related to tenderness and to the 'emotions of love and beauty'.[19] Like Hetty's his life is seen 'hardening and narrowing itself' into what may be called a syndrome of dehumanization. George Eliot uses figurative language, but she is also strictly diagnostic:

> Strangely Marner's face and figure shrank and bent themselves
> into a constant mechanical relation to the objects of his life, so
> that he produced the same sort of impression as a handle or a
> crooked tube, which has no meaning standing apart. The promin-
> ent eyes that used to look trusting and dreamy, now looked as if
> they had been made to see only one kind of thing that was very
> small, like a tiny grain, for which they hunted everywhere: and
> he was so withered and yellow, that, though he was not yet forty,
> the children always called him 'Old Master Marner' (ch. 2).

His soul and body wither because, with only things and not people
to feel for and to touch, their functions are seriously diminished. He
is literally and physically no longer a man, but an organism for
weaving and hoarding, 'his muscles moving with such even repetition that their pause seemed almost as much a constraint as the
holding of his breath'. One gets a similar sense of a mind and body
being chemically fused with an 'external fatality' when the gold
gathers his 'power of loving together into a hard isolation like its
own' (ch. 5).

A similar technical precision characterizes the account of Silas's
restoration. Again the elements of a legendary tale are intermixed
with the principles of case-book psychology and Positivist theory.
The contrast between the hardness of Silas's gold coins and the
softness of Eppie's gold hair is a case in point. Seeing and touching
the 'soft yellow rings all over [Eppie's] head' (ch. 12) have a specific
neurological effect on Silas's associative processes: 'fibres that had
never been moved in Raveloe – old quiverings of tenderness' are
aroused at last. The image of Eppie's golden hair has of course a
purely legendary appropriateness, but the magic of Silas's transformations remains the magic of physiological process, and it is this
which keeps the book's moral teaching realistic.

This attention to process is especially evident in the treatment of
'fetishism' in *Silas Marner*. The incident of the broken pot is one
example. The pot is associated with some of the few fresh and clear
sensations in Silas's life, and for this reason he comes to love it as a
'companion', its form having 'an expression for him of willing
helpfulness, and the impress of its handle on his palm [giving] a
satisfaction mingled with that of having the fresh clear water' (ch. 2).
This, and his habit of thinking of his loom and his money as his
'familiars', show that 'the sap of affection was not all gone'. More
importantly, they are clear instances of a childish and so redemptive
impulse towards animism, which the Positivist reader would instantly have recognized. Silas's creative talent for enlivening his little

world during the years of his loneliness in effect prevents his sympathies from becoming atrophied. He comes to share this talent with Eppie, who, as Dolly Winthrop correctly prophesies, takes great pleasure in playing with bits of red rag and chattering 'to 'em as if they was alive' (ch. 14). Together Silas and Eppie create 'fibres' of sympathy and love between themselves and the world, 'from men and women with parental looks and tones, to the red lady-birds and the round pebbles'. In their imagination and affections, physical things become alive, just as Comte believed they should even in the imagination and affectations of civilized adults. These distinctively Comtist ideas are explicitly defended in the text. Of Silas's preservation of the hearth by which he found Eppie, George Eliot writes with full-toned assurance: 'The gods of the hearth exist for us still; and let all new faith be tolerant of that fetishism, lest it bruise its own roots' (ch. 16). *Silas Marner* is the work of a thorough-going Positivist.

The fullest deployment of contemporary ideas on the subjects of heredity and psychology in George Eliot's novels, however, is to be found in *The Mill on the Floss*. Even Henry James welcomed the 'attempt to classify the Dodsons socially in a scientific manner'.[20] This attempt can be documented fairly precisely. Thus the family's 'inalienable habit of saving, as an end in itself' (Bk I, ch. 12) alludes to the body of theoretical discussion about states such as miserliness which we have already considered in the cases of Silas and Bardi. The prejudices of Maggie's maternal aunts about the bleaching of linen rather than its use, about curing rather than eating ham, and about bequeathing rather than enjoying their fortunes, similarly exemplify the tendency of ideas and feelings associated with a particular end to become ends in themselves and as such to be transmitted to succeeding generations. The Dodsons, in other words, illustrate a general, inheritable tendency in human nature which in the English middle classes takes the particular form of identifying wealth with respectability. Spencer described this tendency as 'growing with their growth, and strengthening with their strength' until it 'becomes at last almost what we may call an organic conviction'.[21] Among the Dodsons' other organic convictions is a strong sense of that family pride which Comte described as 'aggregate selfishness',[22] and which he regarded as a source of the great practical strength of bourgeois domesticity. However, practical success of the kind which the Dodsons exemplify depended, in his view, far more on what he called 'character' than on 'intellect or affection' – 'poverty of thought and feeling' being, he felt, in many cases pre-requisites of worldly success.[23]

But George Eliot's thinking about heredity and psychology is most clearly in evidence not in her semi-facetious descriptions of the Dodsons but in her treatment of Tom and Maggie Tulliver. The account of their childhood, adolescence, and young adulthood is comprehensively influenced by the thought of Comte, Bain and Spencer. Tom, for example, is presented as the physical and mental inheritor of a store of associations acquired in gradually increasing mass by his mother's family. 'Character' in precisely Comte's sense is his most striking Dodson quality. His 'wonderful, instinctive discernment of what would turn to his advantage' (Bk I, ch. 7), his primitive sense of justice, and his coldness in punishing Maggie point both to the impoverishment of feeling and to the concentration of purpose which Comte regarded as the essential mental equipment of the capitalist and entrepreneur. Thus from a comic representation of the Dodsons as 'characters' we are imperceptibly led through their most impressive representative to a consideration of the psycho-dynamics of Political Economy itself.

Tom's cruelty has a special place in this conception. Gratuitous it may be, but it is not a sign of viciousness. Like most other boys Tom has to pass through what Spencer called 'that phase of character exhibited by the barbarous race from which he is descended'.[24] In accordance with this principle the young Tom has one of those 'average . . . physiognomies' which nature turns out 'by the gross' (Bk I, ch. 5), and which is in such marked contrast to the heavy-browed distinction of his features as a man; but then a 'high degree of individualization in features and expression', as George Eliot herself had suggested, necessarily occurs late in the growth of men and nations alike.[25] Spencer agreed,[26] and argued that in this respect mental and physical development were similar: a boy's instincts and talents were properly those of a practical-minded, self-centred savage whose work and pleasures were hunting and fighting; in both individuals and the race, however, this practical activity eventually became more rational. The transition from the immature Tom Tulliver killing cats and playing with Mr Poulter's sword to the earnest apprentice of his uncle Deane typifies in its modest, English way the transition from militarism to industrialism which was the basis of Comte's historical optimism.[27] The core of soundness which George Eliot discovers in the Dodson ethos is a real if limited victory over an inhuman past.

Tom's cruelty, however, is not rationalized out of existence. It connects, as Lewes was later to observe in an interesting comparison of the cruelties practised by British 'roughs', American Indians, and Tom himself, with his ruling and most historically resonant passion,

love of power.[28] Love of power was a key Associationist concept.
'Intolerance has its firmest root in the passion for the exercise of
power', Bain wrote. 'It is not enough', he pointed out, 'that people
form opinions and contract likings or aversions . . . they must also
impose the same line of conduct upon all around them'. Love of
power, he suggested, also shows itself 'in the exercise of ascetic
self-restraint', in which those committed to self-denial frequently
require 'the concurrence of everyone else'. Its opposite is the
response of tenderness. Bain argued, for example, that love of power
is developed in active temperaments while 'tender emotion allies
itself to repose'.[29] He also saw 'the pleasure of power' as a factor in
the urge to inflict pain retributively and so to console 'the wounded
feelings of the agent'; grief, on the other hand, he described as 'a
resort to the assuaging efficacy of the tender emotion'. Tenderness
and love of power, he believed, are aroused by opposite physical
stimuli: tender, passive responses by sensations such as 'agreeable
warmth, balmy odours, soft music and the like',[30] active, power-
seeking responses by volitional or appetitive pleasures which are a
spur to action.

Maggie's temperament is as relevant here as Tom's since the inner
lives of both children correspond in some detail to this polarization
of tenderness and power. However, neither in Bain's work nor in
George Eliot's is the polarity mechanically complete. Self-
complacency, Bain notes, can associate with both.[31] Nevertheless,
Bain's explanation of the two distinct masses of thought and feeling
which constitute love of home or a particular place tellingly corres-
ponds with the quite distinct feelings of attachment to the Mill felt
by Tom and Maggie. Thus Tom bears out Bain's belief that
'Egotistic and selfish emotion diffuses itself over all matters related
to self' and that 'Possessions, office, the fruits of one's labour, the
symbols of rank, are all overgrown with this connexion, and radiate
feelings of self-complacency and importance to the mind'; members
of one's family, Bain adds, 'are objects . . . of affection and egotism
combined'.[32] Maggie, by way of contrast, illustrates his belief that
'Natural Tenderness . . . overflows from sentient beings upon
places and things' and that the 'associations with home, with one's
native spot . . . are made powerful by all the causes that give force to
the contiguous bond'.[33]

An opposition similar to that between tenderness and love of
power in the work of Bain underlies the larger conflict between Tom
and Maggie which arises out of the opposed traditions and personalities of the Dodson and Tulliver families. The Tullivers lack
'character' or 'personality' in the Comtist sense. Typically Aunt

Moss marries for love and fecklessly bears an endless succession of children. And though they are intelligent, the Tullivers are not consecutive or practical in their thinking, and this makes them characteristically ignorant of the ways of the world. Unlike Tom, Mr Tulliver lives on the edges of certainty; one of his earliest remarks in the novel – 'it's puzzling work, talking is' (Bk I, ch. 2) – is unimaginable from his son. But this imprecise sense of causality gives a wider scope to his moral imagination: his decision not to press his brother-in-law for payment is grounded in superstitious concern for the future of his little girl, a talent for moral imagination which Maggie inherits from him. It allows her innate tenderness to flourish, even if, like Mr Tulliver, she is made to suffer for her lack of worldliness. Thoughts, for Maggie, are there to be played with: among the gypsies she fancies herself being rescued by Jack the Giant-killer, Mr Greatheart and St George as well as by her father. Imaginatively and emotionally she is thus what Tom is practically, a savage. This accounts for her fetishism, as a result of which her emotional responsiveness, like Silas Marner's, is kept alive and active even in the absence of a human object: when Tom is away she can kiss her doll oblivious of its emotional inertness. Of course the darker side of her nature is similarly liberated – hence her savagery to the Fetish in the attic – but by and large her animistic thinking is morally enriching: the mill-stones give her 'a dim delicious awe as at the presence of an uncontrollable force' (Bk I, ch. 4); floury spiders rouse her to complex speculations about social life; and pictures and stories make her vividly aware of other people: her concern that Luke should see that he has a duty to his fellow-creatures is an imaginatively felt conviction grounded in primitive animism.

Allusions such as these to evolutionary anthropology turn Maggie and Tom's growing up into a representative process. Their primitive feelings, egoistic savagery and animistic emotionalism are not destroyed but transformed. As Comte put it:

> The development of the individual exhibits to us in little . . . the chief phases of social development. In both cases, the end is to subordinate . . . all our passions to rules imposed by an ever-strengthening intelligence, with the view of identifying the individual more and more with the species.[34]

Though in no way diagrammatic in its approach to this or any other process, the novel also lends support to two other Comtist positions, the centrality of family life in transforming egoism into altruism and, once again, the importance of Submission. Tom's practicality and Maggie's need of love are both explicitly connected with

Submission: 'It is a wonderful subduer', George Eliot notes, 'this need of love – this hunger of the heart – as peremptory as that other hunger by which Nature forces us to submit to the yoke, and change the face of the world'. (Bk I, ch. 5). The Submission which hunger for food enforces issues in practical Dodson perspectives. The Submission arising out of the hunger of the heart is what Maggie must and can learn – 'that knowledge of the irreversible laws within and without her, which, governing the habits, becomes morality, and developing the feelings of submission and dependence, becomes religion' (Bk IV, ch. 3).

George Eliot's treatment of these concepts is convincing and unstrained because the categories on which she relies to illustrate them – Dodson and Tulliver, lover of power and tenderness, altruism and selfishness, the moral and the practical – are notably flexible. In Tom, for instance, there are 'tender fibres that . . . answer to Maggie's fondling' (Bk I, ch. 5) and soften his Dodson stiffness. One feels that a tiny shift in the balance of forces within him might transform his relations with the world. However we may judge the culmination of this effect in the flood, we are prepared for Tom's transformation with tact and urgency.

Similarly subtle is George Eliot's presentation of the most contentious polarity in the novel between Tom's emerging manhood and Maggie's emerging womanhood. The area is a difficult one. Comte's attitude to women is notorious. Maggie, we are told, is 'quite equal to . . . peculiarly masculine studies' (Bk IV, ch. 3), whereas Comte was convinced that women were 'constitutionally in a state of perpetual infancy', their 'more lively moral and physical sensibility' being 'hostile to scientific abstraction and concentration'.[35] Nevertheless, George Eliot accepted his assertion that women had a 'more lively moral and physical sensibility' and were 'superior to men in a spontaneous expansion of sympathy and sociality',[36] or, as Feuerbach put it, that 'Love is . . . essentially feminine'.[37] She seems also to have accepted that the sexes had differing social functions, the relations of a hard, actively practical, outwardly motivated brother with his tender, passively imaginative, passionately motivated sister having for her a greater representativeness than the private and possibly fleeting intensities of love.

Her ideas about maleness and femaleness become especially obvious in her treatment of Philip Wakem's disability, which prevents him from developing the character-building talent for masculine action: forced into passivity, he develops an 'extreme sensitiveness', and even a feminine appearance (Bk II, ch. 3). His reaction to Tom – a 'bitter complacency in the promising stupidity of this well-made active-looking boy' – sensitively defines the mutual misunderstandings to which 'masculine' and 'feminine' tempera-ments are liable. The consequences of these two ways of feeling and acting are carefully stated. Tom's boyish nature, we are told, 'conceals some of [nature's] most rigid, inflexible purposes, some of her most unmodifiable characters' (Bk I, ch. 5), while Maggie reminds Philip of 'the stories about princesses being turned into animals' (Bk II, ch. 5). Both, obviously, are candidates for painful, representative transitions, which is why as children they must be seen as typically boy and girl. This is why Lucy Deane and Bob Jakins are so important in the early chapters. The conspiratorial intimacy of Maggie and Lucy is excellently suggested. Lucy confirms Maggie's authentic young femaleness and highlights her brilliance: far from deviating from the norm she intensifies it. The passages involving Tom and Bob have the same effect, particularly the incident of the pocket-knife. Bob is as cruel as Tom, as 'masculine' in George Eliot's terms, but he is also clumsy and humble. This gives great subtlety to the impression Tom makes as a 'Rhadamanthine personage' with an unusual 'share of boy's justice in him' (Bk I, ch. 6).

George Eliot handles Tom's young masculinity with particular delicacy after he is sent away to the Stellings'. The resulting violation of his boyishness makes him as complex and vulnerable as Maggie. Education was much discussed in George Eliot's circle. She herself believed that a teacher should aim 'less at perfecting specific acquirements than at producing that mental condition which renders acquirements easy, and leads to their useful application'.[38] 'In this free-trade era,' Spencer wrote, '. . . we are learning that there is . . . a natural process of mental evolution [in children] which is not to be disturbed without injury'.[39] Latin grammar forced into Tom's mind by rote violates this fine principle of pedagogic *laissez-faire*. Spencer, in fact, would have allowed Tom to choose his own school-work, not only because he thought 'youthful happiness [to be] . . . in itself a worthy aim',[40] but also because in his judgment 'an appetite for any kind of information implies that the unfolding mind . . . needs it for the purpose of growth.'[41] He would undoubtedly have recognized Tom's ability to tell 'a pointer from a setter . . . [to] predict with accuracy what number of horses were cantering behind him . . . [and to] guess to a fraction how many lengths of his stick it would take to reach across the playground' (Bk II, ch. 1) as legitimate modes of intelligence. But Tom's natural powers, as a boy and as a Dodson, are painfully frustrated at the Stellings'; he even temporarily acquires 'something of the girl's susceptibility', a reaction carefully distinguished from his appropriately manly readiness to look after the Stellings' little girl.

After Tom's return from the Stellings' both children enter the world of adolescence. Maggie's self-education at this period has essentially to do with the solitary religious feelings which her fetishistic and impulsively emotional childhood prepared her for. Thus the fourth book describes her discovery of a higher level of religious sensitivity than had ever been experienced in St Ogg's before. As she approaches womanhood she has to confront in a particularly intense way the 'great problem of the shifting relation between passion and duty' (Bk VII, ch. 2). Under the inspiration of Thomas à Kempis (Comte called Catholicism 'the religion of our adolescence'),[42] she at first hopes to resolve the tensions between passion and duty by abolishing passion, by submitting, in Comte's phrase, to the 'Necessity without us' so that 'the check which it places on the whole of [her] personal desires' can assist 'the spontaneous expansion of [her] sympathetic instincts'.[43] 'Our life', she says, 'is determined for us – and it makes the mind very free when we give up wishing' (Bk V, ch. 1). But Philip rejects this over-simplification: 'we can never give up longing and wishing while we are thoroughly alive,' he says, pointing to a Necessity within us which also demands our submission. The famous struggle between these two points of view conceals, of course, an emotional conflict in which their positions are reversed. In condemning self-repression, Philip unwittingly argues against his own aspirations as a lover, for it is in the very spirit of renunciation which he denounces that Maggie tearfully lowers 'her tall head to kiss [his] pale face that was full of pleading love – like a woman's' (Bk V, ch. 4). After the quarrel with Tom she even feels 'a certain relief' (Bk V, ch. 5) at the end of the relationship. This she attributes to 'the sense of deliverance from concealment', but it is not only that. With Maggie moral and personal issues are never pecisely differentiated.

Tom's entry into adulthood is by contrast almost entirely without mystery or ambiguity. His manliness is normative to the point of being classical. He is like Hector, Tamer of Horses, engaging 'in a dustier, noisier warfare [than Maggie], grappling with more substantial obstacles, and gaining more definite conquests' (Bk V, ch. 2). The boy who delighted in the blinding of Polypheme now embodies that very history which Philip, the detached intellectual, can only know from books. For if Tom's masculinity is rooted in a savage past, he has to face life in a modern St Ogg's. His sense of the male role has to mature from his boyish idealization of his father as 'a substantial man . . . who used to go hunting when he was younger'

(Bk II, ch. 1) into an essentially modern recognition that work in a warehouse is the truly 'manly business' (Bk III, ch. 5). Business, however, gives him scope for the mixed motives of his historically representative manliness. His strong will successfully binds together 'integrity . . . pride . . . family regrets and . . . personal ambition' (Bk V, ch. 2) into that combination of personal qualities called character. 'Self-command and practical judgement' Tom certainly has when he ensures the destruction of Moss's promissory note on the ground that 'I ought to obey my father's wishes about his property' (Bk III, ch. 3). He exemplifies, in this magnificent scene, not his father's muddled generosity but the harsher classical virtue of piety, modified by a hard-headed bourgeois conception of probity, trust, reputation and accountability as being concerned primarily with a man's property. It is a disturbing view of life because it modernizes the eccentric, provincial and therefore acceptably comic Dodson system of values, and aggressively asserts its representative centrality. Tom exemplifies the strength and exposes the weakness of entrepreneurial capitalism by taking its purported values with absolute seriousness. He expects nothing from others but what presents 'itself to him as a right to be demanded' (Bk III, ch. 5).

For this reason he is a major test of George Eliot's theoretical clearheadedness. The narrow-minded, dictatorial young man has to be granted his place in life. That is why the scene in which he announces the full repayment of his father's debts is moving and terrible. His cruelty to Maggie makes the tact and compassion with which his triumph is nonetheless presented an exemplary instance of authorial integrity. For Tom is at least right in this: life has to be lived, decisions doggedly, even blindly taken. The tragedy of both Tom and his father is thus that in different ways they are right, yet the rightness of each is also massive error. The coherence of the first two volumes is largely the result of the integration of this tragic theme with George Eliot's endlessly inventive comedy and her own wisdom as story-teller and commentator. The comedy is of a piece with the tragedy; the commentary points to the common ground between them and places itself on that common ground as well. There is nothing excessive or question-begging about Mr Tulliver's death; tragic emotion does not cut arbitrarily into the Gordian complexity of theme. On the contrary Mr Tulliver's hopeless last words – 'This world's . . . too many . . . honest man . . . puzzling' – his final hour of 'loud hard breathing', and at last the 'total stillness . . . [when his] dimly lighted soul had forever ceased to be vexed by the painful riddle of this world' (Bk V, ch. 7), faithfully reinforce our sense of the price humanity pays for its strength as well as for its weakness. It is no easy sentimentality that Tom and Maggie should cling and weep together.

From this point on, however, the characterization of Tom – that is, George Eliot's analysis of his character and his own personal development, the two being identical – is effectively complete. All that remains to be achieved in his case is his moment of illumination in 'The Final Rescue'. He consequently plays a minor role in the sixth book. Nevertheless the 'positive and negative qualities' (Bk VI, ch. 12) in his personality continue to be presented with insight, sympathy and an exacting sense of justice. His loneliness as he stares at the fire, 'as if he was watchin' folks at work in it' (Bk VI, ch. 6), his indignation over Maggie's erratic behaviour, softening clumsily into 'the tone of a kind pedagogue' when he puts his hand gently on her arm, and the vulnerable self-righteousness of his earnestly tender lecture to her, expertly marshal the case for and against him. Even when, in the desolation of his ruined repossession of the Mill, he rebuffs Maggie's plea for help with uncompromising cruelty, his positive and negative qualities stand out like light and shade in an angular sculpture harshly lit.

Maggie, by way of deliberate contrast, is like G. F. Watts's 'Eurydice', brilliantly illuminated and yet diffuse in outline. If Tom represents a view of life as transparent, susceptible to definitive interpretation and to decisive action, Maggie exemplifies Philip Wakem's belief that 'there are stores laid up in our human nature that our understandings can make no complete inventory of' (Bk V, ch. 1). Philip cites some reactions to music as an example of this mysteriousness, but the example given by Bain is nothing less than the aggregrate of tender feeling in women like Maggie Tulliver and men like Philip himself: 'The feminine constitution on the whole', Bain writes,

> and certain well-recognised varieties of the constitution of the male sex, are favourable to the emotion; circumstances tending to show that the sense organs by themselves are not the exclusive foundation of it, but that the interior organic functions participate in a way that cannot be precisely described. The analogy of the sexual feeling strongly supports the assumption.[44]

This is to introduce into Associationist theory a conception of physiological and psychological interaction so specific and so detailed as to prohibit scrutiny, and it is in accordance with precisely this conception that Maggie's feelings are observed with an attention to detail which makes their interpretation impossible. Her feelings *in* love, for example, are not just feelings *of* love; because 'her whole nature' dissolves all her experiences into each other, they also include

> the half remote presence of a world of love and beauty and delight, made up of vague, mingled images from all the poetry and romance she had ever read, or had ever woven into her dream reveries (Bk VI, ch. 3).

Her actions, therefore, are as closed to interpretations as Tom's are open to it:

> 'Do take my arm,' [Stephen] said, in a low voice, as if it were a secret. There is something strangely winning to most women in that offer of a firm arm: the help is not wanted physically at that moment, but the sense of help – the presence of strength that is outside them and yet theirs – meets a continual want of the imagination. Either on that ground or some other, Maggie took the arm (Bk VI, ch. 6).

This inherent mysteriousness of the mental life makes for irony of almost Jamesian subtlety. Particularly in her love-relationships, Maggie's psychological and moral ambivalence is represented as a (theoretically defensible) sign of the richness of her physical and moral being. This is especially true of her most morally compromising action, her journey with Stephen on the river, which is something far richer than a mere moral lapse, though a lapse it undoubtedly is. Tenderness, Bain writes, is a 'passive emotion' which flourishes in 'the quiescence of the moving members . . . gentle sensations . . . [owing] to it the luxuriousness of their character as feelings'.[45] Just such a view of her heroine's surrender to the movement of the river enables George Eliot to suffuse Maggie's greatest sin with her noblest moral resource.

Whether the results of this deployment of Associationist conceptions and rhetoric in Maggie's case, and of Positivist and Spencerian conceptions in Tom's, are entirely satisfactory may of course be questioned. What these two deeply considered characterizations illuminate, however, are the intentions underlying the structure of *The Mill on the Floss*. It is intellectually a highly ambitious work. Through its two central characters it explores the tension of human experience between the need to know and the inevitability of ignorance, between discipline and passion, work and joy, male and female, perhaps even ego, will and idea on the one hand, and the unbounded territory of subjectivity on the other. Moreover, in its closing movement it apparently seeks to represent a successful if momentary reconciliation of all these opposites, and because the perspectives it takes are not only psychological but evolutionary as well, its projected reconciliations are given historical, not to say political, significance. No account of the way in which the novel organizes its ideas can be complete, therefore, until proper account is taken of George Eliot's ideas about social history as an aspect of evolution; but this is a topic which requires treatment in a separate chapter.

Meanwhile we can sum up the account of heredity and the mental life which have been the subject of the present chapter by emphasizing once again the principle of fluidity linking both sets of phenomena and operating within each of them. Mind and body are conceived of by George Eliot as being both objectively and subjectively in a state of flux, of permanent instability, which makes the language used to elucidate them inherently provisional and as it were soluble also. Mind-body states, ideas, images and feelings are continually melting into each other and so are the metaphors used to describe them. This principle of fluidity, moreover, transcends the individual life. The conjuctions and fusions, the tensions and disjunctions in the individual, develop out of, and contribute to, those in society at large. It is not a mere metaphor in other words that represents society in personal terms or the individual as a paradigm of the social structure. Structures common to each are transmitted to future generations internally in the mysteries of inheritance and externally in the institutions of family and society. Not surprisingly, therefore, the river, perpetually in movement and yet always the same, carries a wealth of significance in *The Mill on the Floss* which will repay further analysis.

3 History and evolution

FEUERBACH saw history in terms of the evolution of man's religious consciousness. Comte, as we have seen, represented it as a series of intellectual transitions. Human culture, in Comte's view, passes initially through the various stages of theological belief, from fetishism to monotheism; thence it moves into a negative phase, in which men become increasingly critical of theological premises, but are unable to replace them with anything more concrete or precise than abstract principles; finally negation and abstraction yield to the concrete systematic and positive analyses of science. But this evolutionary process, as we have also seen, is not merely an intellectual one. Men develop in their feelings as well as their thinking from barbaric self-centredness to civilized altruism, and there are corresponding developments in social organization from the violence of the primitive hunting group to the complex structures of interdependence in a modern industrial state. Spencer's views on psycho-social evolution were similar. He was frequently annoyed by their being confused with Comte's. Both of them, however, together with Feuerbach and George Eliot, saw history as an integral organic process, a self-propelled realization of human potentialities according to laws which did not have to be understood by those affected by them to be effective, at least until the process of development was nearing completion. History was thus a form of natural history. 'The study of men, as they have appeared in different ages, and under various social conditions,' George Eliot wrote in an early essay, 'may be considered as the natural history of the race.'[1]

It is in some respects appropriate, therefore, that her most frequently quoted essay on this topic should be 'The Natural History of German Life'. In it she takes a distinctly 'anthropological' attitude towards European social history, an attitude which was in fact very characteristic of the period. The founder of the recently established Anthropological Society of London believed that even 'Political Economy must be based on anthropology',[2] and it is therefore hardly surprising to find Spencer in *The Principles of Psychology* and George Eliot in 'The Natural History of German Life' describing the savage and the peasant from a similarly anthropological viewpoint. Spencer's savage is characterized by his lack of foresight, his hand-to-mouth living, his inability to generalize, his lack of individuality, and his primitive moral sense; the Australian aborigine, he notes, has no words for 'justice', 'sin', or 'guilt'.[3] Of the German peasantry George Eliot writes:

> A painter who wants to draw mediaeval characters with historic truth, must seek his models among the peasantry. This explains why the old German painters gave the heads of their subjects a greater uniformity of type than the painters of our day: the race had not attained to a high degree of individualization in features and expression. It indicates, too, that the cultured man acts more as an individual; the peasant, more as one of a group. Hans drives the plough, lives and thinks just as Kunz does; and it is this fact, that many thousands of men are as like each other in thoughts and habits as so many sheep or oysters, which constitutes the weight of the peasantry in the social and political scale.[4]

Implicit in this perspective on race and class is a conception of progress which is evolutionary, not revolutionary, in character: 'What has grown up historically', George Eliot writes,

> can only die out historically, by the gradual operation of necessary laws. The external conditions which society has inherited from the past are but the manifestation of inherited internal conditions in the human beings who compose it . . . and development can take place only by the gradual consentaneous development of both.[5]

George Eliot's view on the historical process, however, are perhaps less clear than critics who rely on this essay have generally recognized. It is also too easy to emphasize the conservative aspects of Comte's thought, to quote the Positivist slogan *'Progress is the development of order'*,[6] for example, in contexts which highlight order at the expense of development. It is on both equally that the emphasis falls in George Eliot's treatment of historical change in her fiction. It is no accident, for example, that so many of her narratives deal with cultural innovation and historical transition. Worlds on the brink of dramatic transformation, but as yet ignorant of them – Italy just before the Reformation, a Midlands town just before the coming of the railways – had a special interest for her, because the tension between holding on to the past in such situations and moving into the future created the psychological space in which her characters could develop.

This tension was also built into Positivist historiography. History, Comte believed, begins in subjectivity: 'our first steps', he wrote, 'are the result of a purely subjective logic',[7] but since man is drawn into this primitive fetishistic speculation because of the ambitious nature of the problems apparently solved by it,[8] primitive subjectivity is as limited morally as it is intellectually. Fear, for example, as Feuerbach observed, 'inevitably intermingles itself'[9] with primitive religion, and as we have seen, its wilfulness issues in an egoistical reliance on miracle like that of Lantern Yard. In the area of moral evolution, however, progress can never be simple or direct, since 'the subordination of the Subjective to the Objective' in which it essentially consists[10] will have to yield in the final stages of human development to the criteria of a perfected Subjectivity. All change is therefore ambivalent. Every advance from subjectivity, wilfulness and fear is a step from man's final destiny as well as towards it. The task of evaluating an age of transition is therefore a very delicate one.

George Eliot shared this cautious approach to the mental and moral emancpation of mankind, notably on the subject of fear. In her essay on 'The Influence of Rationalism', which appeared three years after *Romola*, she wrote:

> Fear is earlier born than hope . . . and remains master of a larger
> group of involuntary actions. A chief aspect of man's moral
> development is the slow subduing of fear by the gradual growth
> of intelligence, and its suppression as a motive by the presence of
> impulses less animally selfish; so that in relation to invisible
> Power, fear ceases to exist, save in that interfusion with higher
> faculties which we call awe.[11]

In *Romola*, it is precisely this process which operates in the plague-stricken village after Romola's arrival there. Initially the *pievano* expects only to be punished, but Romola tells him with 'encouraging authority' that he 'will fear, no longer', and he and Jacopo then set about helping the villagers, convinced that Romola has been sent 'over the sea to command them' (ch. 68). Fear interfused in this way with higher faculties to become awe has not been destroyed but transcended, and rightly so, for without fear man is morally very much at risk. Tito, for example, lacks not only 'that awe of Divine Nemesis which was felt by religious pagans', but also that 'vague fear at anything which is called wrong-doing' which is 'still felt by the mass of mankind' (ch. 11). The old Eumenides of Aeschylus were right: 'fear should sit as the guardian of the soul'.

A comparable ambiguity attaches to the subjective emotionalism of much of Florentine life. Admittedly George Eliot is rather tight-lipped about the grossness of the Carnival, the practical jokes of the street-idlers, and the humour enjoyed by the grey-haired Domenico Cennini, but in general she refuses to view her Florentine world with the envious, disparaging eye of the Northern European Protestant tourist. The dull-witted, the superstitious and the poor are given their due in *Romola*. In particular, the crude devotions of the *contadini* to the Virgin command earnest respect. But primitive values influence the lives of others besides peasants and middle-aged widows like Monna Brigida. When the City Fathers hear Tito's news of supplies reaching Leghorn, they stand 'bare-headed in the presence of a rescue which has come from outside the limit of their own power – from that region of trust and resignation which has been in all ages called divine' (ch. 43). Angelo Poloziano talks significantly of 'the gods awaking from their long sleep and making the woods and streams vital once more' (ch. 3), while Romola herself not only becomes a second Virgin-Mother figure, but – at least for Tito before he altogether loses his capacity for awe – she seems comparable with 'a great nature-goddess [or old], who was not all-knowing, but whose life and power were something deeper and more primordial than knowledge' (ch. 9).

In principle, then, George Eliot's attitude to the 'strange web of belief and unbelief, of Epicurean levity and fetishistic dread' (Proem) of the Renaissance world of *Romola*, was necessarily a cautious one, if only because the fifteenth century was a period of change. The Italian city states, in Comte's view, had pioneered man's emancipation from the false subjectivity of medieval theology. In Italy, he claimed, 'we observe the spirit of Art gradually growing up on the traces of industry, and preparing the way for science and philosophy',[12] but no easy conceptions of progress are written into George Eliot's account of the period. Even its intellectual culture, which by any standards was not only very high but the basis for many other kinds of emancipation, is presented in a characteristically ambiguous manner. The Apostles, Feuerbach wrote,

> were men of the people; the people live only in themselves, in their feelings; therefore Christianity took possession of the people . . . The classic spirit, the spirit of culture . . . is the objective spirit. In place of this, there entered with Christianity the principle of unlimited, extravagant, fanatical, supranaturalistic subjectivity; a principle intrinsically opposed to that of science, of culture.[13]

The idiom is that of post-Hegelian Higher Criticism, the sentiments those of Romola's father, for whom the opposition between classical and Christian values is simple and complete. But as we have seen already Bardi's limitation is his isolation from the common life he despises. He has freed himself from primitive enslavement to subjectivity and fear but not from self-will, and consequently his lonely pursuit of fame issues only in impotence and ultimate oblivion. The principle of science, of culture, is insufficient on its own.

A similar balancing of issues marks George Eliot's treatment of the other great achievements of Renaissance Italy, art and commerce. An interest in art, Comte wrote, is 'the commonest sympton of the birth of the spiritual life';[14] it brings out 'our highest emotions in order to regulate our ruling motives'.[15] It is an extension of language, which arises 'spontaneously in the Affections'[16] ('gestures and cries . . . communicating feelings, rather than ideas'),[17] and is extended first to activities, then to speculation. The arts 'give utterance to all our deepest impressions.'[18] In *Romola*, Piero di Cosimo's deepest impressions are clearly formed at this level. He objectifies but is not objective. Bain is interesting in this connexion: 'the sense of colour . . . is not only identical with a facility of remembering scenes and pictures, and shades of colour; it also generates a strong interest in the concrete, pictorial, and poetic aspects of the world, and a repulsion from the scientific point of view'.[19] Piero would agree: 'the only passionate life', he declares, 'is in form and colour' (ch. 8). Admittedly Bain argues that such a feeling for form is rarely associated with one for colour, but his contention that painters are in general deeply anti-scientific is certainly borne out in the portrait of Piero, with his extreme sensitivity to noise, his intuitive insights into personality, and his contempt for philosophers. 'I find it enough to live,' he declares, 'without spinning lies to account for life' (ch. 18). In his chaotic and uninhibitedly frank lack of deliberation, he is manifestly free of the tyranny of will which is Bardi's curse. But art too has to face the scrutiny of George Eliot's agnosticism. Its limitations are suggested by Piero's exclamation, '*Va!* your human talk and doings are a tame jest' (ch. 8). Significantly his intuitions are of little practical help to Romola or to Florence. He is also rather too hasty in his condemnation of the Pyramid of Vanities. Romola, on the other hand, is hesitant about condemning the Pyramid because in her the 'subtle result of culture which we call Taste [is] subdued by the need for deeper motive' (ch. 49). Many of the passages about art in the novel also have ironic implications. Giotto's campanile may seem 'a prophetic symbol' (ch. 3) of how human life must some day shape itself, but the gates of San Giovanni have lost their gilt, the marble has faded, and the inlaying and statued niches are never to be completed. Art speaks, therefore, with a kind of impotence. It reminds us of how slowly history moves towards its appointed perfection.

In important respects, therefore, Bardi's narrow intelligence and Piero's impractical sensitivity compare poorly with the civic and domestic effectiveness of Romola's godfather, Bernardo del Nero, the embodiment of an aristocratic ideal sanctioned by Comte, whose description of Cosimo de Medici – 'a worthy type of the industrial patriciat'[20] – could also be applied to Bernardo. He is the first of George Eliot's public men: his successors, Philip Debarry and Sir Hugo Mallinger, share his acute judgment, cautious openness of mind and sense of tradition. He is quick to see through Tito, although his reactions derive in part from patrician prejudice. At the same time, as a man of affairs he knows that traditionless men like Tito can be useful even to men like himself, 'enabling those who [have] . . . scruples to keep their hands tolerably clean' (ch. 57). Like the Ghost of the Proem, Bernardo is 'a man of public spirit, and public spirit', George Eliot insists, 'can never be wholly immoral, since its essence is care for a common good'. The negative terms in which this defence is couched, however, are noteworthy. They are reinforced throughout *Romola* by the choric comments of Machiavelli. It is one of the quiet ironies of the book that the Signoria employ Tito and not Machiavelli as Secretary. In fact just as the qualities of objectivity in Bardi, of insight in Piero, and of practicality in Bernardo are of little help to Romola in private life, so in the public affairs of Florence and Europe, the right men and the right ideas never make contact. This is why so much political discussion in the novel, supremely important to those involved, seems as random and trivial as Bardi's frantic concern for his reputation. From the historical perspectives established by the commentary, history is seen to evade control. An effective synthesis of social forces and human powers seems impossible to achieve.

This is a thoroughly Positivist conception. The influence of Comte on the novel is most obvious and least hedged about with qualification in George Eliot's treatment of Florentine public life. The very Victorian debate about the franchise, for example, is represented as 'a question of boiled or roast' (ch. 35). In similar vein Comte suggested that constitutional problems were insignificant; 'in general, the thing wanted', he thought, was 'a preparatory reformation of principles and manners'.[21] This task, he suggested, had originally been performed by the Catholic Church, the political independence of which he believed to be 'the greatest advance ever made in the general theory of the social organism'.[22] By 'constituting a moral power wholly independent of the political', the medieval church, he argued, had 'infused morality into political government'.[23] Its chief tasks had been popular education and the maintenance in practice of 'the principles which education had prepared for the guidance of [man's] life'[24] – hence the importance of the confessional, and possibly George Eliot's surprising emphasis on Romola's resort to it. In general, the medieval Church had made it possible both for 'political action . . . to assume, in its intellectual relations a character of wisdom, extent, and even rationality which had never existed before',[25] and for the mass of the people to be 'lifted above the narrow circle of their material life'.[26] But though this obviously gave the clergy considerable influence, Comte disapproved of their direct involvement in politics. 'Command of any kind', he insisted, 'is fatal to the Priestly functions . . . [disturbing] the breadth of view they need, whilst the employment of force . . . corrupts the feeling'.[27]

The relevance of this analysis to Savonarola's situation in *Romola* is obvious. His relationship with the masses, for example, works on precisely Positivist principles. While the politicians debate, his preaching gives 'the vague desires of [the] majority the character of a determinate will' (ch. 35). Comte believed passionately in the 'irresistible power of public opinion . . . because', he argued, 'men submit to it, apart from any sense of wrong in the conscience or the understanding.'[28] The function of the spiritual power, therefore, was to transform society through public opinion. Savonarola's achievements follow this pattern exactly. Exploiting 'the great wave of feeling which gathered its force from sympathies that lay deeper than all theory' (ch. 24), he brings people of all classes into moral and practical agreement. Tito believes that 'no wise man would take as a guide' the 'mere tangle of anomalous traditions and opinions' which constitute the 'sentiment of society' (ch. 11), but Machiavelli knows otherwise, and by the end of the novel Tito has to admit the 'power over men's minds' (ch. 62) exercised by a man like Savonarola. That power ensures that the starving country people are not shut out during the siege, and is responsible, more ambiguously, for the Pyramid of Vanities. And Savonarola also succeeds in influencing the young Florentine boys who are to be the heroes of 'the last struggle of their Republic' (ch. 49). The nearest Florence ever comes to an effective synthesis of its powers is under his leadership. He is the supreme manifestation of effective spiritual power.

The synthesis was not, of course, sustained. Despite his protestations, Savonarola does 'meddle . . . with the functions of the State' (ch. 59). The very fact that justifies his rebellion, the papacy's failure to maintain its non-political character, gives brute force, embodied in Dolfo Spini, a crucial advantage over the Frate's purely moral authority. He is thus forced to indulge in compromising *Realpolitik* himself, notably when he refuses to save Romola's godfather from execution. He thereby experiences in his own person the very contradictions which had already undermined the spiritual power of the papacy and so justified his own disobedience.

As well as exemplifying the historic decline of Catholicism, however, Savonarola also exemplifies the emergence of the Protestant spirit. Comte's attitude to the Reformation was ambivalent. It heralded the imminence of metaphysical modes of thought, yet as a negative moment in European history, it initiated also a period of dangerous anarchy by democratizing inspiration and thereby undermining authority and law. In effect, the Reformers referred all political or social events to God's direct involvement in human affairs, that is 'to Will, divine or human'.[29] In this respect Savonarola is both an arch proto-Protestant and an anti-progressive force: 'believing in great ends, and longing to achieve those ends by the exertion of [his] own strong will', he makes 'faith in a supreme and righteous Ruler' (ch. 21) indistinguishable from faith in direct divine intervention. He asserts first that his mission is prophetic and the Florentines 'a second chosen people', then that God will 'attest the truth of his prophetic preaching by a miracle' (ch. 52), and finally that the cause of his party '*is* the cause of God's kingdom' (ch. 59). This is precisely what Feuerbach condemned as 'religious utilitarianism';[30] any claim to special revelation, he contended, 'poisons, nay . . . destroys . . . the sense of truth.'[31]

From one point of view, then *Romola* apparently takes a thoroughly pessimistic view of the historical process. Scholarship, art, commerce, politics and religion – Bardi, Piero, Machiavelli and Savonarola – are all deflected from their courses, reduced to ineffectiveness, condemned to death; and though the novel attempts to balance this record of defeat by means of the narrative of Romola's moral development and triumph, the results are too obviously both speculative and extra-historical. But one cannot ignore the fact that the present in which *Romola* was written to be read is a crucially important aspect of its meaning. Once allowance is made for the recognitions which the text assumes in the reader, the novel loses much of its cautious pessimism. The Victorian liberal to whom it is addressed would know, after all, as Machiavelli could not, that not only would his name survive as one of the pioneers of modern political theory, but that a fully scientific theory of the state, and one far more optimistic than his own, would eventually become a possibility. Again, unlike Bernardo, such a reader would know that commerce and industry would flourish on a scale inconceivable from the perspectives of a city state. He would enjoy, as Piero could not, the full range and variety of European art from the work of Piero's great contemporaries, through the Dutch masters celebrated in *Adam Bede* to the ambitious Romantics whose aspirations excite Will Ladislaw in *Middlemarch*. And finally, unlike Savonarola, he would know that the corrupt political power of the papacy would be drastically reduced, and that an authentic cleansing of Christendom would be effected, not by the armies of the French king, but by Luther and his successors, down to Wesley and the Evangelicals. In other words, George Eliot's conviction that human beings act blindly, that statesmen and scholars are as tragically in the dark as Mr Tulliver and Dolly Winthrop, and that the pattern only becomes visible with hindsight, has to be seen in the light of her other conviction, that the pattern does indeed become visible in the end, and that progress is real precisely because it is achieved not by policy but by process.

In these terms *The Mill on the Floss* must be read as an historical novel also, since it is about the real forces of change in society, namely the organic development of mind and society. It is true that the impressive image with which the novel opens, of black ships, laden with fir-planks, seed, and 'the dark glitter of coal' being carried to St Ogg's on a 'mighty tide', quickly dissolves into the dream-figure of a small girl by Dorlecote Mill, and that the large ideas of the opening paragraph apparently disappear in the domestic comedy arising out of Mr Tulliver's plans for Tom's education; but this skilfully controlled narrative is carefully interrupted by the account of St Ogg's social history near the end of the first book, and again at the mid-point of the novel by the intrusive autobiographical description of the 'narrow, ugly, grovelling' image of life on the Rhone (Bk IV, ch. 1), the two chapters of this brief, important book being similarly discursive. These interruptions of the narrative clearly emphasize the narrator's determination to make her characters 'belong to the universe' in a highly specific way. The shifts of attention between 'the moral, the intellectual world' on the one hand, and 'the personal spectacle' on the other, are more ambitious than those in *Scenes of Clerical Life* and more historically particular than was possible in the pastoral world of *Adam Bede*. *The Mill on the Floss* is certainly not an *abstracted* natural history of English life. It is about a moment of cultural transformation, significantly preceding the economic transformations of the railway age, a moment in which modern consciousness is born.

Hence the importance of the fourth book with its description of Maggie discovering a higher level of religious sensitivity than had ever been experienced in St Ogg's before. In a half-ironic concession to the reader's spiritual susceptibilities, George Eliot admits that the novel has been 'irradiated by no sublime principles, no romantic visions, no active, self-renouncing faith' (Bk IV, ch. 1); now, however, Maggie is to attempt such a life. This is important, George Eliot insists, because 'the small pulse of [an] old English town' is linked 'with the beating of the world's mighty heart', not only by the Floss and its commerce, but also by a great tide of evolving mental activity which lifts Tom and Maggie 'in the onward tendency of human things . . . above the mental level of the generations before them, to which they have been nevertheless tied by the strongest fibres of their hearts'. The Tulliver children are thus in the vanguard of history yet are tied to the past by complicated emotions of love and duty. This past will prevent them from fulfilling a destiny which in a sense belongs as much to mankind as to themselves, yet, in the form of intimate personal memories, it makes possible the moment of reconciliation in the last book towards which the entire work is directed.

Stephen Guest is a key figure in this evaluation of the past. The antipathy felt towards him by many critics, notably Swinburne and F.R. Leavis, is usually accounted for by our not having seen him as a child. His late appearance is in fact well judged. He represents something new, not just in the narrative, but historically. The pre-industrial, provincial culture of St Ogg's has only recently become involved in national economic and intellectual life. Stephen's references to *The Divine Comedy* and *The Creation* are therefore appropriately lacking in urbanity and as such are histor-ically significant. He *is* shallow, egoistical and naively self-approving; his culture *is* a late, uneasily acquired accomplishment. Yet as Joan Bennett observes, he becomes 'capable of tragic suffering'.[32] His praise of Dr Kenn indicates a basic soundness in his sense of values, and his reading of Buckland's *Geology and Mineralogy* a creditably modern-minded outlook. Certainly his contribution to the debate about Maggie's decision to leave him is not negligible. If his role in the novel is to be questioned it should be as Lucy's 'half-ardent, half-sarcastic' lover (Bk VI, ch. 1) rather than the focus of Maggie's passionate longings, which, as we have seen, are not just for sexual and personal fulfilment, but for the intellectual and emotional emancipation that wealth, ease and refinement can, apparently, bring. Whether Swinburne knew it or not, economic and cultural changes which the young Mary Anne Evans herself experienced had created naive but still touching ambitions in clever girls from provincial market towns for a spacious and affluent life of intellectual and emotional refinement, for sweetness and light as they understood them. George Eliot could also see, as Stephen's denigrators could not, that he represents more than adequately the superficially conscious yet profoundly unknowing stream of modern life, and that Maggie's rejection of him expresses an uncompromising repudiation of a cultural modernity which was, and is, genuinely seductive. What Stephen stands for is certainly not to be lightly dismissed. He speaks out, after all, in defence of an ethic of honesty and spontaneity in personal relations which the obliteration of Christian norms and sanctions would appear to justify. 'Would Philip and Lucy have thanked us', he asks Maggie when she proposes leaving him and returning to St Ogg's, 'for anything so hollow as constancy without love?' (Bk VI, ch. 14). This not only anticipates the voice of Bloomsbury, it also, apparently, reiterates the trenchant remarks made earlier by George Eliot herself on Maggie's decision to go on seeing Philip in the Red Deeps: 'we can always find some point of view,' she suggests, 'in the combination of results' to justify our actions; adopting a providential or a philosophical perspective, makes it too easy 'to obtain a perfect complacency' in choosing to please ourselves (Bk V, ch. 3). The 'mysterious complexity of our life', she writes later, 'is not to be embraced by maxims, and . . . to lace ourselves up in formulas' is to cripple the sympathetic life (Bk VII, ch. 2). It is hard not to see Stephen's arguments as following logically and imaginatively from the position thus advanced by the author herself. In insisting on leaving him Maggie is apparently missing an historically created and humanly important opportunity for genuine emancipation.

In fact, of course, Stephen's views do not follow from George Eliot's. When Maggie declares that we 'can't choose happiness either for ourselves or for another . . . We can only choose . . . whether we will renounce [indulgence] for the sake of obeying the divine voice within us', she is not in fact lacing herself up in another formula, since her declaration takes fully into account the fluidity or instability of human connexion on which Stephen has based his case. Precisely because the world is in a state of continual flux, improvisation is no more adequate than principle. Nor are calculations about happiness, our own or other people's: George Eliot was never a utilitarian. The only moral resource available to us in memory, the divine voice within us, our constituted selves. But as we noted at the conclusion of the last chapter, the self itself is an unstable category; the individual and society are constituted in each other's structures. It follows that in sanctioning Maggie's loyalty to her own past, George Eliot is making an important judgment about history as well as about the moral life.

This is evident from the novel's structure. As a narrative it is carefully constructed round two false climaxes, one centring on Tom, one on Maggie and both conventionally familiar. The resulting sense of unfinished business makes the need for a true climax involving both all the greater. Tom's release from debt is the hero's traditional triumph, confirming his manhood and his right to love. But he has no one to marry, and such sadly omniscient comments as, 'Tom never lived to taste another moment so delicious as that' (Bk V, ch. 6), and 'Tom . . . got up and made the single speech of his life' (Bk V, ch. 7), confirm that for him things have climaxed too soon. The ending of Maggie's love affair in earnest debate and a clumsy return home similarly disrupts conventional literary as well as social expectations. Most readers must begin the last book, therefore, feeling that a flood of the kind so frequently mentioned in the commentary and by the characters is the only event which could bring brother and sister together and the novel to a fitting conclusion; and when at last it comes, its speed, scope and turmoil provide a compelling climax to the action. Yet this very excitement, and sense of expectation fulfilled, tends to exacerbate the feeling of our being manipulated as well. The Floss has never really been part of the story, only of the background. The anticipations of its flooding, therefore, 'strike us as artificial',[33] and the catastrophe itself as a mere device.

This effect of arbitrariness has even more serious implications in the context of the novel's concern with the larger patterns of psycho-social history. Maggie early develops 'a blind unconscious yearning for something that would link together the wonderful impressions of this mysterious life' (Bk III, ch. 5), and we legitimately expect this yearning to reach some kind of conclusion. But more than a private revelation is promised. 'Time,' we are told, 'with ever-unrelenting purpose, still hides [the] secret [of universal well-being] in his own mighty, slow-beating heart' (Bk II, ch. 2); and in the important passage which presents Tom and Maggie as victims of 'the onward tendency of human things', the claim that theirs are representative lives is justified by a comparison of the author's point of view with a scientist's: 'does not science tell us,' George Eliot asks, 'that its highest striving is after the ascertainment of a unity which shall bind the smallest things with the greatest?' (Bk II, ch. 1). The reader is clearly encouraged by such questions to speculate about the novel's own capacity to resolve the theoretical and historical problems which permeate it. Its ambitious deployment of symbols is certainly consistent with such a synthesis being in preparation.

The most important of these symbols, of course, is that of the river itself. In an early essay George Eliot compared the mind of a great scholar to 'some mighty river, which, in its long windings through unfrequented regions, gathers minerals and earthly treasures only more effectually to enrich and fertilize the cultivated valleys and busy cities which form the habitation of man.'[34] More than the mental development of a scholar, however, is suggested by this image, since the true historian embodies that human development in which he believes so passionately, and consequently the movement of the river expresses the evolution of culture itself, as well as that of an individual mind. The Floss bears a similar double meaning – with results that might be thought confusing. On the one hand it represents the flow of sensation, emotion and thought through the minds of the characters; yet it is also the physical link between St Ogg's and the commerce of Europe and so with history in broad and concrete terms. Consequently when the river sweeps Tom and Maggie into climactic reunion and revelation, it is hard not to feel that George Eliot is allowing social and personal reconciliations to become confused, that she is trying to bind the smallest things with the greatest in a flurry of illogical excitement.

Paradoxically, however, the flood can be defended *because* it is illogical. Integration of the dénouement with events preceding it was not, after all, impossible. The failure of some dykes, for example, could have been made to result from family misunderstandings. Instead the arbitrariness of the flood is emphasized. It sweeps in on Maggie at the very moment when she has accepted life. Her prayer, 'O God, if my life is to be long, let me live to bless and comfort' (Bk VII, ch. 5) is not 'instantly answered' as Barbara Hardy suggests,[35] nor is the ending providential. Rather it preserves the crucial distinction between psychological and historical events on which the novel's intellectual integrity depends. Clearly the broader reconciliations between man and woman, duty and desire, and submission and power to which the text alludes will not be achieved by means such as these. The flood is a device deliberately chosen to take Tom and Maggie outside history; the feeling of issues unresolved, of raw dissatisfaction with events, with which most readers close the book, is thus entirely consistent with its teaching. Far from engineering the suppression of 'ideological conflict',[36] as Terry Eagleton alleges, the conclusion of *The Mill on the Floss* deliberately and explicitly leaves issues painfully open since it was, and could only be, in death that Tom and Maggie were not divided.

The river imagery in the last two books decisively supports this reading. As a child, when her father's suffering had made Maggie demand 'some explanation of this hard, real life' (Bk IV, ch. 3), she had discovered the inadequacy of the dream-world. On the river with Stephen, however, she allows herself to be temporarily isolated from reason and from the past in an 'enchanted haze' (Bk VI, ch. 13). I have discussed her reasons for returning to the hard, real world again, but when the Floss sweeps in on her with sudden and arbitary force, she relinquishes her hold on it once more, although this time under compulsion. For Maggie, as for Hetty, Silas and Baldassare, exclusion from society involves loss of human status, death. The mind's practical relation with reality, 'the threads of ordinary association', are 'broken', and only 'God' is left (Bk VII, ch. 5). Insofar as this involves loss of contact with society, it is truly death, but for Tom and Maggie, simply because they are together, it is also a liberation, a momentary and therefore legitimate precipitation of all the tensions of the novel into their most universal form, 'when all the artificial vesture of our life is gone, and we are all one with each other in primitive mortal needs'. In such a condition it is also legitimate (though only because no more is allowed them) for Tom and Maggie, not just as individuals but as representatives of their kind, to glimpse the promise in their shared past and miraculously revealed mutual need.

The Tito narrative in *Romola* has an exactly comparable structure. Like *Silas Marner* and the short story 'Brother Jacob', Tito's history has many of the characteristics of fable. In all three narratives the misappropriation of gold or jewels is central to a story concerned with Providence and Nemesis. In Tito's case, Nemesis has two forms, objective and subjective. When he sells his jewels an 'importunate thought, of which he had till now refused to see more than the shadow as it dogged his footsteps' (ch. 9), rushes in and grasps him: he has finally to make up his mind about ransoming his adoptive father. Later this thought comes startlingly alive when Baldassare literally dogs his footsteps and rushes in to grasp hold of him. Their situations are symmetrically reversed at the end of the novel. On the night of Spini's *coup d'état*, Tito brilliantly evades pursuit and leaps into the river. By chance, however, Baldassare, his desire for vengeance now reduced to a formless will to live, is waiting downstream. Suddenly he sees something in the water, a possible 'fortunate chance for him' (ch. 67). Tito is washed up beside him and Baldassare dies killing him. This stylized conclusion is starkly fortuitous; it therefore takes on a specific meaning. As in *The Mill on the Floss*, flood waters symbolically sweep two major characters out of 'history' and into 'vision'. 'Justice', George Eliot concludes, 'is like the kingdom of God – it is not without us as a fact, it is within us as a great yearning.'

The conclusions of both narratives therefore have a consistency and coherence that is easily denied them. This does not mean that the organization of either novel is finally defensible. But what can be said, at least in partial defence of both, is that they register, in the overtness and explicitness with which they deploy arbitrary and chance developments, the fundamental difficulty of seeing history, and therefore of acting within it, inherent in George Eliot's determinist and organicist principles. In particular, critics of *The Mill on the Floss* have mistakenly read the climax of the novel as purporting to offer a solution of some sort to the problems raised in the text. It does not. Rather it states a problem. George Eliot's historical perspectives are realistic as well as melioristic. As a meliorist she represents an organic unfolding of human potentialities in history, which seems to have its effect without significant reference being made to choice or effort. As a realist, however, she scrupulously identifies the point at which historical optimism has to recognize the gap between hope and fulfilment, the point at which it is necessary to regard the ends of history as dreams rather than certainties. Only in death are Tom and Maggie united. Justice, like the kingdom of God, is within.

4 Politics and class

THE ENDINGS of both *The Mill on the Floss* and *Romola* develop out of clearly apprehended historiographical principles. At the same time, however, they highlight a serious problem in George Eliot's thought, namely the uncertain status of politics in the modern world. Maggie gives her allegiance to the past, though the full cost of her doing so is certainly not understated – if George Eliot was conservative, she was never complacently so. More seriously, in *Romola*, political consciousness and political action are shown to be utterly nugatory. The most convincing suggestions of hope in the novel derive from its implicit suggestion that though the future is opaque, as it seems demonstrably to be to the characters in the action, looking back on the past from the privileged position of the modern reader reveals limited but specific patterns of amelioration in the human lot. However, if in principle the future from any given historical present is inherently unpredictable, at least in terms of the kind of predictability required for concrete action, political activity itself becomes highly anomalous. Yet Positivism offered a precise account of the statics and dynamics of contemporary society. While never organized as a political movement, it was intensely conscious of political developments, and passionately committed to social transformation. And George Eliot was a Positivist.

This has been disputed, of course. Prominent scholars, notably Gordon Haight, have doubted if she ever took Comte very seriously. Lord Acton, on the other hand, was convinced that 'the scorn for Liberality and Utilitarianism which appears in *Felix Holt*' was directly due to Comte's influence.[1] The 'Address to Working Men, by Felix Holt', moreover – George Eliot's response to the passage of the 1867 Reform Bill, published early in 1868 – reaffirms her continuing belief in the beneficent power of public opinion, the premise on which, as we have seen, Comte's defence of the spiritual power was based. 'Each class', it declares, 'should be urged by the surrounding conditions to perform its particular work under the strong pressure of responsibility to the nation at large',[2] and provided only that public order is preserved, 'there can be no government in the future that will not be determined' by the insistence of the working-class on 'fair and practicable demands'.[3]

The most satisfying evidence, however, for George Eliot's continuing fidelity to broadly Positivist perspectives in *Felix Holt* is provided by the casual good humour with which she feels free to treat them. There is a felicitous touch of farce, for example, in the way she depicts the 'Militarism' of the medieval Debarrys giving way to the 'Industrialism' of 'Wace & Co., brewers of the celebrated Treby beer', who use the local castle's sheltering northern wall as 'an excellent strawyard for the pigs' (ch. 3). The 'new conditions complicating [Treby Magna's] relations with the rest of the world, and gradually awakening in it that higher consciousness which is known to bring higher pains' have less connexion with the French or industrial revolutions, it seems, than with Lawyer Jermyn's youthful efforts to set the town up as a fashionable spa, efforts which result only in the establishment of a tape factory. Meanwhile the intellectual crisis which Comte supposed had followed on the failure of the Enlightenment seems in Treby Magna to have taken the homely form of a new breed of Dissenters who 'without meaning to be in the least abusive, spoke of the high-bred rector as a blind leader of the blind.' 'Western anarchy', Comte wrote anxiously, 'bears most upon the intellect, the disorder in which is the main source of the impaired tone of feeling and the waywardness of activity'[4] – a situation apparently represented in North Loamshire by the stolid complacencies of Wace and Nolan, and young Joyce's unfeeling proposal to muster the country's trades union delegates 'for our yeomanry to go into' (ch. 20).

This humorous Englishing of continental melodramas, however, is in fact carefully calculated to point up the relevance of Positivist perspectives to North Loamshire's case. For Comte the 'great question of modern times' was 'the incorporation of the proletariat into society.'[5] In accordance with this view, the miners and stonemasons of North Loamshire are represented in the 'Introduction' to *Felix Holt* as interlopers, hidden for the most part, but dangerously unassimilated into 'the large-spaced, slow-moving life' of the Midlands Plain, with its 'homesteads and far-away cottages and oak-sheltered parks.' However, 'riots and trades-union meetings' cannot be forever confined to villages 'dingy with coal-dust, noisy with the shaking of looms'. As the narrative goes on to show, there are 'sharp-visaged men' abroad, ready to set up the cry, 'Let us go to Treby Manor' (ch. 33), and so to attack the seat of both local authority and local culture, 'that treasure of knowledge, science, poetry, refinement of thought, feeling, and manners . . . which is carried on from the minds of one generation to the minds of another.'[6] An unassimilated working-class, therefore, threatens not just the order of present society, but the social and possibly even the genetic transmission of values into the future. Disordered class relations constitute a new and specific threat to the humanization of man, and clearly specific action is called for.

But not political action. The pursuit of liberal freedoms, Comte believed, of equality, popular sovereignty and national independence, had performed useful negative service in undermining monarchical and aristocratic government, but they provided no positive basis for a modern social order.[7] He was particularly suspicious, as we have seen, of all schemes for constitutional reform. A limited franchise, he maintained – and the Reform bills of 1832 and 1867 could both have been cited to prove this – might help to 'regulate, by protracting, the political conflict';[8] but such measures only irritated the unenfranchized, and were dangerously unstable and superficial. Society, he argued, needed not constitutional but moral reorganization. Hence his dislike of liberalism and his consistent complaints about the declining political morality associated with sterile liberal principles.[9] Only mediocre men, he thought, would appeal to the people's self-interest. He also objected both to 'demogogues and sophists, who have alienated the working class from their natural industrial leaders' (the employers), and to employers who used their power to coerce the allegiance of their workers.[10] It is no accident that these three evils are successively dramatized in the scenes in Sproxton. Johnson corrupts the workers with treating and sly talk about their forgetting 'Jack at Newcastle' and thinking of themselves (ch. 11); the trades union man wants the workers to give their loyalty not to their employers but exclusively to their own class; and the Whig mine-owner's agent, Spratt, 'hated manager of Sproxton colliery', assumes that the miners' 'voteless enthusiasm' belongs to his master by right.

Further evidence of the Positivist scepticism with which George Eliot regarded the political process as she was writing *Felix Holt* is provided by the opinions and actions of the middle-class voters in the novel. Mr Nolan's complacent pontifications, for example, suggest, if not the dangers, at least the futility of freedom of opinion, even when those opinions echo an important truth, namely that the 'prosperity of the country is one web' (ch. 20), while the nervous fair-mindedness with which Mr Rose allows his two votes to cancel each other out tolerantly exposes the practical insignificance of political liberties. Nor are the legislators treated with more sympathy than the men who elect them. The successes of reform legislation were supposed to be a matter of record – the 'Introduction' actually specifies some of the more notorious abuses that had been put right since 1832 – but this does not deter George Eliot from asserting later in a much-quoted passage that 'faith in the efficacy of political change' has been succeeded by 'a time of doubt and despondency'. Reform has not made men wiser but has produced 'rather a more abundant breeding of the foolish and unhappy' (ch. 16). Politics have failed, as Comte said they would, and we are left with the only politicians of which he approved. 'Our official conservatives are behind hand,' he wrote '. . . yet, the mere revolutionist seems to me still more alien to the spirit of the time.'[11] The very word *conservateur* was changing its meaning and now designated 'the party . . . endeavouring to reconcile order and progress.'[12] Peel's appropriation of the French term is carefully emphasized in the comparison between Philip Debarry and his father. George Eliot's effective endorsement of the latter's election to Parliament is thus a very precise reflection of the Positivist principles which Acton detected in the novel.

The task of conservative politicians, however, was, in Comte's judgment, provisional only. They were to hold society together while a successor to the old Catholic spiritual power, the new Priesthood of Positivism, brought about the only kind of change that mattered, through direct action on 'the affections, the propensities [and] the passions', that is on 'the great springs of human life',[13] in the population at large. Through the educating function of its priests, he suggested, the ideals of Positivism would work their way freely into men's minds and hearts, and so mould the institutions of the future. The emergence of this 'wholly new class' from all orders of society would, he believed, be 'essentially spontaneous, since its social sway [could] arise from nothing else than the voluntary assent of men's minds.'[14] There can be little doubt that Positivists would have been justified in regarding *Felix Holt* as an appropriately tentative study of how under English conditions this process might conceivably have already begun.

Particularly relevant in this respect are the clergymen in the novel. Mr Debarry, for example, is unmistakably a representative of the moribund spiritual power of feudalism, while Mr Lyon represents the negative or transitional phase of its evolution. Both belong to the past, but there are differences between them. Mr Debarry is the more hidebound in his views, seeing nothing in Mr Lyon but 'a crazy little firefly' (ch. 23). Mr Lyon, however, can recognize a kindred spirit in the unbelieving Felix. His sanctioning of Felix's work symbolizes a legitimizing continuity – a kind of apostolic succession – in the evolution of a secularized spiritual power. Certainly the life to which Felix commits himself is unambiguously a priestly one. He weds himself to poverty and for a time to chastity, withdrawing himself (in contrast to Adam Bede) from a respectable ambition. (George Eliot believed strongly in the need for a working-class clergy.)[15] He sets himself up as a watchmaker – St Paul made tents – and as a teacher follows an even more venerable precedent, by planning to take one of the miners' children 'and set him in the midst' (ch. 11). He dissociates himself from politics, except to admonish those responsible for abuses, to give general warnings about the limitations of the political process, and to moderate the excesses of the rioters. He is unmistakably a prototype of the Positivist priest. His speech on nomination day in particular, with its insistence on public opinion as 'the greatest power under heaven', is quintessentially Comtist.

Peter Coveney, however, interprets Felix Holt's radicalism very differently. His reading is implicitly but directly anti-Comtist. The novel's radicalism, he suggests, is grounded not in theory but in Nature, in a 'rejection of the money-world of the mid-nineteenth century, in favour of values of an "unremarketable" kind.'[16] Comte, of course, believed firmly that Industry and Science were authentic sources of value in the modern world. 'A course of industrial and scientific growth,' he wrote, 'ending ultimately in the complete establishment of [a] universal moral standard . . . was the obvious programme' arising from modern conditions.[17] If comparable views do not find their way into *Felix Holt*, then Acton's judgment on it must be set aside.

Fundamental to Coveney's case, however, is his reading of the 'Introduction'. George Eliot, he maintains, describes the rural village communities which were threatened by the new manufacturing towns in strongly approving terms. He suggests, for example, that there is a 'wealth of intention' lying 'behind the symbolism of . . . hedgerows'. They represent 'a natural world entirely separate from the Victorian world with its political economy.' They are 'part of a *society*', in which there 'is no sense of a romanticized Nature apart from men . . . no antithesis between social Man and Nature.'[18] But in fact there is a great deal of soft-voiced satire against this rural world both in the Introduction and the novel generally, satire which is interestingly connected with attacks on the Church of England. George Eliot was to describe the English Church as the 'least morally dignified form of Christianity'[19] and Comte, too, doubted if Anglicanism could 'generate very deep convictions[20] – a conclusion he would have found trenchantly confirmed in George Eliot's account not only of the religious ideas and religious practice of Mrs Transome and the Debarry girls, but also of the rural population generally, whose low level of religious life, we are told, keeps them 'safely in the *via media* of indifference.' The Shepherd of the 'Introduction' may obey the rhythms of earth and season, as Coveney suggests, but he also feels 'no bitterness except in the matter of pauper labourers and the bad-luck that sent contrarious seasons and the sheep rot'. Here, surely, an 'antithesis between social Man and Nature' is urgently required. Deeply attached as George Eliot was to the rich traditions of the English countryside, she does not look to village life in *Felix Holt* to provide those values and feelings which she thinks appropriate to the modern world.

Instead she turns to the manufacturing towns, and specifically to Rufus Lyon's Independent chapel in Malthouse Yard. This is where important modern values have taken root rather than in the splendid rectories of the countryside, 'bulwarks of our venerable institutions – which arrest disintegrating doubt, [and] serve as a double embankment against Popery and Dissent' (ch. 23). For there are continuities in English life other than those of the countryside. As Valentine Cunningham has shown, Rufus Lyon is the self-conscious heir of the seventeenth-century traditions of root and branch Dissent.[21] It is true that Cunningham also suggests that Mr Lyon is in fact too radical for a congregationalist minister of his type and period, since old-fashioned Congregationalism which flourished in the 1830s was far more apolitical than Mr Lyon seems to be.[22] But Mr Lyon is not in fact meant to be typical. Rather he is the point at which George Eliot attempts to graft her Positivist convictions on to existing English traditions.

Mr Lyon's political significance is perhaps particularly evident in the contrast which an amused George Eliot draws between his 'worn look of intellectual eagerness, slight frame and rusty attire' and the 'flourishing persons, unblemished costume, and comfortable freedom from excitement' of Harold Transome and Mr Jermyn. This difference, she suggests is typical of that between 'the men who are animated by ideas, and the men who are expected to apply them' (ch. 16). Mr Lyon's eccentricities, in other words, preserve precisely that 'distinction between theory and practice'[23] which provided the fundamental justification for Comte's differentiation of the spiritual and temporal powers. Mr Lyon's political and religious convictions are no less Comtist – though they take an appropriately Dissenting form. Like Comte, he admits the need for expediency and cries woe on those through whom it comes. The text of his sermon – 'And all the people said, Amen' – touches on the Comtist theme of irresistible public opinion, and his laboured prosing about music anticipating 'the millenial reign when . . . one law shall be written on all hearts, and be the structure of all thought and . . . the principle of all action' (ch. 13) implicitly anticipates a time when law will be socially and psychologically organic through the agency of the spiritual power.

In a sense, of course, this deliberate deflection of the English radical tradition away from that intense preoccupation with central and local government which was in fact to characterize it in the mid-nineteenth century towards a Positivist concentration on education of the mind and heart, is quite as unhistorical as Coveney's organicist conception of retrospective radicalism. However, the novel's overt progressivism, and specifically its acceptance of the manufacturing town as a source of value, ensures that the admittedly hypothetical radicalism of *Felix Holt* at least has authentic roots in English history which Coveney's reading denies it. This applies in particular to what Coveney rightly sees as the focal point of the novel's radicalism (it is also the key to its difficult and contentious organization as a narrative), namely Esther Lyon's decision to forgo her claim on the Transome estate.

As Barbara Hardy rightly observes, George Eliot does all she can to free this choice of Esther's from 'the desires of the heart',[24] to make it a uniquely special case. Specifically, Esther's claim is one 'with which equity has nothing to do',[25] the elaborate, improbable, and tedious plot being carefully organized to deny it broadly significant legal or social implications, and so to prevent it from setting any generally applicable precedents. Esther's obligations to Mr Lyon, for example, turn out to be far less pressing than those of Eppie to Silas Marner: her adoptive father has proved himself capable of living alone, and he did, however forgivably, deceive her. The moral claims of the Transomes are even more strictly limited. Harold's involvement in the estate has no element of piety in it; he is not even his father's heir; and the possibility of his marrying Esther softens her moral dilemma as far as his family is concerned by making a decent compromise at least possible. The sole issue confronting Esther, therefore, is none other than whether the inheritance of a landed estate has real moral value, and this in turn demands a re-evaluation, not of political goals, but of the governing class itself.

This central and historically extremely important issue is first raised in the introduction, when George Eliot writes of 'fine old woods' which allow the passer-by 'only peeps at the park and mansion which they shut in from the working-day world', a passage which has been interpreted by Coveney as an exposure of the 'social irrelevance'[26] of well-timbered country estates. But this is to take too simple a view of the matter. Mrs Transome has a point when she remarks that Radical houses stand 'staring above poor sticks of young trees and iron hurdles' (ch. 1), naked, new, without deep roots. So has Harold, of course, when he replies 'with gay careless-ness' that 'the Radical sticks are growing . . . and half the Tory oaks are rotting.' The truth and the superficiality in both their judgments in fact constitute the problem. How are the competing and equally legitimate claims of young trees and fine old woods to be dealt with? Harold's 'gay carelessness', moreover, is precisely what makes Esther feel decidedly anxious some months later when she notes how the superficiality of his personal responses is reflected in political views that blend 'pride in his family and position, with the adhesion to changes that were to obliterate tradition and melt down enchased gold heirlooms into plating for the eggspoons of "the people"' (ch. 43). The need to preserve all that is represented by fine old woods and enchased gold heirlooms is in fact consistently asserted in *Felix Holt*. Similarly, in the 'Address', George Eliot was to express considerable anxiety about the dangers to which demo-cracy would expose that 'wealth of a . . . delicate kind, that . . . refinement of thought and feeling, and manners . . . which is carried on from the minds of one generation to the minds of another'. In particular, she feared that if 'the classes who hold the treasures of knowledge . . . [and] refined needs' were abruptly denied access to 'the sources by which their leisure and ease are furnished', they would 'withdraw from public affairs' and so endanger the whole social order.[27] In other words she was happy to leave the ordinary direction of society to 'gentlemen', and she thought that such men should be maintained in the style to which they were accustomed. The radicalism of *Felix Holt*, therefore, whatever its precise content, has to encompass George Eliot's endorsement of a way of life which the novel's heroine finally repudiates.

This important tension underlies the debate between Esther and Felix on 'fine-ladyism' and the theme's subsequent development. The Byronic vacuity of Esther's reading (so neatly recalling the pleasures of Mrs Transome's young womanhood) is sharply con-demned, but not all that Esther stands for is so easily disposed of. George Eliot may seem to endorse Felix's heavy-handed attack on Esther's position, but even when he suggests that by 'opinions' Esther means 'men's thoughts about great subjects, and by taste . . . their thoughts about small ones' (ch. 10), her choice of the word 'sensibilities' for 'opinions' has a certain force. Admittedly he is right again when he insists that opinion is really a form of sensibility, and 'taste' a pettier kind of sensibility than 'opinion'; but Esther's instinctive attachment to refinement may still have a value Felix cannot appreciate. Both words figure interestingly in the passages just quoted from the 'Address'. More important is the reference in the Introduction to the 'unmarketable beauty' of honeysuckle with its 'charm more subtle and penetrating than beauty', which apparently endorses in advance Esther's attachment to reticence and tact. Moreover, when she moves into Transome Court, that reticence and tact (which are significantly appropriate to her surroundings) enable her to perform an invaluable service to Harold and his mother. But even though delicate instinct wins important victories in *Felix Holt*, Esther finally opts for the 'dim life of the back street, the contact with sordid vulgarity, the lack of refinement for the senses, the summons to the daily task' (ch. 48), a setting in other words which puts delicacy and refinement in real danger, as Felix recognizes when he fondles her curls (they interestingly recall the 'tendrilled strength' of the convolvuluses in the "Introduction"), and reminds her that she is 'a delicate creature'. Thus the radicalism of *Felix Holt* consists in George Eliot's determined but reluctant acceptance of the need to transplant some of the unmarketable beauty of delicacy and refinement out of its liberal pre-industrial homes in hedgerow and country house into the sordid vulgarity of the back street. Esther's choice is not simply a retrospectively based rejection of Victorian money values, but a forward-looking sacrifice of truly enriching social and class contexts as well.

Moreover, through Harold Transome, George Eliot establishes the moral importance of gentlemanliness in a way which emphasizes the sacrificial character of this choice. At first both Harold and gentility are seen in decidedly unflattering terms. He is, we are told,

> not stringently consistent, but without any disposition to falsity; proud, . . . unspeculative, unsentimental, unsympathetic; fond of sensual pleasures, but disinclined to all vice, and attached as a healthy, clear-sighted person, to all conventional morality, construed with a certain freedom, like doctrinal articles to which public order may require subscription (ch. 8).

What this unflattering allusion to Anglican Church discipline means in practice becomes apparent when we are informed that he still maintains a mistress 'brought with him from the East' (ch. 36). He is symptomatically dependent on 'external Reason' for the maintenance of any sort of moral order in his life; cut off from it in the East, he actually buys himself a wife, and he only rejects Christian's offer to disappear because things would look black for him if the matter came to light later. The nearest he comes to moral feeling before the great crisis in his life is the subtle dislike he experiences when he thinks of the social humiliation likely to result from his having to give evidence at Felix Holt's trial. Yet there is more to Harold's gentlemanliness than is at first apparent. At the trial he has 'generosity and candour enough' not to resent Felix's rejection of his help. He also has 'all the susceptibilities of a gentleman; and these moral qualities [give] the right direction to his acumen, in judging of the behaviour that would best secure his dignity' (ch. 46). The phrasing is trenchant; but if Harold's dominant impulse is intelligent self-regard, his resulting behaviour is nonetheless practically beneficial to others, and grounded in sensibilities which, though selfish, are supple and alert. Gentlemanliness begins to emerge as a significant value at this point, and its importance is confirmed in the developing contrast between Harold and Matthew Jermyn.

This contrast is carefully worked out in class terms. The prospect of shame and loss stimulates Harold to behave precisely as his sense of gentlemanly honour dictates. On the evening after his parentage is revealed his always courteous manner towards Esther is morally transformed. He does not of course become wholly altruistic. To look for such purity would be to ignore the strong-willed, cultivated, intelligent courage of his address to her. But he does become 'occupied with resolute thoughts, determining to do what he knew that perfect honour demanded, let it cost him what it would' (ch. 49). Beside this finely controlled study in moral regeneration there is the degeneration of Matthew Jermyn. George Eliot wrote of few characters with such understanding or such distaste:

> A man of sixty, with an unsuspicious wife and daughters capable of shrieking and fainting at a sudden revelation, and of looking at him reproachfully in their daily misery under a shabby lot to which he had reduced them – with a mind and with habits dried hard by the years – with no glimpse of an endurable standing-ground except where he could domineer and be prosperous according to the ambitions of pushing middle-class gentility, – such a man is likely to find the prospect of worldly ruin ghastly enough to drive him to the most uninviting means of escape (ch. 42);

'pushing middle-class gentility' is a gross, ugly phrase, but so is Jermyn's behaviour when he asks Mrs Transome to confess her shame to her son. Finally, however, Jermyn's feelings override even the external Reason of his type and class. A primitive violence possesses him in his last confrontation with Harold: he has 'words within him that [are] fangs to clutch [Harold's] obstinate strength, and wring forth the blood and compel submission' (ch. 47). There follows the public revelation of Harold's paternity. At this climactic moment, however, the nearly fainting Harold is physically and morally supported by Sir Maximus Debarry, who orders Jermyn to leave the room on the grounds that he is not a gentleman. Harold, by implication, is. In effect, just as Rufus Lyon acknowledges the 'ministry' of the unbeliever, Felix Holt, so Sir Maximus acknowledges the lawyer's bastard as his social equal. Esther is thus not the only character in the novel to recognize the insignificance of a merely legal right; Sir Maximus Debarry, reactionary old baronet as he is, does so as well. There are values and loyalties which are superior to facts. Gentlemanliness is one of them.

Harold's moral growth has important political implications. As a boy, he was a type of simple male aggressiveness, rather like Tom Tulliver, 'bright, active, good-tempered . . . with sharp eyes and a good aim [who] delighted in success and in predominance' and who developed 'the energetic will and muscle, the self-confidence, the quick perception, and the narrow imagination which make what is admiringly called the practical mind' (ch. 8). And like Tom Tulliver he is insensitive, in adulthood, to the needs and feelings of women, though Esther observes and enjoys his 'practical cleverness – the masculine ease with which he governed everybody and administered everything' (ch. 43). It is of some importance to the novel's political theme that suffering finally enables him to integrate this masculine practicality and authority with a new receptiveness to the needs of others, particularly his mother. It is worth noting, also, that after a period away from North Loamshire, he reassumes the semi-public responsibilities of a landed proprietor. He becomes, in fact, the kind of man to whom the ordinary direction of society could safely be entrusted. Yet there is no suggestion of his ever again entering public life. Originally a brutal usurper and innovator, he becomes the authentic embodiment of traditional gentlemanly virtue, and yet is left functionless, almost impotent, at the end of the novel. Having brilliantly refined the gentlemanly ideal, George Eliot chooses to subordinate it aesthetically to her sense of a very different kind of heroism, a kind of secular sanctity, in the person of Felix Holt, who is the antitype of gentlemanly virtues, and who therefore constitutes a truly radical critique of the role of class in public life.

He is certainly not the 'fragment'[28] described by Henry James, but in some ways a thoroughly convincing character. His 'priggishness and pedantry', as Arnold Kettle suggests, 'are by and large "placed", and a genuine strength and simplicity emerges.'[29] There is something slightly Lawrentian, in fact, in the way in which, as an overbearing, self-educated, working-class lover, he attacks fastidiousness in the woman to whom he is strongly drawn sexually. His humourless self-preoccupation is also proto-Lawrentian. In his first interview with Mr Lyon he makes the following statements about himself: 'I am not a mouse'; 'I'm not one of your subtle fellows'; 'I was converted by six weeks debauchery'; 'I can live on bran porridge'; 'I'm perhaps a little too fond of banging and smashing' (ch. 5). With Esther he adds impulsive bad manners to this 'young heartiness' and not surprisingly they quarrel about gentility. 'I hate your gentle-manly speakers,' he declares, and 'One sort of fine ladyism is as good as another.' 'A real fine lady,' Esther replies, '. . . is something refined, and graceful, and charming, and never obtrusive.' But Felix relishes the graceless and obtrusive – he would like to scold Esther 'every day, and make her cry and cut her fine hair off'. Even at his trial he indulges his psychologically convincing if unattractive taste for self-definition;

> 'I consider that I should be making an unworthy defence' [he declares], 'if I let the court infer . . . that because I am a man who hates drunken disorder, or any wanton harm, therefore I am a man who would never fight against authority . . . there is no great religion and no great freedom that has not done it, in the beginning' (ch. 46).

This declaration (including the question-begging last phrase) is characteristic. Felix's lack of control on the subject of himself verges on the socially stupid. Henry James complains of the 'want of tact' with which George Eliot indulged her 'taste for general con-siderations'.[30] Her hero shares this shortcoming. He does so, however, only because his commitment to moral absolutes is such that it could never be tactfully adapted to social conventions. To grasp the point George Eliot is making through him, in other words, it is not necessary for middle-class readers to like Felix Holt – indeed it may help if they do not.

This is not to suggest that his ideas, as distinct from his personality, are unimportant. There is a drawing together of occasion, character, incident and theme towards the end of his nomination day speech, for instance, when he touches on the corruptions of the electoral process, which brings his English to life and gives lasting relevance to what he has to say: 'I'll tell you what sort of men would get the power' in a democracy, he declares –

> 'They would be men who would undertake to do the business for

a candidate, and return him, men who have no real opinions, but who pilfer the words of every opinion, and turn them into a cant which will serve their purpose at the moment; men who look out for dirty work to make their fortunes by, because dirty work wants little talent and no conscience' (ch. 30).

As a direct result of this outburst, and the laugh at Johnson's expense which Felix draws from the crowd, Christian and Johnson, declined gentleman and rising attorney, are brought together. Politically the speech makes sense: corruption and cynicism are demonstrably more serious dangers in a democracy than a drunken electorate, and imaginatively the subsequent sense of dirt gathering in the dusk is very effective. In this accurately analysed and vividly felt moral twilight, Felix, as the awkward embodiment of an impracticable and uncomfortable idealism, offers, if not practical hope, then at least genuine illumination.

But in politics illumination is not enough. It is also necessary, at least for the radical, to reach decisions and to act on them. For this reason, Esther's decision to marry Felix is of the first importance. By it we can measure George Eliot's commitment to change not as a hope but as a choice. It must be said at once that this commitment, while undoubtedly serious, is nonetheless limited – but at least it is not ignored: the whole problem of choosing, of making radically innovatory decisions, is more extensively and carefully discussed in *Felix Holt* than it is in *The Mill on the Floss*. At the same time it is given thematic status in certain key images. The issue is first raised when Felix and Esther compare her decision to read romantic literature instead of accompanying Mr Lyon to chapel with Felix's decision also to absent himself from religious observance. He would sink himself, he says, by doing anything but what he saw to be best. Esther bridles at the implication that she is 'a lower kind of being' who would not be similarly degraded by compromise. 'If a woman really believes herself to be a lower kind of being . . .' Felix replies, 'she should be ruled by the thoughts of her father or husband. If not, let her show her power of choosing something better' (ch. 14). In the earlier novels choosing (as against long-term willing) is the suddenly revealed consequence of habitual, consciously cultivated mental attitudes, and only those decisions grounded in established feeling are trustworthy. But Felix seems to be talking about authentic moral innovation. Esther, however, doubts her power to choose. Harold tells her glibly that she is 'empress of [her] own fortunes', but she is uncertain about 'what to do with [her] empire' (ch. 40). At this point the problem of choice is justifiably interwoven with that of a

woman's right to moral independence: Esther may be prevented
from making 'her own lot', not because choice is impossible, but
because as a woman her 'lot is made for her by the love she accepts'
(ch. 43). In any case it would seem that the opportunity for making
choices is both rare and morally subject to the past if not determined
by it. ('It is only in [the] freshness of our time', George Eliot
suggests, 'that the choice is possible which gives unity to life, and
makes the memory a temple where . . . all worship and all grateful
joys, are an unbroken history sanctified by one religion' – ch. 44.)
The specific problem of free choice, however, remains prominent.
Esther has real freedom compared with the hunger for power which
gives Mrs Transome her imprisoned queenliness. 'Unlike that
Semiramis who made laws to suit her practical license' – the
reference is to Catherine the Great as well as to Semiramis herself –
Mrs Transome lives 'in the midst of desecrated sanctities, and of
honours . . . tarnished in the light of montonous and weary suns'
(ch. 40). Esther, by way of contrast, can feel a 'succession of
influences that modify the being', and can therefore undergo
something 'little short of an inward revolution'. This 'revolutionary
struggle' (ch. 39) in fact continues until she leaves Transome Court.
The fact that the notion of revolution is so carefully emphasized at
this point, even though it is inconsistent with the ideal of 'an
unbroken history sanctified by one religion', deserves careful consideration. It is the culmination of a series of references to queens and
empresses (Marie-Antoinette has a shadowy presence in the novel)
surrounding Esther and Mrs Transome. The possibility of Esther's
making a revolutionary act of the will is clearly being examined.
Unfortunately the decision she reaches, however broadly radical its
implications socially, is safely conservative in personal terms. If she
had accepted her inheritance and remained unmarried her choice
would have been unmistakably other than any that a father or a
husband would have made for her. As it is, the issue of whether she
chooses for herself, or is acted on by established structures of
feeling, goes unobtrusively out of focus. George Eliot's determinism
allows her to envisage profound if evolutionary transformations in
people and therefore in society, but at this stage she will not
contemplate a specifically revolutionary act of the will.

What she affirms, however, in spite of this abdication of responsibility, is nonetheless important. She seems to envisage social
transformations radical enough to be described as a cultural revolution. Nor can this be dismissed simply as an attempt to defuse the
challenge of revolutionary politics. It is a real and uncompromising
attack on the dominant assumptions and evaluations of a class-

dominated society, an attack all the more impressive for the strength of the case made out in defence of the existing balance of cultural forces. Within a framework of conventional political thinking in the 1860s, this is in key respects a more authentically radical position than that taken by the political radicals of the period, who were, after all, to end up as Unionists in alliance with the Conservative party and proponents of the aggressively self-confident class ethos of Imperialism. No subsequent writer in English, not even Hale White, Butler or Wells, was so radically to attack the ideology of class, until Lawrence. That is why it is worth re-emphasizing the connexion between Felix Holt and Rupert Birkin.

Nevertheless George Eliot's rejection of political action in *Felix Holt* brings us to the *terminus ad quem* of her political thinking, at least until she came to write her last novel. It returns us also to the point at which she was compelled to close her narratives in *The Mill on the Floss* and *Romola*, the point at which the impulse and the need for change became incompatible with the impulse and the need for continuity. The continuities in question are primarily psychological and social, and they prohibit certain kinds of emotional, intellectual and institutional fractures with the past. History for George Eliot sets limits on the realization of human potentialities, limits which theory and narrative alike must respect, theory on the ground that science is a structure of thought based on *sequence*, narrative because it is the artist's duty to be realistic. Discovering the manifold connexion of event and character, after all, is one of the major pleasures of reading George Eliot. There can be intimations in the smallest image or the most inconspicuous phrase, of complex, consistent, yet ultimately incalculable possibilities in the ordered worlds of physical, mental and social contingency. Hers is the kind of fiction from which conclusions are drawn – she continually draws them herself – and consequently it is the kind of fiction which imposes a responsibility on its author to do without opium. But if Positivism puts the mind in a cage, it does not limit vision. If Comte had wished to do that he would have been content with the respected *Cours de Philosophie Positive*. But he went on to write the despised *Système de Politique Positive*, in itself a massive demonstration of how Positivism was capable of resisting if not of overcoming its own structural imprisonment. For precisely similar reasons George Eliot's fiction could never limit itself to the realistic perspectives by which it was formally structured. She could not accept the limitations imposed on her by the moment of death or retreat into the past to which she was led by the logic of her narrative. Her historical and political realism are consequently compromised and fractured by vision and symbol, just as Positivism itself was compromised by prophecy and dogma. It is for this reason that her thinking on the nature of art and its relation to the real world is of the first importance in coming to an adequate understanding of her teaching.

5 Art and vision

ONE of the most noticeable and initially puzzling contrasts in George Eliot's work is that between *Silas Marner* and *Romola*. They have many features in common and are obviously the work of the same author, but the first is an exemplary performance, modest, profound and realistic, while the second is ambitious, wooden, and romanticized. Both certainly struck contemporary reviewers as verging on opposite extremes. *Silas Marner* was thought to be a particularly brutal example of realism. E. S. Dallas, for example, described the people of Raveloe as 'boors' to whom George Eliot had *given* moral dignity. 'We see [them],' he wrote, 'amid all their grovelling cares, with all their coarseness, ignorance, and prejudice – poor, paltry, stupid, wretched, well-nigh despicable.'[1] To Henry James, the world of the novel was 'doubly, brutally, morbidly English.'[2] The following dialogue indicates what they meant:

> 'Some folks 'ud say that was a fine beast you druv in yesterday, Bob?'
>
> The butcher, a jolly, smiling red-haired man, was not disposed to answer rashly. He gave a few puffs before he spat and replied, 'And they wouldn't be fur wrong, John' (ch. 6).

Romola, not surprisingly, seemed an excessively artificial work by contrast. Even the *Westminster Review* complained of its 'facile opportuneness' of plot,[3] while the *Saturday Review* thought it a pity that such a book should have been written 'by the authoress of *Adam Bede*'.[4]

These extremes of realism and romanticism in George Eliot's work are in fact united by a conception of how art functions which is of fundamental importance to an understanding of her own perform-ance as an artist. In 1856, she began 'The Natural History of German Life' with an attack on painters of the countryside who

> treat their subjects under the influence of traditions and preposes-sions rather than of direct observation. The notion that
> peasants are joyous, that the typical moment to represent a man

in a smock-frock is when he is cracking a joke and showing a row
of sound teeth, that cottage matrons are usually buxom, and
village children necessarily rosy and merry, are prejudices difficult to dislodge from the artistic mind, which looks for its
subjects into literature instead of life.[5]

The conventions of opera were acceptable – 'a chorus of colliers in
their pit costume, or a ballet of char-women and stocking-weavers'
would be incongruous – but the novel was different:

> our social novels profess to represent the people as they are, and
> the unreality of their representations is a grave evil. The greatest
> benefit we owe to the artist, whether painter, poet, or novelist, is
> the extension of our sympathies.[6]

However, it is precisely this principle of extending the sympathies
which elsewhere is adduced in favour of art other than the realistic,
and specifically of art produced 'under the influence of traditions and
prepossessions rather than of direct observation.' For example, in a
review of the third volume of *Modern Painters*, also in 1856, George
Eliot wrote:

> The fundamental principles of all just thought and beautiful
> action or erection are the same, and in making clear to ourselves
> what is best and noblest in art, we are making clear to ourselves
> what is best and noblest in morals; in learning how to estimate the
> artistic products of a particular age according to the mental
> attitude and external life of that age, we are widening our
> sympathy and deepening the basis of our tolerance and charity.[7]

Art, in other words, incites us to two different kinds of imaginative
sympathy. Realistic art breaks through class and social barriers in
current society; other art forms stimulate and enrich the historical
imagination. Thus even if it is true, as the commentary of *Adam Bede*
asserts, that George Eliot turns 'without shrinking, from cloud-
borne angels, from prophets, sibyls and heroic warriors, to an old
woman bending over her flower-pot' (ch. 17), she has an obligation
nonetheless at some point to turn back again, and engage like
Dorothea Brooke in Rome with the morally necessary task of
extending her sympathies by trying to understand works of art that
seem bewildering and even distasteful.

There is a contradiction lurking in this principle of sympathy,
however, to which George Eliot was particularly sensitive at quite
an early stage in her career. The uneasy reference to char-women
and stocking-weavers in 'The Natural History of German Life', for

example, contains an implicit recognition that, while in general art may enlarge the sympathies, some art at least is class-based and therefore socially divisive. This, as we have already seen, is one of the most important tensions in *Felix Holt*, but it first receives explicit recognition in as early a work as 'Mr Gilfil's Love-story', the principal theme of which is precisely the contrast between a cultured cold-heartedness on the one hand and coarse rustic humanity on the other, and which attempts to integrate into a single text the art of cloud-borne angels and that of old women bending over their flower-pots. It does so in full consciousness of the human and historical contradictions implied by the very existence of these two artistic modes. Its opening in the safe, uncomplicated world which preceded Amos Barton's curacy is reassuringly realistic without being reductive. It is relaxing to move among country-people with interest centred in this second narrative on a parson who, unlike Amos Barton, has settled comfortably for an undoctrinal care of souls, based on his knowledge of the local dialect and of human nature rather than on strict scriptural exegesis and a precise doctrine of justification. The authorial voice participates in the narration with a freedom and relevance it lacked in the earlier story – the intellectual humour in particular is enriched with relevant local imagery:

> For Shepperton, you observe, was in a state of Attic culture
> compared with Knebly; it had turnpike roads and a public
> opinion, whereas, in the Boetian Knebly, men's minds and
> waggons alike moved in the deepest ruts, and the landlord was
> only grumbled at as a necessary and unalterable evil, like the
> weather, the weevils, and the turnip-fly (ch. 1).

The Times rightly reported this first chapter to be especially admirable, and if a false note of unearned intimacy with lady-readers warns us of difficulties ahead, the developing perspectives of the story's opening are an impressive conception. This makes all the more disturbing the sudden move through the closed doors of the dead Caterina's room: the sense that reductive emotional intimacies are imminent can be felt almost at once, and the narrative is undoubtedly unsettled at this point, if not actually betrayed. But the move is a revealing and a necessary one, for without such a transition there would have been no need to develop the story further, to turn the sketch of Mr Gilfil's ministry into a narrative; there would have been no problem for George Eliot to solve. And the problem with which the subsequent narrative has to engage is that Mr Gilfil is not a product of the richly human world in which he ministers. He has a private life, symbolized by Caterina's room, of which his parishioners are wholly ignorant. Nor, on consideration, could it be otherwise. What is disturbing, however, is that ostensibly he is the product of precisely the kind of privileged aristocratic culture with which George Eliot herself seems to be thoroughly out of sympathy. The limiting artificiality of this life is certainly emphasized in the second chapter, which begins with Lady Cheverel treading the lawn 'as is she were one of Sir Joshua Reynolds's stately ladies, who has suddenly stepped from her frame.' Behind her, the manor gives a similarly artificial impression – it would make 'a charming picture for an English Watteau'. And so does Captain Wybrow: asleep at the end of the chapter, he looks 'like a fine cameo in high relief on the slightly indented pillow.' The human and moral limitations of late eighteenth-century country-house culture clearly operate within, and are expressed by, the aesthetic conventions it finds acceptable. Thus the awkward stylistic transitions in the text of 'Mr Gilfil's Love-story' from shapeless realism to the ornamental and the formal reflect and express a fundamental ambiguity in the social functions of art as George Eliot perceives them.

And the problem is not a simple one, in spite of the seductive attractiveness of the simple life and richly realistic representations of it. The high culture of Cheverel Manor, after all, enables us to recognize the very real limitations of life without adequate education. Sir Christopher's tenants and estate-workers, for example, no more understand his neo-gothic ornamentatiion of the Manor (so like the elaborate play of fanciful imagery worked into George Eliot's own narration) than Caterina's father is able to assimilate the glories of Milan cathedral; and the fact that his attention focusses instead on a 'tinsel Madonna as the symbol of divine mercy and protection' (ch. 3) is explicitly represented as a sign of his childishness as well as of his good-heartedness. Thus while the arts may promote and confirm divisions, estrangements and even immoralities in human society, they also and far more importantly enlarge human knowledge and extend human sympathy.

The task George Eliot has undertaken in 'Mr Gilfil's Love-story' is apparently to identify a principle of unity in art by which all these contradictions might be transcended, and she finds it, tentatively, hypothetically as it were, in Caterina's singing, the aesthetic complexity of which is appropriaate to the Cheverels' drawing-room, while its immediate and intense emotional yield relates it to the spontaneity and warmth of common life. Vulnerable and socially isolated though she may be, therefore, Caterina embodies unique, even revolutionary possibilities of integration in the world of the novel. For that very reason, of course, she is also a threat to the class divisions and suppressions of feeling on which it depends. Her story therefore develops into a symbolic representation of major social divisions and historical collisions.

As such, however, it cannot be decisively resolved. Her complete destruction would have been improperly pessimistic. On the other hand, final and successful integration into English life would have been mere romantic self-indulgence. She therefore recovers from the crisis of Wybrow's rejection of her and his subsequent death, but only for a while. Appropriately she finds refuge first of all with the common country-people with whom she has always felt at ease. Later she is roused from her torpor by the accidental sounding of 'a deep bass note' on the harpsichord brought by Maynard Gilfil to the Foxholm parsonage:

> The vibration rushed through Caterina like an electric shock: it seemed as if at that instant a new soul were entering into her, and filling her with a deeper, more significant life. She looked round, rose from the sofa, and walked to the harpsichord. In a moment her fingers were wandering with their old sweet method among the keys, and her soul was floating in its true familiar element of delicious sound, as the water-plant that lies withered and shrunken on the ground expands into freedom and beauty when once more bathed in its native flood (ch. 20).

Soon she is singing the air from *Orfeo* which she had sung at the beginning of her sorrows, the 'long happy days of childhood and girlhood [have] recovered their rightful predominance over the short interval of sin and sorrow', and in Maynard Gilfil's arms the 'soul that was born anew to music' is 'born anew to love'. But only for a time. She dies and her room is sealed off from the world. But we now know what it is Mr Gilfil treasures there – it is the memory of that transcendence of division which the intense but exquisite musicality of his young wife was able briefly to embody.

Two aspects of George Eliot's aesthetic theory emerge with particular clarity from this narrative – the physiological and psychological basis of artistic gifts on the one hand, and what may be called their historical teleology on the other. The first, of course, derives from Associationism, and it enables George Eliot to hypothesize structural correspondence between Caterina's *physique*, her moral condition, and the music she plays:

> Caterina, thinking she was not wanted, went away and sat down to the harpsichord in the sitting-room. It seemed as if playing

massive chords – bringing out volumes of sound, would be the easiest way of passing the long feverish moments before twelve o'clock. Handel's *Messiah* stood open on the desk, at the chorus 'All we like sheep', and Caterina threw herself at once into the impetuous intricacies of that magnificent fugue. In her happiest moments she could never have played it so well: for now all the passion that made her misery was hurled by a convulsive effort into the music, just as pain gives new force to the clutch of the sinking wrestler, and as terror gives far-sounding intensity to the shriek of the feeble (ch. 13).

Similar correspondences between situation, *physique*, and music inform the rather subtler descriptions of Maggie Tulliver's responsiveness in *The Mill on the Floss*. One such moment is her reaction to the duet in *Masaniello*:

When the strain passed into the minor, she half started from her seat with the sudden thrill of that change. Poor Maggie! She looked very beautiful when her soul was being played on in this way by the inexorable power of sound. You might have seen the slightest perceptible quivering of her whole frame as she leaned foward to steady herself; while her eyes dilated and brightened into that wide-open, childish expression of wondering delight, which always came back in her happiest moments (Bk VI, ch. 7).

The singers are Philip and Stephen. The words 'thrill', 'beautiful', 'soul', 'quivering', and even 'childish', therefore, have considerable connotative range, suggesting complex but unstateable connexions between Maggie's reactions to the music and her reactions to those making it. Her external problems are thus painfully internalized through the action of the music on her susceptible frame, but at the same time the music gives external expression to the intimate movements of her inner life. What we confront through music, therefore, in Maggie's case and in Caterina's, is the mystery of subjectivity as the vulnerable locus of authentic values in the living world.

But music also enables us to gain access in a certain sense to the future. The action of music on Fidalma in *The Spanish Gypsy* is in this respect characteristic. The long notes, we are told

> With subtle penetration enter all
> The myriad corridors of the passionate soul,
> Messenger-like spread, and answering action rouse . . .
> To soft andante strains pitched plaintively. (pp. 62–3)

The word 'plaintively' here is typical and significant. Like the similar word 'yearning' it is highly suggestive of the relations George Eliot detected between music and history. In 'Jubal', for example, we are told that the hero's body is

> Fashioned to finer senses, which became
> A yearning for some hidden soul of things (p.10)

Music, and the musical *physique*, express a straining away from the present, often back into the past, but also forward towards the future, a straining which seems to be built organically into the human constitution. Even the tone-deaf Mr Lyon in *Felix Holt* can recognize the implicitly historical thrust of musical experience:

> 'though I am not [he says], endowed with an ear to seize those
> earthly harmonies which to some devout souls have seemed, as it
> were the broken echoes of the heavenly choir – I apprehend there
> is a law in music disobedience whereunto would bring us in our
> singing to the level of shrieking maniacs or howling beasts . . .
> And even as in music, where all obey and concur to one end, so
> that each has the joy of contributing to a whole whereby he is
> ravished and lifted up into the courts of heaven, so it will be in
> that crowning time of the millenial reign, when our daily prayer
> will be fulfilled, and one law shall be written on all hearts, and be
> the structure of all thought, and be the principle of all action'
> (ch. 13).

Mr Lyon is here indulging in an eschatalogical fantasy, but in Positivist terms his speech clearly anticipates that normative assimilation of moral and scientific law into the organic life of the individual and of society which is the apparent goal or purpose of history. Thus in the idiom of 'Jubal', the hidden soul of *man* is identical with the hidden soul of *things*, and both are given indirect but passionate expression in the yearning harmonies of music.

Effects comparable with these were, of course, attributed to the other arts, and particularly to architecture. Religious buildings, Comte wrote, 'are the most perfect monumental expression of the ideas and feelings of our moral nature',[8] while in a review of Owen Jones's *The Grammar of Ornament* in 1865, George Eliot declared that architects modify 'men's moods and habits, which are the mothers of opinion, having quite as much to do with their formation as the responsible father – Reason.'[9] It is certainy not an accident that architecture figures in intricate association with music in 'Mr Gilfil's Love-story', for like music, architecture is prophetic. Allusion has already been made to Giotto's campanile in the Florence of *Romola*, which

> in all its harmonious variety of colour and form led their eyes
> upward, high into the clear air of this April morning, [and]
> seemed a prophetic symbol, telling that human life must some-
> how and some time shape itself into accord with that pure
> aspiring beauty (ch. 3).

The emphasis in this passage is clearly away from the present; beauty aspires, it reaches upwards. But perhaps as important as the prophetic implications of music and architecture is their lack of specificity, their inarticulateness. The measure of our remoteness from the goals of history which the forms and harmonies of music and architecture so exquisitely sybolize, is precisely the high level of abstraction in both art forms. Art conceals the future which it expresses.

Comte for one seems to have recognized the implicit defeatism in this idea: 'The principal function of art', he wrote,

> is to construct types on the basis furnished by Science . . . In the
> early periods of Polytheism, Poetry repaired the defects of the
> system viewed dogmatically . . . [In] dealing with a system
> founded, not upon the imagination, but upon observation of fact
> . . . the Positivist poet will naturally be led to form prophetic
> pictures of the regeneration of man.[10]

The important word in this passage is 'pictures'. Comte seems to be implying a need to bring the abstracted intuitions of music and architecture towards the more specific if still inarticulate condition of the image – but not the realistic image. 'That the portraiture should be exaggerated', he writes, 'follows from the definition of art; it should surpass realities so as to stimulate us to amend them.'[11] Elsewhere he argues that 'art rises above science, as better adapted to promote the development of true unity, by idealizing the future and the past, the combination of which must more and more control human existence.'[12] The Positivist artist, in short, breaks out of the merely realistic as a kind of moral provocation; he synthesizes and idealizes the past and the present; and finally his work strives away from the condition of music and towards that of the image if not of the word. In setting *Romola* in fifteenth-century Florence, yet at the same time trying, as she told Frederic Harrison, to depict 'some out of the normal relations',[13] and doing so in an intensely pictorial manner, George Eliot was obviously and probably consciously assuming the mantle of the Positivist artist.

As George Levine has shown, *Romola* is carefully and overtly constructed as a fable.[14] The effect is of pictorial symmetry and variation comparable with Piero di Cosimo's strange allegorical paintings. Very much more elaborately than 'Mr Gilfil's Love-story', in other words, *Romola* is about its own method of construction: it is an artificial fiction in which the status of artifice is a principle theme. Unlike the 'inartistic' Miss Irwines in *Adam Bede* (ch. 5), therefore, whose significance is precisely that they cannot be included in the picture, the significance of Tito and Romola can only be grasped if the reader sees them – and realizes that he is meant to see them – as figures formally and symbolically placed in a context which with sustained specificity insists on its own historically realistic status. *Romola* is thus in a very precise way the fictional equivalent of a Pre-Raphaelite painting, a minutely realistic and elaborately allegorical composition. Romola herself is a literary hybrid, a symbolic figure who responds in a deeply normative way to the images and symbols with which as a fifteenth-century Florentine she is realistically surrounded, and in developing the tensions between these two conditions, George Eliot is in effect defining in a highly complex fashion her own sense of the relationship of art to reality, that is of art to history.

Initially Romola is presented to us through a series of images and allusions which suggest immaturity and promise. The immaturity is largely the result of inexperience – she is in a state of 'girlish simplicity and ignorance concerning the world' (ch. 5). This, however, is concealed behind the majestic self-possession of her manner, and though she is highly susceptible – at 'the slightest touch on the fibres of affection or pity' she becomes 'passionate with tenderness' – her emotional life generally is hidden and undeveloped, the promise of her nature being visible only in her eyes. Even memory lies dormant within her until it is 'kindled . . . by the torch of some known joy' (ch. 6). She is thus in a complex sense virginal – both as a living personality awaiting translation out of potentiality into reality, and as a symbol awaiting interpretation. It is entirely appropriate, therefore, that symbols initially seem more important to her than actualities and that they have accordingly greater importance also in the narrative. In her first love-scene, for example, she is preoccupied not so much with what is happening to her for its own sake as with the three images of young manhood which have now been revealed to her, Dino's yearning 'look at the crucifix', an imaginary scholar-bridegroom with 'deep lines in his face . . . and with rather grey hair', and finally Tito himself, with his 'rich dark beauty which [seems] to gather round it all images of joy' (ch. 17). In the subsequent chapters various attempts are made

to reconcile the conflicts between sorrow, faith, reason and joy
implicit in these images, but the reconciliations are again all
symbolic. The first is the crudest. Romola and Tito simply bury the
images of sorrow represented by Dino's crucifix in the 'tomb of joy'
(ch. 20) represented by Piero's tryptich, but the futility of this
simple response is promptly indicated in the 'huge and ghastly image
of Winged Time' which bears down on them after the betrothal, and
later by the disillusionment which follows their marriage. Romola is
thus forced back upon that very asceticism which she had thought
buried in the tryptich. She labours 'to subdue her nature to her
husband's' (ch. 27); inwardly 'very far from . . . quiet endurance',
she courts 'rude sensations' (ch. 36) since pleasure and ease are now
associated with Tito's broken promises. But suppression either of
joy or of sorrow is also self-suppression, and consequently the 'larger
possibilities of her nature' remain hidden, 'folded and crushed like
embryonic wings' (ch. 27) within her. She is still morally a virgin,
still trapped in the world of symbol. This state is graphically
represented when, as she prepares to flee from Florence for the first
time, she removes Dino's crucifix from its tomb of joy and is
confronted with two images of herself, in the tryptich and in the
looking-glass. In one she is Ariadne, in the other a nun, in neither
simply herself.

The integration and actualization of Romola's personality begins
when she meets Savonarola on the road to Bologna. She has always
'lived apart' from the 'actual life of the mixed multitude' (ch. 15).
When she returns to Florence, however, she begins at last, in her
works of womanly sympathy for the poor, to enact rather than to
visualize that reconciliation of joy and sorrow for which she has been
searching. However, she herself then becomes that visible madonna
who embodies in her own person the meanings and values which the
contadini honour in the invisible *Madonna del Impruneta*. In leaving
the world of symbol, Romola paradoxically becomes one; in engaging with reality, she acquires the status of an ideal. This significantly
is the exact reverse of an effect which George Eliot had aimed at in
those of her early fictions in which art is represented as being under
a fundamental obligation to conform to observed truth. In *Romola*, a
narrative which is itself almost ostentatiously artificial, life as
embodied with psychological specificity in the heroine's self-
actualization finally conforms itself to potentialities which only art
can symbolize. And as George Eliot's letter to Harrison makes clear,
the Positivist reader at least was expected to recognize what this
development implies. The cult of the Virgin, Comte believed,
offered 'as the feminine type the beautiful mystic reconciliation of

purity with maternity', and this made it, he thought, 'a better representative than God of the one final object of all Western aspirations – Humanity.'[15] It would be excessive to suggest that Romola as the visible madonna is George Eliot's version of Comte's Virgin-Mother, but she is almost that: the image with which the novel ends, of a beautiful widow instructing a young boy about the virtues of a dead religious leader is iconographically an ample and exact statement of Positivist aspirations for humanity in general.

Precisely this orientation towards the future in a work of historical fiction, however, is in itself highly problematical. The difficulties would have been fewer if George Eliot had been concerned simply with transformations in a more or less timeless sphere of universal morality, as she had been, in effect, in *Silas Marner*. Her Florence, however, for all its frantic indulgence in prophetic fantasies, is so demonstrably ignorant of its own fate and the fates of Europe and the Church, that it seems a particularly anomalous setting in which to develop prophetic images on one's own account. But that of course is why George Eliot chose it. If she were to make a case for prophecy, she would have to acknowledge the strength of the case against it. Her visionaries, therefore, are frankly represented precisely according to the prejudices and presuppositions of her readers, as celibate fanatics. They encourage superstition and repression. They create conditions of mass hysteria. They are incapable of self-criticism. On a narrow front, their powers and obsessions make them seriously inattentive to the real world. Dino's desire for 'a life of perfect love and purity . . . in which there would be no tormenting questions, no fear of suffering' (ch. 15) is naive, simplistic and potentially selfish, and even though his prophetic dream arouses 'a strange awe' in Romola, there is considerable force in her question, 'What is this religion of yours, that places visions before natural duties?' and he is explicitly condemned for failing to give her the information necessary to save her from marrying Tito.

Having made these admissions, however, George Eliot is free to suggest what a great deal of successful prognostication goes on in ordinary life. Piero the artist is a prophet in his way; so is Bernardo, the man of affairs. Both are intuitively right about Tito, while even Baldassare can recognize in Tessa a 'creature who would need to be avenged' (ch. 33). More difficult to defend are visions themselves, and the uncertain status of their predictions. Particularly anomalous in this respect are Dino's visionary experiences, because they are not based on actual reported experiences like those of Savonarola, but are invented by George Eliot herself, and therefore have a purely factitious accuracy. The same, however, could be said of Piero di

Cosimo's tryptich, and that, of course, is the point. Dino's visions
are the ocular equivalents of music heard in the head; they are
instantaneous works of subjective art; and this accounts for their
predictive accuracy, for as we saw in an earlier chapter, the
structures and processes of individual lives reproduce those of the
surrounding social medium, just as the surrounding social medium
develops out of the structures of the individual mind and heart. It
follows that if it is possible for a particular personality to understand
intuitively, and to represent itself in symbols, the *potentialities* of its
own being as well as its present reality, then it must also be possible,
perhaps even in the self-same act, for such a mind to grasp and
represent a future inhering in quite specific social situations, so long
as they correspond in some way to the structures of its own inner
life. Thus Baldassare can confusedly sense his own situation in
Tessa's; Piero, slowly, can build up symbolic anticipations of Romola's developing life; and Dino, with that greater intensity of imagination that goes with his constitution and monastic asceticism, can
literally see in his dreams something of the fate awaiting Romola in
her marriage. In Savonarola's case, however, the internal life which
is the source of such images is exceptionally rich and noble, and
consequently his visionary experiences have a relevance to the major
structural transformations that are about to take place in Italy and
the world. Thus in spite of the great dangers involved in surrender-
ing to the gift of vision, in spite of its proximity to superstition,
hysteria and a kind of moral solipsism, it is incomparably more
significant than shallow objectivity like Tito's. 'Man is governed and
made happy by images,' Feuerbach writes. An 'inward necessity
. . . impels him to present moral and philosophical doctrines in the
form of narratives and fables', and even if this impulse is misrepre-
sented as revelation, the motive behind the representation is
nonetheless to make men 'good and wise'.[16] The inward necessity in
the true visionary simply concentrates and intensifies this process.

But this does not mean that George Eliot sanctions uncritical
acceptance even of the greatest visionary. Once again the time and
place in which she sets the novel are important in establishing her
meaning. Clearly the circumstances of pre-Reformation Florence are
far from ideal, and the function of the city's visionaries is correspondingly provisional. Like Poetry in the early periods of Polytheism,
they repair the defects of current belief viewed dogmatically, and
that is why they fall continually into error, in spite of the great
truths latent in what they see. Their failure is not one of seeing but
of interpreting. In Comte's account of the Positivist order, however,
the poet will no longer correct error intuitively; he will have a

precise and rational understanding of the relations of his work to current belief, and he will share with his readers a modern and coherent view of the prophetic nature of literary activity. At the end of *Romola*, therefore, the visionaries of Florence are all either dead or discredited, overcome like Caterina by natural and historical forces, disease, mental pressures, politics and war, with which they are unable to cope. But the novel does not therefore imply that the age of vision as such is past. On the contrary, in its closing stages, the task of 'seeing' is handed on to the reader. It is we, with our scientific psychology and our developed historical, moral and aesthetic perspectives, who have to compose in our own minds a vision of the normal state as embodied in the novel's principal character. Thus Romola herself, not simply as the visible madonna, but precisely as one who is *seen*, is the goal to which George Eliot has been led by the logic as well as the aesthetics of Positivism. It is not, unfortunately, a particularly happy point on which to conclude so ample a meditation.

There is no doubt but that in principle *Romola* is a progressive work. Starting from the belief that all aesthetic and emotional experiences have a common source in the structures of subjectivity, George Eliot, as we have seen, seriously attempts to extend her sense of those structures and the promise she believes they contain beyond the wordless condition of music to the clearer and more definitive condition of the image. Her effort, however, serves only to reveal the limitations rather than the authority of the image, for precisely as vision rather than realistic report, images expose the gap between what might be and what is. They are thus expressions of the frustration of human potentialities as well as of their possible fulfilment, and are consequently as incapable of transcending the imprisoning logic of Positivism as music is. This is a conclusion which George Eliot herself clearly recognizes. At the end of the novel Romola has to accommodate her sense of values to the complex fact of Savonarola's failure, and because she constitutes the substance of what we for our part are permitted to see of 'the normal relations', we, as modern visionaries, have simply to accept that accommodation as exemplary. Greater emphasis is thereby given to a moral task in the present, that of interpreting limitation and defeat, than to the promise inherent in the perspective which images in principle can open on the future. Art, having emerged from subjectivity to do battle with the processes of history, is forced finally to retreat from the future back to the present and its origins in subjectivity. Of all George Eliot's novels, therefore, *Romola* is the one which most strongly suggests that her efforts to teach were nothing more than a vastly ambitious exercise in self-defeating rationalization. It is therefore also the work which confirms the inadequacy of merely surveying that teaching. What it requires and deserves is a depth of analysis and criticism which hitherto it has been denied.

Part Two: Confusions

6 Theory and practice

The challenge of Marx's 'Theses on Feuerbach'

MARX'S 'Theses on Feuerbach' constitute a fundamental attack on the whole tradition in which Comte and Feuerbach worked. They are consequently of direct relevance to a study of George Eliot's teaching, particularly so, perhaps, because of their anomalous status as early posthumously published jottings (they are written in 1845) which are nonetheless important enough to be quoted on his tombstone. We are not, after all, engaged on anything so ambitious as a 'Marxist' study of George Eliot's writings, but at most on what might serve as part of the first stage in such an undertaking. Since George Eliot's teaching is no more than one component of what she produced, its analysis must logically precede any examination of how that production related to a determining historical context. Moreover, to the extent that the 'Theses' are the conditions or premises of Marx's enterprise, they cannot be identified with dialectical materialism as such. Their application to George Eliot's world-view, therefore, does not imply any endorsement or any repudiation of Marxist positions. But they do lay down the conditions for an approach to the problems addressed in the novels which is very different from George Eliot's but which has subsequently proved far more influential than hers.

Marx argues in the 'Theses' that works such as *The Essence of Christianity* regard 'the theoretical as the only genuine human attitude.'[1] They fail to grasp the significance of 'practical-critical' activity, that is activity informed by a consciousness which enjoys a full awareness of its own formation within the activity which it serves and its dependence on it. Theory divorced from practice attributes objectivity to its own conceptions. Theory united to practice defines truth in terms of 'the reality, and power, the this-sidedness' of thought in the practice to which it is united and this, for Marx, provides the sole measure of its truthfulness. This is because consciousness is externally determined by circumstances and upbringing, and that of course includes the consciousness of the theorist as he goes about his theorizing. Feuerbach, Marx alleges, fails to take this into account and so falls into the trap of *contemplative* materialism: in demonstrating the fact of religious self-alienation he fails to examine either the determinants of this alienation or the factors which made it possible for men like himself to diagnose it at a specific point in time. Instead he assumes that it is enough simply to make the diagnosis and to educate one's fellow-men in its truth. But this is to divide society into the educators and the educated, and to make the former 'superior to society'. It is also to identify the human essence with the individual human subject, to invent a notional individual by whom the indirect self-knowledge of religion is experienced, and who can be changed by being given new thoughts on the matter, that is instruction in the arguments advanced in Feuerbach's own works. The contemplative materialist, Marx suggests, thinks in terms of single individuals in 'civil society'. The alternative is to recognize that the human essence is not an 'abstraction inherent in each single individual', but 'the ensemble of the social relations', that is, the historically specific and changing social and class structures in and by which human beings actually live. It is to recognize also that the factors which determine the formation of a religious interpretation of experience are to be found in this same 'secular foundation' and that, therefore, a true, this-sided, world-changing consciousness can only be developed by means of an active engagement in the collective practical struggles of history.

As the work of recent critics in the Marxist tradition demonstrates – I am thinking of both Louis Althusser and E. P. Thompson – it is very difficult for any writer to avoid the contemplative trap described in the 'Theses'. The standpoint from which this present analysis of George Eliot's teaching is being written, for example, is itself contemplative and so unwittingly subject to all the historically determined limitations and ideological contradictions of such a stance. Even on its own terms, however, theory remains capable of self-criticism (if only on the level of theory). It can therefore deploy key concepts in the 'Theses', notably on the question of epistemological confusions and political conservatism of Positivist and Feuerbachian principles, to explain the unease which is generally felt about George Eliot's treatment of political, social and historical fact.

The fundamentally Feuerbachian character of George Eliot's thinking is evident in her earliest published work. As we have already observed, the perspectives of the Riehl review are very much those of contemporary anthropology, a discipline then thoroughly embued with the contemplative spirit. Specifically George Eliot is absolutely confident that the 'landholder, the clergyman, the mill-owner, the mining agent',[2] can be relied on to observe their

work-people without bias. The notion of the biassed observer, or of
the observer who changes what he sees simply by observing it, had
occurred to thinkers concerned with the basic principles of
psychology,[3] but it had not been considered in relation to sociology.
George Eliot fails to recognize that the educator himself needs
educating. The observer who is effectively superior to society is a
noticeable feature of her early fiction.

The role of the reliable observer is most frequently assumed by
her clergymen, such as Mr Cleves in 'Amos Barton', Mr Irwine in
Adam Bede, and Dr Kenn in *The Mill on the Floss*. Mr Irwine's
relations with his parishioners are particularly revealing: 'If he had
been in the habit of speaking theoretically', we are told,

> he would perhaps have said that the only healthy form religion
> could take in [their] minds was that of certain dim but strong
> emotions, suffusing themselves as a hallowing influence over the
> family affections and neighbourly duties. He thought the custom
> of baptism more important than its doctrine, and that the
> religious benefits the peasant drew from the church where his
> fathers worshipped and the sacred piece of turf where they lay
> buried, were but slightly dependent on a clear understanding of
> the Liturgy or the sermon (ch. 5).

These intuitive insights of a middle-aged country gentleman anticipate themes which Feuerbach and Comte were to make explicit. A
second embodiment of sociological objectivity in *Adam Bede* is the
passing horseman through whose eyes we observe Dinah's preaching
and who later exercises his powers as a magistrate to ensure her
admission to Hetty's prison. His function is to provide an objective
view of Dinah's performance as a preacher, and to protect it from the
charges of unwomanliness and hysteria. In her, we are told, he
encounters for the first time a form of Methodism that is neither
'ecstatic' nor 'bilious' (ch. 2); her quiet depth of conviction strikes
him as being 'in itself an evidence for the truth of her message.' He is
thus moved and possibly changed by the experience, as his later
behaviour shows, but he leaves the scene wholly in command of
himself. In this he is notably unlike the villagers, who are confused
and in one or two cases upset by the sermon, but largely unchanged
by it. The horse-rider can thus learn more from his experiences but
is less determined than the peasants. As wise social observers, he
and the Rector can recognize Dinah's moral importance and her
political innocence: her sphere of operations is not 'civil society' but
the individual heart.

In itself, the device of the neutral observer is not a factor of major importance in George Eliot's novels. In any case, none of her later fictions has such characters – Mr Debarry in *Felix Holt* and Mr Gascoigne in *Daniel Deronda* are very different from the clergymen in *Adam Bede* and *The Mill on the Floss*. (It is one of the important if surprising strengths of *Silas Marner* that interest in Mr Crackenthorp is limited to his cravats.) However, the assumptions underlying the introduction of such characters into the early novels were bound also to affect George Eliot's presentation of herself in the role of narrator. 'Amos Barton' is revealingly full of quotations from Sophocles, facetious adaptations of theological jargon and slightly wordy refusals to quote Virgil, and in the first sentence of *Adam Bede* we are made aware of an author whose temporal point of view may be that of her readers as together they look back to 'the roomy workshop of Mr. Jonathan Burge, carpenter and builder, in the village of Hayslope, as it appeared on the eighteenth of June, in the year of our Lord 1799', but whose intellectual perspectives, as indicated in the laboured allusion to the Egyptian sorcerer, are undoubtedly superior to those of the public she is addressing. George Eliot is more than the omniscient recorder of her narrative; she is also the privileged intellectual commentator upon it. According to her own aesthetic principles, however, this is not an entirely satisfactory position from which to write. Specifically, it runs counter to her belief that art should stimulate an unrestrained flow of feeling. In the early essays she argues that Harriet Beecher Stowe's *Dred* succeeds through its 'energetic sympathy, and not by conscious artifice'[4] and that in Elizabeth Barrett Browning's *Aurora Leigh* 'there is simply a full mind pouring itself out in song.'[5] George Eliot's own fiction therefore has itself to negotiate the tension between a stance of sympathetic identification with her characters and her readers alike, and one of theoretical superiority to both. It was a difficulty, however, which her Feuerbachian principles enabled her to resolve, for, as Marx observed in the 'Theses': 'Feuerbach, not satisfied with *abstract thinking*, appeals to *sensuous contemplation*.' George Eliot makes a similar appeal. She solemnly relinquishes her position as an intellectual observing the human condition from a position of privileged objectivity, and explicitly relocates herself in an ethically and emotionally simplified relation with her characters, from which she can in turn invite her readers to join her in contemplating them.

   This is particularly noticeable in *Scenes of Clerical Life*. The reader of 'Amos Barton' is assured, for example, that all he has to do is to 'look' and he will see what the author sees. 'But I, for one,' we read, 'do not grudge Amos Barton his sweet wife. I have all my life had a sympathy for mongrel ungainly dogs, who are nobody's pets' (ch. 2)

– the implication being that whatever differences there may be between them intellectually, author and readers can at least occupy the same uncontentiously 'human' ground with respect to feelings and values. The only issue of real importance is sympathy, discerning and loving 'sincerity of purpose amid all the bungling feebleness of achievement'. The notorious moralizing in the fifth chapter of 'Amos Barton' is offensive primarily because in urging the female reader to 'learn with me to see some of the poetry and the pathos, the tragedy and the comedy, lying in the experience of a human soul that looks out through dull grey eyes', George Eliot disingenuously ignores the connexion between poetry, pathos, tragedy and comedy on the one hand, and all that information and intelligence on the other which are so readily to hand when she wishes to write humorously or discursively. It was a tactic, however, implicit in her Feuerbachian principles.

A comparable development occurs in 'Mr Gilfil's Love-story'. Tina is presented in the shallow stereotypes of contemporary anthropology so that the reader can see her and feel for her without effort. But the imperative 'See how she rushes noiselessly, like a pale meteor, along the passages and up the gallery stairs!' (ch. 13) diminishes Tina herself, trivializes the reader's involvement in her suffering, and invalidates the understanding which both George Eliot as author, and Maynard Gilfil as clergyman and lover bring to bear on Tina's situation. 'Our thoughts are often worse than we are,' Maynard tells her, 'just as they are often better than we are. And God sees us as we are altogether, not in separate feelings or actions, as our fellowmen see us' (ch. 20). What is false here is not the reliance on God by an author who did not believe in him, but her emotionally loaded appeal to a conception of the whole man which is explicitly acknowledged to be invisible even to the theoretically privileged spectator. The human essence is identified with a completely abstracted concept of human individuality which the reader can never know but with which, as an individual subject himself, he can have a simple moral relationship based not upon historically specific, and therefore complicated, possibly incomprehensible, circumstance, but on personal, that is essential or universal, reactivity.

This reliance on sensuous contemplation is especially evident in 'Janet's Repentance', notably in the fifth chapter where there is a new explicitness about the supposed memories of the 'narrator' as an average boy among boys. His facetiously described sheepishness acts as a prelude first to some sententious moralizing – 'The golden moments in the stream of life rush past us, and we see nothing but sand; the angels come to visit us, and we only know them when they are gone' – and then to Janet's second appearance – 'And who is this bright-looking woman walking with hasty step along Orchard Street . . . Can it be Janet Dempster?' Yet again the authorial commentary gratuitously assumes that reader and author can share a point of view in uncomplicated intimacy. In the subsequent narrative there are occasions when such sensuous contemplation seems like a kind of treason against intelligence and art:

> Janet had that endearing beauty which belongs to pure majestic outline and depth of tint. Sorrow and neglect leave their traces on such beauty, but it thrills us to the last, like a glorious Greek temple, which, for all the loss it has suffered from time and barbarous hands, has gained a solemn history, and fills our imagination the more because it is incomplete to the sense (ch. 14).

Aesthetic experience, which in 'Mr Gilfil's Love-story' was seen to be inherently problematical, is here deployed to foreclose on thought. These anti-intellectual strategies can be quite explicit. Ideas, we are told,

> are often poor ghosts; . . . they pass athwart us in thin vapour . . . But sometimes they are made flesh; they breathe upon us the warm breath, they touch us with soft responsive hands, they look at us with sad sincere eyes, and speak to us in appealing tones; they are clothed in a living human soul, with all its conflicts, its faith, and its love. Then their presence is a power . . . and we are drawn after them with a gentle compulsion, as flame is drawn to flame (ch. 19).

Just such a compulsive drawing together of 'author', reader and character, compromises the literary composure of 'Janet's Repentance'. 'We' are coerced, for example, into hoping with 'him' that 'there is a saving grace' (ch. 5), into condemning ourselves if 'the thought of a man's death . . . hallows him anew to us' since 'life is sacred too' (ch. 11), and into assenting to the proposition that the 'wrong that rouses our angry passions . . . passes through us like a vibration, and we inflict what we have suffered' (ch. 13). Finally there is the almost notorious identification of the author's point of view with that of Mr Tryan, the Evangelical curate. Refusing to place herself on the 'lofty height' of critical detachment, George Eliot insists on remaining 'on the level and in the press with him, as he struggles his way along the stony road, through the crowd of unloving fellow-men' (ch. 10). This self-abstraction from 'the crowd', and renunciation at the same time of so many important authorial responsibilities, largely account for the general unpopularity of 'Janet's Repentance'.

Even in *Scenes of Clerical Life*, however, appeals to simple, universal and abstractly personal criteria of perception and judgment are relatively rare, and though they recur in key chapters of *Adam Bede* and *The Mill on the Floss*, thereafter they largely disappear from George Eliot's fiction. But this does not mean that her work ceases to be damagingly contemplative, at least in certain respects. She may be a more tactful narrator in her later work, but she continues to insist that theoretical understanding and sensuous contemplation not only make it possible to understand human history but are the principal agents of change within it. Hence her justification for dismissing revolutionary politics. In 'The Natural History of German Life' she endorses Riehl's opinion that the peasants lacked any true understanding of the events of 1848 on the grounds that they were innately incapable of that 'provisional subordination of egoism, to which even the artisans of the town [had] rarely shown themselves equal'.[6] Bemused by communist propaganda, the average peasant was in the end utterly degraded; 'corrupted into bestiality by the disturbance of his instincts', he provided, 'the worst example of ignorance intoxicated by theory.'[7] In the 1860s George Eliot's political scepticism seems to have been particularly intense. The gap between her humanist hopes and convictions and the actual conditions of life around her appears to have greatly depressed her. 'A Word for the Germans', for example, published at this time, is openly contemptuous of stolid, uncomprehending English philistines, while 'Servants' Logic' makes unpleasant fun of the foibles of the semi-educated – 'They have a vast number of certainties which are deep by reason of their groundlessness'.[8] More seriously, in 'The Influence of Rationalism', she complains of the 'spongy texture'[9] of the general reader's mind, dwells at length on the history of magic, witchcraft and persecution, and ignores other chapters in the book she is reviewing – W.E.H. Lecky's *History of Rationalism in Europe* – on topics altogether less bleak. Her principal preoccupation seems to be the massive irrationality of human opinion and behaviour. Similar attitudes are apparent in Felix Holt's 'Address to Working Men'. The Positivist belief in the power of public opinion, for example, becomes a ground for blaming the vices of the oppressors – 'the commercial lying and swindling, and poisonous adulteration of goods, the retail cheating, and the political bribery' – on the voteless majority who lack the moral elevation to groan and hiss 'in the right place'.[10] Any 'large body of men', Felix asserts, 'is likely to have more of stupidity, narrowness, and greed than of farsightedness and generosity'.[11] In addition, there are 'sots, libertines, knaves, or else mere sensual simpletons and victims . . . the multiplying brood begotten by parents who have been left without all teaching save that of a too craving body.'[12] This is the rhetoric of fear, and it is hardly surprising to find one of the most striking images of regeneration in *Silas Marner*, that of 'the old winter-flies that came crawling forth in the early spring sunshine' (ch. 14), representing in the 'Address' 'a despicable old man, a superannuated nuisance'[13] who has wasted his life with perverse deliberation. George Eliot undoubtedly found it hard at times to sustain even her modest faith in organic evolution, and in party terms, as Haight points out, her position in the mid-1860s was a 'thoroughly conservative' one.[14] Her treatment of the election in *Felix Holt*, for example, is demonstrably biassed. Quite apart from the fact that it was the Tories who engineered the disorders in the original Nuneaton election on which the events in *Felix Holt* are based,[15] she treats Tory corrupt practices – the coercion of tenant farmers by their landlords – with superficial humour, while her reaction to the less serious abuse of treating the unenfranchized poor is one of contrived horror.

But reaction and fear were not the true basis either of Positivism or of George Eliot's art. Despite her occasional reliance on sceptical arguments and her tendency to indulge her own sceptical moods she rejected a merely sceptical Conservatism. Thus the only thoroughly sceptical character in her late poem 'A College Breakfast Party', the student Rosencranz, is also the most firmly repudiated. Unfortunately this felt obligation to sustain an optimistic view of history in spite of pressures in the opposite direction, and to do so without abandoning her contemplative perspective on society, is ultimately responsible for the strained plotting in her novels.

Connexions between plot structure and ideological contradiction are particularly evident in *Adam Bede*. One major problem with *Adam Bede*, as both George Eliot and Lewes recognized as it was being written, is that its hero has too little to do. The fight with Arthur was introduced at Lewes's suggestion to counter this effect, though in fact it does not do so, since the crucial question about whether Arthur and Hetty have actually become lovers is finally answered in the same scene, and this, rather than Adam's fury, makes the true climax of the first part of the narrative. Adam consequently plays a subordinate role in a chapter intended to emphasize his centrality, and in spite of George Eliot's efforts in the commentary to secure his moral pre-eminence. Later the need to enhance Adam's claim to our attention forced George Eliot into making extra problems for herself over the timing of Hetty's pregnancy. It is true that no solution was possible for some of the difficulties arising out of this element in the story. Mrs Poyser has to be notoriously blind to Hetty's condition; Hetty has to leave for Windsor before she is near to term; she has therefore to give birth prematurely, even though this effectively destroys the legal case against her – a premature baby might well have appeared dead before it was buried. Yet almost perversely George Eliot makes this plotting weaker. The betrothal, which has no point except to intensify Adam's involvement in Hetty's case, happens when Hetty is at least two months pregnant; she is nonetheless made to feel 'something of contentment' in Adam's love (ch. 34), and so must be inexplicably ignorant of her condition. Later the presentation of the trial through Adam's eyes is too evidently intended to highlight his personal agony and seems almost impertinently to demand sympathy for him at the expense of the reader's concern for Hetty.

The unsatisfactory plotting of *Adam Bede* is thus directly related to George Eliot's inability to provide her hero with anything positive to do, but this in its turn is logically entailed in the kind of depoliticized transformations which the novel's conclusion proposes in the marriage of Adam and Dinah. John Goode makes this point very well. He analyses the novel 'as a process of transforming historical realities into ideological fable'.[16] Initially, he argues, 'the massively established world of Hayslope is threatened by three major possibilities of change, Methodism, the death of Thias Bede, and the affair between Arthur and Hetty'.[17] However, he finds the 'seduction theme . . . severed from the social portrayal';[18] 'the ideological pattern of the novel,' he suggests, 'prevents us from carrying the limits of moral enquiry beyond the merely individual to the social.'[19] Possibly under the influence of Spencer and Riehl, George Eliot allows natural history to replace real history. She fails to see 'the historical and human basis of human institutions', and so confines herself to 'a metaphysical scheme justified by natural [i.e. by organic evolutionary] law.'[20] But, as we observed earlier, Goode also believes that Dinah's dreaming is represented 'as a limited response to reality', and this surely is mistaken. George Eliot unambiguously represents Dinah's dreaming as the one really strong response to reality which is also legitimate because it initiates dramatic transformations in the only sphere in which she finds profound change tolerable. That is why Dinah can be active when Adam must be passive, for Adam lives in the world, not of contemplation, but of work: 'we must have something beside Gospel i' this world,' he declares. 'Look at the

canals, an'th' coal-pit engines, and Arkwright's mills . . . there's the
sperrit o' God in all things and all times . . . i' the great works and
inventions, and i' the figuring and mechanics' (ch. 1). Change in this
world is possible, but it must be slow and steady: a well-lived life
like Adam's, therefore, while it undoubtedly issues in practical,
material progress – 'some good piece of road, some buildings . . .
some reform of parish abuses' (ch. 19) – derives ultimately from a
synthesis of faculties and affections which are inherited rather than
achieved. Moral sensitivities are 'given to us'; all we have to do is 'to
obey and to trust'. Adam is therefore properly and inevitably
passive.

Adam embodies, in the end, the Positivist ideal of Submission.
But Submission is always in danger of seeming logically redundant,
even within the framework of an evolutionary view of history; for if
trusting the processes of human development is the first and greatest
moral imperative, and if the end of evolution is complete responsiveness to moral imperatives, then Submission becomes its own cause
and effect. We are confronted at best with a useless category, at
worst with an evasion of responsibility. Man, it seems, must learn to
be acted on, rather than make deliberate if hazardous interventions
in the world about him. Thus the changes which Adam as the
embodiment of practical energy is permitted to introduce into the
world of the novel are in no way comparable with the subjective
transformations introduced by Dinah. The union of 'practice' with
'sensuous contemplation', which their marriage might appear to
symbolize, does not in fact compromise the latter's essential detachment from society. It is not just the authorial viewpoint, therefore,
but the story itself which lacks a practical and necessary connexion
with the world in which it is set. The result is a dehistoricization not
just of the principal characters in the narrative, but also of the
society in which they are supposed to live but from which they are
ultimately detached. Thus, as Ian Gregor has shown,[21] time in *Adam
Bede* is registered in seasonal or pastoral terms, not as history. The
great set-piece descriptions, the Church-going, the Coming of Age,
and the Harvest Home, suggest recurrence not change. Moreover,
on the evidence of the very different impression made by *Silas
Marner*, and some fairly explicit remarks in *Impressions of Theophrastus
Such*,[22] George Eliot herself knew well enough that her picture of
Hayslope was an idealized one. The logic of her position, however,
is quite clear. If minds are determined by natural rather than
historical forces, then the material and historical order of a fictional
society may be chosen for its capacity to highlight a psycho-drama,
rather than seriously to account for it.

This is to deny any degree of autonomy to the social and economic spheres, and in no work is this more evident than in *Romola*. No aspect of Florentine life has historical significance in its own right. Customs, festivities, art, jewellery, even trade are all given the status of a symbolic grammar, a kind of occult virtue such as the Florentines anyway attribute to their precious stones. Florence in its essence is a condition of mind to which its carnivals and fiestas above all give us access. Yet brilliant and varied as George Eliot's accounts of those festivals are, they prevent us from understanding the city as a practical reality. None of the characters simply works for a living. Nello shaves in order to talk; Bratti peddles in the street for pleasure; even the iron-worker, Caparra, becomes 'an unconscious model to Domenico Ghirlandajo' (ch. 1). One has only to compare this with Scott's presentation of lawyers and salmon-fishers in *Redgauntlet* to see how George Eliot's sense of historical relevance lacks balance. She never lets anything simply be itself; everything is always open to interpretation, and the meaning is always felt to be more significant than the shell of fact surrounding it. Even the 'Art' of money-changing becomes one of the 'usages of our city' (ch. 8), which Pietro Cennini for one holds sacrosanct, and overtly 'historical' events such as the French invasions and the executions of Bernardo and Savonarola are denied intrinsic importance. They are mere signifiers, like Noah's flood, a text to be read. Public events are thus made subordinate to the mind observing them; Savonarola the protagonist yields to Machiavelli the observer, the ensemble of Florentine social relations to Romola the embodiment of sensuous contemplation. Each becomes an educator – Machiavelli when he writes *The Prince*, Romola when she solemnly instructs Lillo about the Frate in the final chapter. History is seen exclusively as a form of emotional education. 'After all has been said that can be said about the widening influence of ideas,' George Eliot writes, 'it remains true that they would hardly be such strong agents unless they were taken in a solvent of feeling' (ch. 52). It does not occur to her to consider the relations of both feelings and ideas to work and money, both of which may be more amenable to definitive exploration than symbols and visions ever could be.

In so overtly pictorial a work, however, there may be a certain logic in George Eliot's representing the Florence of *Romola* as a background, but such a defence is not available in the case of *Felix Holt*, the protagonists of which are quite as detached from their environment as Dinah and Romola are from theirs. It is impossible to imagine, for example, what it is going to be like at the end of the novel for someone as 'quick and sensitive' as Esther, as 'alive to . . .

the nicest distinction of tone and accent' (ch. 6), to live among the Sproxton miners, nor what it will be like for them to live near her. This is largely because George Eliot can only allude to the brutalization of the Loamshire working-class; she cannot show it. Dredge and his companions are mere stage louts, who sup ale, beat their wives, and call Felix Holt 'Master'. By glossing over the actual conditions of working-class life in this way George Eliot avoids having to deal with basic economic and political questions, and specifically with the problem of how Felix can hope to make his educational programme effective. Obviously, these are serious omissions in a novel which is committed to the view that history is determined by the cultural influences that make class differences visible rather than by the material conditions which may be thought to cause them.

The emphasis on culture as the essence of class, moreover, reveals the fundamental flaw in the logic of Positivism itself, as becomes tangibly obvious when one compares Felix with the trades-union man. The latter's speech, as David Craig rightly points out, is 'plausible and telling',[23] and it is also historically accurate. Its main points, that the Reform Bill is a trick, that religion has become a commodity, and that only accountability of Parliament to people can set matters right, constitute the essence of Chartism. In view of the coming defeat of Chartism the bitterness and incipient cynicism of the trades-union man are also authentic. He is convincing because he is typical. George Eliot knew that Esther and Felix would also have to seem typical if her solution to the social problems depicted in *Felix Holt* were to appear viable. Hence her assertion that the lives of Felix and Esther were 'rooted in the common earth, having to endure all the ordinary chances of past and present weather' (ch. 3). But even as she announces how 'ordinary' her hero and heroine are, she has to warn us about improbabilities of plot that lie ahead. Her narrative is grounded in 'circumstance', but not, in the event, in 'ordinary' circumstance. There is no 'ordinary' way, after all, for the clever son of a quack-doctor to emancipate himself intellectually, nor do 'ordinary' means exist by which he can become an effective alternative to workers' representatives in Parliament. Comte solved a similar difficulty by asserting that the advent of his spiritual power would be 'essentially spontaneous' – an unseemly reliance on sociological miracle, but one which arises inexorably out of his belief in the power of thought to initiate its own advances, and then to stimulate social action. Such a premise leads logically to a dehumanizing isolation of teacher and thinker from ordinary social pressures. This certainly seems to have been Comte's own personal experience, and George Eliot has made it Felix Holt's. He is utterly alone, magically free (until he meets Esther) of any need for companionship, and George Eliot has to work very hard in consequence to give him any social impact at all, notoriously so when she suggests that since 'lions and dogs know a distinction between man's glances', doubtless the Duffield audience was '*unconsciously* influenced by the grandeur' of Felix's appearance (ch. 30 – my emphasis). As for his speech, its 'prearranged syntax and smoothly sequential linking of the sentences' do not, David Craig points out, 'suggest any kind of utterable English'.[24] The intellectual, artistic, and political emasculation that follows from the separation of theory from practice has rarely been more plainly illustrated.

This inability of contemplative materialism to engage with political, social, and economic reality is of course particularly noticeable in a work like *Felix Holt* which is explicitly concerned with problems in these areas. Even in *Middlemarch*, however, it can threaten the coherence of the novel's characterizations and of the narrative. This is especially obvious in the case of the over-plotted connexions between Bulstrode, Ladislaw and Casaubon, and the unconvincing intrusion of Raffles into the action. In many respects the characterization of Bulstrode, particularly in his relations with Lydgate and with his wife as well as with Raffles, is very impressive, but his life-story is unsatisfactory and it detracts from the significance attaching to him. He fails, for example, as a 'representative of Evangelicalism in . . . its relation to capitalism'[25] because George Eliot has had to substitute a melodramatic intrigue antedating the main action for a convincing account of his record as a banker at a period when banking operations like his had considerable historical significance. This is consistent with the peripheral status accorded to public issues generally in *Middlemarch*; the casual references to national events suggest a Positivist contempt for formal politics, and though the 'landscape of opinion' in the town of Middlemarch is well filled in with references to 'shoddy cloth, inferior dye-stuffs, oppressed weavers, ill-housed tenants,'[26] we see nothing of its people at work, never mind hear the thoughts of 'the wretched handloom weavers in Tipton and Freshitt' (ch. 34). As 'a reinterpretation of Whig history',[27] which presents progress in terms of altruism rather than reform, *Middlemarch* dematerializes local English history. The *London Quarterly Review* described Bulstrode as 'an integer in the triply-embodied conception of the futility of exclusively self-seeking efforts.' Featherstone, Casaubon and Bulstrode, the reviewer suggests, are each frustrated through 'narrow-minded egoism' that has 'no eye for the inexorable influences of external circumstances.'[28] But in fact the restricted sense of external circumstance is George Eliot's.

She it is who gives Bulstrode's egoism a power which is melodramatic rather than typical of the relations between bankers and their clients in provincial commerce. Evil is thereby denied a social dimension in *Middlemarch* except in the safely non-economic form of opinion, gossip and prejudice.

Comparable weaknesses attach to Caleb Garth and to Ladislaw. As a family the Garths are refreshing and convincing, but the moral standing accorded to them is rendered nugatory by the theoretical contradictions inhering in George Eliot's perspectives on her provincial world with which as a man of 'Business' Caleb Garth refuses to be merged even though he is supposed to embody the novel's answer to the problems posed by Political Economy. This is especially regrettable because in two great scenes between Mr Brooke and Dagley, and between Caleb and the labourers, George Eliot reveals a grasp of the problem of poverty which was missing from *Felix Holt*. The first of these scenes, in which Dagley, 'a figure in the landscape' (ch. 39) who steps out of his frame and thrusts his despair in his landlord's face, raises important questions about the social impotence of the poor as well as 'the midnight darkness' of their minds. In the dispute with the labourers, Caleb is similarly unable to match Timothy Cooper's argument that the railways will 'only leave the poor mon furder behind' (ch. 56). Timothy, in fact, opposes violence, but only because this 'is the big folks's world', and he adds, accurately enough, that Caleb himself is 'for the big folks'. Caleb, we are told, in a fine passage which is a far cry from the cheap sneers of 'Servant's Logic', is unable to reply to these protests because it is impossible to 'reason with rustics who are in possession of an undeniable truth which they know through a hard process of feeling and can let fall like a giant's club on [a] neatly carved argument for a social benefit they do not feel.' The ambiguities here are intelligent and urgent. Is the truth undeniable only to coarse rustic intelligence, or because it is in effect *identical* with a 'hard process of feeling' which only the poor can know? Felix Holt could refer glibly to 'the force that ignorant numbers have' to smash and destroy. That force is morally transformed when it becomes a giant club of emotional truth that may, or may not, be true. In *Middlemarch*, poverty is not smoothly subsumed into a general theory of progress. Caleb's debate with the labourers, however, is significantly about the railway which by 1870 had proved of undoubted benefit even to the poor. The reader is thus in a conveniently privileged position from which to judge the correctness of his ideas. This puts out of focus, however, the whole problem of how he came by them. His adolescent vision of 'Business', after all, which is apparently so like

Lydgate's of medicine, is not documented and located as Lydgate's is. Not that Caleb's ideal is meaningless. Work is indeed degraded if it becomes a commodity. But the implication that this problem can be solved simply by our thinking about it as Caleb does, is naive and disingenuous. We are never given a convincing account of how such an alteration of perspective can be achieved. Alone of all the characters in the novel, Caleb is simply granted a liberating vision.

Ladislaw's renunciation of Bulstrode's money is similarly unsatisfactory. Money is an important theme in *Middlemarch*. On the one hand Mr Farebrother and Mrs Garth rightly insist that 'Business', family and integrity of life depend on money. As David Daiches observes, Lydgate's 'refusal to see the economic realities that underlie class distinctions' is 'a sort of vulgarity'.[29] Dorothea and Will, on the other hand, refuse the fortunes which fate puts at their disposal and which social and literary convention would have permitted them to accept. But defying a cruel, eccentric codicil, has little connexion with Dorothea's more generalized conviction that while their tenants live in sties, the rich 'deserve to be beaten out of their fine houses with a scourge of small cords' (ch. 3). Similarly Will's rejection of Bulstrode's money leaves the reader happily undisturbed by his own legacies and settlements (except, of course, those obtained by forgery and theft). Both renunciations are thus little more than signs of personal fastidiousness, romantic, desocialized gestures made possible by the conventions of fiction rather than the pressures of life.

In a novel as copious and controlled as *Middlemarch*, these are minor discordances compared with the strategic weaknesses of plotting and characterization in *Adam Bede*, *Romola* and *Felix Holt*. They remain significant, however, because they show the continuing pressure on George Eliot's imagination of the political and economic quietism implicit in contemplative materialism. The minds of Bulstrode, Caleb Garth and even those of Ladislaw and Dorothea are cut off from anything that could be called a typical relationship with the social and economic pressures of their society. Bulstrode's history is over-plotted, Caleb's not plotted at all, and Ladislaw is burdened with a highly improbable ancestry; none has a normative relationship with wealth and work in a provincial society, and consequently the decisions they take do not reflect any kind of judgment, favourable or otherwise, on the structure of that world. They have moral or personal implications only. Yet to secure this result George Eliot has to abandon the very principles on which the novel was founded. She set out, by her own account, 'to show the gradual action of ordinary causes . . . and to show them in some directions which have not been from time immemorial the beaten paths – Cremorne walks and shows of fiction.'[30] But spontaneously virtuous countrymen and Blifil-like intriguers belong precisely to the Cremorne walks of the romance tradition. The intellectual perspectives of the novel are thus in one crucial respect distorted. To the end of her writing life, George Eliot was unable to establish unimpeded contact with the secular foundation of the worlds on which she based her fictions.

We may conclude, therefore, that the logical and epistemological weaknesses in George Eliot's speculative materialism derive from her acceptance of the legitimacy of separating theory and practice, that they invalidate much of her thinking on its own terms, and that they lead her to adopt narrative strategies which distort her aesthetic structures and weaken her teaching. A more general and fundamental difficulty remains, however. The entire project apparently informing the novels and recognized as doing so by her contemporaries, the project of communicating an intellectually consistent and morally coherent view of the world, seems deeply suspect in itself. Indeed the steady deflection of attention away from George Eliot's didactic purposes almost certainly reflects the unease of a later generation at the mere thought of so grand a project. Conviction, we feel, almost always involves rationalization, corruptly motivated thinking, and, in the case of a novelist, corruptly motivated imagining. The problem is one not of error, ideological distortion or class bias, but of deep-seated bad faith of a kind that falls outside the conceptual framework of the 'Theses on Feuerbach'. To examine possible failures of this kind in George Eliot's work we must turn to Nietzsche, and *The Genealogy of Morals*.

7 Malady of conscience

The challenge of Nietzsche's *The Genealogy of Morals*

NIETZSCHE explicitly condemned George Eliot as a 'little moralistic' female but then excused her on the grounds that in this respect
she was simply being 'English'.[1] The Englishness he disliked was that
of agnostics and psychologists like Spencer and Bain who refused to
jettison religion with God, and Christianity with Christ, who were
in effect Feuerbachians. Nietzsche proclaimed the 'true' atheism
which Feuerbach denied, that is he repudiated not only the notion of
God as a real being, but also the value of the divine predicates as
qualities in man. This involved him in an epistemological revolution
at least as radical as that initiated by Marx's 'Theses on Feuerbach'.

A key to understanding Nietzsche's position is his treatment of
the subject of Judaism in *The Genealogy of Morals*. The book begins
with a brutal sneer at the damage allegedly done by the Jews, 'that
priestly people', to 'the powerful and great of this earth'.[2] Nietzsche's justification for this attitude is his belief that 'priests' are the
instruments and vehicles of the instinct he most hated, the will to
pain represented by a moral order based on punishment of the guilty
and self-denial by the virtuous. But he has something far more
fundamental to express in *The Genealogy of Morals* than a mere
opinion about asceticism. What he works towards is a moment in
which all opinions, even his own, are obliterated, and he does so by
means of a series of brilliantly organized reversals of view. Having
thoroughly savaged the ascetic priest, for example, he makes a
carefully judged concession concerning the priest's pastoral functions in controlling the internalized, self-mutilating aggression for
which the priestly ethos is allegedly responsible: 'the aescetic priest,'
he writes, 'seemingly life's enemy and great negator, is in truth one
of the major conserving and affirmative forces';[3] he directs the
resentment of the weak and the sick away from the strong and the
healthy back on to themselves, 'for the purposes of self-discipline,
self-surveillance, self-conquest.'[4] It should not come as a surprise,
therefore, when later Nietzsche turns on 'those newest speculators
in idealism called anti-Semites, who parade as Christian-Aryan

worthies and endeavour to stir up all the asinine elements of the nation by that cheapest of propaganda tricks, a moral attitude',[5] nor when he attacks the whole process of modern, post-Christian critical philosophizing as the work of 'proud solitaries, absolutely intransigent in their insistence on intellectual precision . . . hard, strict, continent, heroic minds . . . wan atheists, Antichrists, immoralists, nihilists, sceptics, suspenders of judgement', amongst whom he might almost have been counted himself. More unexpectedly, perhaps, what he finds wrong with modern intellectual culture is its 'restless activity' which 'thinly veils a lack of ideals, the want of a great love',[6] but this he explains as the consequence of a continuing and still essentially Christian reverence for the 'truth'. Real freedom can only exist among those who assert 'Nothing is true; everything is permitted.'[7]

Thus having identified asceticism as the enemy of life, analysis finds that it is itself ascetic: the intellect hunts itself down in *The Genealogy of Morals* and is in at the death: all that remains is the will. But where, according to Nietzsche, has the will been hiding throughout the long history of man's enslavement to the 'divine' and the 'true'? Where else but in the self-destructive energy of the ascetic ideal itself? The ascetic ideal, he concludes, 'signifies . . . a will to nothingness, a revulsion from life, a rebellion against the principal conditions of living. And yet, despite everything, it is and remains a *will*.'[8] This conclusion is anticipated at the beginning of the second essay, in a description of 'the brutality, tyranny, and stupidity' associated with 'the preparatory task of rendering man up to a certain point regular, uniform, equal among equals, calculable' – everything the aristocratic ideal might be thought to despise. But 'the terminal point of this great process', Nietzsche argues, 'where society and custom finally reveal their true aim . . . [is] the sovereign individual, equal only to himself, all moral custom left far behind. This autonomous, more than moral individual . . . has developed his own, independent, long-range will, which dares to make promises.'[9] This is the point towards which the entire process of evolving morality, art, thought and feeling, has been moving; slavery and priesthood have concealed within themselves the principles of liberty and nobility which they were committed to destroy. The conclusion of the argument is not a moment of illumination, but the obliteration of intellect in a choice, a choice of and for the self.

Obviously an atheism of this kind, which subordinates intelligence to will as Positivism subordinated will to intelligence, is inconsistent with a didactic stance like George Eliot's. Irrespective of its precise doctrinal content, her fiction is manifestly predicated

on the reader's capacity first to envisage, remember, perceive and
sympathize, and only then to choose. But the issue between her and
Nietzsche is not one of broad principle only. There are a number of
more specific instances where his analysis must make all but the
blindest of George Eliot's admirers uncomfortable. She was closely
associated, for example, with those 'English psychologists' whom
Nietzsche attacked for

> pushing into the foreground the nasty part of the psyche, looking
> for the effective motor forces of human development in the very
> last place we would wish to have found them, e.g., in the inertia
> of habit, in forgetfulness, in the blind and fortuitous association
> of ideas: always in something that is purely passive, automatic,
> reflexive, molecular, and, moreover, profoundly stupid.[10]

Admittedly she could have claimed a notable and serious attachment
to remembering rather than forgetting (though as we shall see this
would not have saved her from further Nietzschean scorn), but it is
also the case that habit (if not as a form of inertia) has a crucial
determining function in all her novels, while her attitude to reflexive, even automatic passivity is at the very least indulgent if not
wholly approving. It would also be easy to accuse her – in *Romola* for
example – of abusing those 'more interesting deleterious drugs'
which induce 'extravagance of feeling, the strongest anodyne for a
long, dull enervating pain',[11] and in general of attaching herself, with
Herbert Spencer, to those 'admirers of mystery and the unknown
. . . [who] worship the question mark itself as a god'.[12] Parts of her
fiction, late as well as early, could be confidently offered in evidence
in order to substantiate some of Nietzsche's other insights, for
example his suggestion that in 'prescribing love of one's neighbour,
the ascetic priest really prescribes an excitation of . . . the will to
power . . . albeit in cautious doses',[13] that conscience and altruism
derive from a morbid turning of an aggressive, envious impulse
against the subject, that 'the wellspring of all altruistic values'[14] is a
perversion of instinct, and that it was the transformation of man into
'sociable and pacific creature' which forced him to succumb to bad
conscience as to 'a deep-seated malady'.[15] George Eliot is also
inclined in her fiction to write of her good characters – Dinah
Morris, Adam Bede, Maggie Tulliver, Romola, Felix Holt – as
though they 'were not a goal' (in other words, ends in themselves)
'but a way, an interlude, a bridge, a great promise.'[16] Her villains, on
the other hand, tend to remain for ever unforgiven. In her heart,
without of course believing in Hell as such, she assents to 'man's will
to find himself guilty, and irredeemably so . . . to believe that he

might be punished to all eternity without ever expunging his guilt
. . . to poison the very foundation of things with the problem of
guilt and punishment'.[17] To sum up, the issue between her and
Nietzsche is 'the value of the non-egotistical instincts, the instincts
of compassion, self-denial, and self-sacrifice',[18] and the undoubted
force of his objection to the ascetic ideal weighs very heavily against
her. Always, Nietzsche writes, asceticism has 'fought under a
banner bearing the motto, "triumph in agony." This tempting
riddle, this image of rapturous pain, has always been its source of
illumination, its pledge of final victory.'[19] The unease with which
critics such as James and Leavis have regarded major parts of George
Eliot's writings clearly derives from a sense that she was far too eager
to succumb to this unpleasant temptation.

The pervasiveness of the ascetic morality in George Eliot's fiction,
however, is a consequence of its wide-ranging inner logic. This can
also be illustrated from the novels. The starting point of her intellectual emancipation was Bray's *Philosophy of Necessity*, a work
which decisively finds man irredeemably guilty. The exultant note
sounded by Greg and quoted so approvingly in George Eliot's
review of *The Creed of Christendom* – '*the deed is done* . . . the
consequences . . . *are there*, are written in the annals of the past, and
must reverberate through all time' – echoes through all her subsequent work. The histories of Lawyer Dempster, Hetty and Arthur,
Dunstan and Godfrey Cass, David Faux in 'The Lifted Veil', Tito,
Savonarola, Jermyn, Mrs Transome, Bulstrode and Lapidoth, are
all carefully organized to exemplify the pitiless operation of impersonal retributive justice. Qualitatively they vary greatly – the
story of David Faux is jeeringly and intemperately farcical, that of
Mrs Transome one of the subtlest in the language – but in all there is
that element of satisfaction in the neatness and completeness of the
punishment which Nietzsche so acutely judges to be the real
motivation behind all retributive moralities.

George Eliot's treatment of self-denial also bears out his contention that the altruist is attracted by the idea of pain. Again this has
little to do with the quality of the narrative. In *Scenes of Clerical Life*,
for example, Milly's total selflessness in death is very moving. Even
finer, perhaps, is the reticence of the Conclusion, and in particular
the allusions to the representative fate of the eldest daughter, Patty,
who becomes 'the evening sunshine' of her father's life, a phrase
which exactly suggests the attenuation of her prospects in the
softening of his. Against the delicate handling of self-denial in 'Amos
Barton', however, must be set the description of Janet Dempster's
watch beside her husband's deathbed in 'Janet's Repentance':

Janet sat on the edge of the bed through the long hours of candle-light, watching the unconscious half-closed eyes, wiping the perspiration from the brow and cheeks, and keeping her left hand on the cold unanswering right hand that lay beside her on the bed-clothes. She was almost as pale as her dying husband, and there were dark lines under her eyes, for this was the third night since she had taken off her clothes; but the eager straining gaze of her dark eyes, and the acute sensibility that lay in every line about her mouth, made a strange contrast with the blank unconsciousness and emaciated animalism of the face she was watching (ch. 24).

In both texts the pain and even the intimations of death involved in selfless love seem to be sources of excitement. It can hardly be an accident that in George Eliot's first full-length treatment of altruism, she compares Dinah Morris's 'pale face full of subdued emotion' to that of 'a lovely corpse into which the soul has returned charged with sublimer secrets and a sublimer love' (ch. 15). Her later noble characters all suffer acutely yet exultantly after the fashion of Janet Dempster. Philip Wakem may argue that 'we can never give up longing and wishing while we are thoroughly alive' (Bk V, ch. 1), but, even allowing for the ironies implicit in the description of the kiss between him and Maggie, the fact that his 'pale face' is 'full of pleading, timid love – like a woman's' (Bk V, ch. 4), suggests that there is an exquisite joy to be experienced precisely in the failure of love to find fulfilment. At the end of *The Mill on the Floss*, Stephen marries Lucy, but Philip remains devoted to Maggie's memory; in that sense he has limited if not abolished longing and wishing, yet he is clearly regarded as living more intensely than Stephen because of his greater capacity for suffering. Romola and Dorothea also endure ecstatic pain, but the most striking case is Mirah's in *Daniel Deronda*. Rescued from suicide by Daniel, whom she has heard chanting the gondolier's song from Rossini's *Otello* (the words are Dante's) –

> Nessun maggior dolore
> Che ricordarsi del tempo felice
> Nella miseria

– she says in a kind of low trance, '*Dolore – miseria*, I think those words are alive,' and then of her attempted suicide,

> 'I thought it was not wicked. Death and life are one before the Eternal. I know our fathers slew their children and then slew themselves, to keep their souls pure. I meant it so. But now I am commanded to live. I cannot see how I shall live' (ch. 17).

As in the debates between Philip and Maggie in the Red Deeps, and between Ladislaw and Dorothea in Lowick, the final outcome of this meditation is formally in favour of life and against death, but in all three cases the capacity to feel an ecstatic joy in the prospect of extinction in and for pure emotion is perversely represented as being in effect a qualification for moral fullness in life.

George Eliot, then, implicitly endorses Nietzsche's suggestion that punishment and self-denial are similarly motivated. She also recognizes that that motivation must be kept secret, in what Nietzsche called 'extravagance of feeling', feeling which engrosses discrimination and enforces uncritical assent. The process is well illustrated by George Eliot's hectic preoccupation in 'Janet's Repentance' with intoxication, self-denial, delirium and devotion, in short with images of pain made holy. Comparably reductive emotional extravagance in the presence of self-denial and suffering occurs in all the later novels, in the agonizing over Hetty, the deaths of Tom and Maggie, the prostration of Romola, and the ecstatic death of Mordecai, to whom death comes 'as the divine kiss which is both parting and reunion' (ch. 70); and if the reader wishes to question what this may mean, he is at once confronted with the incontestable solemnity of a quotation from the concluding chorus of *Samson Agonistes*.

Other logical consequences of the ascetic impulse as analysed by Nietzsche can be amply illustrated in George Eliot's fiction. They arise in particular from asceticism's unbreakable attachment to the past. Nietzsche believed in cancelling mankind's indebtedness to its beginnings, in abandoning moral custom, in committing the sovereign individual wholly to the present and the future. George Eliot, on the contrary, believed in roots and rootedness, a belief which lies at the heart of Maggie's decision to leave Stephen. *Prima facie*, of course, there is no reason why such evaluation of memory and the past should be less compelling in fiction or in life than Nietzsche's of the will and the future. Nietzsche, however, contended that the past in fact provides the ascetic impulse with an essentially dishonest excuse for its perverse and secret satisfaction, and if this is a well-founded view, the dangers of memory as a source of moral perspective in a work of fiction become clearer. Nietzsche's case is a strong one. All theories of retributive justice must accord a certain primacy to the past over the present: pain is the price exacted now for wickedness committed then. This must be especially so in any theory of automatic retribution, such as the philosophy of necessity, in which the past has to be represented as controlling the present. A comparable primacy is accorded to the past in theories of duty based on existing relationships or existing promises, and the past becomes even more important if the loyalty it exacts is represented as being its own reward, and promises of heavenly compensation in the future are dismissed as incredible or immoral. Such a logic will have crucial significance in narrative. It means that the self-indulgent and the bad must be deprived of that subjective contact with the past which consoles the self-denying and the good. The contact of the wicked with their former selves must be objective only, retribution being visited on them by the operation of external causes set in motion by their original wickedness. It is true that between these two states there is what may be called internal nemesis or remorse. However, to the extent that remorse is truly contrite it leads to a measure of consolation which invariably involves the memory, so that self-punishment becomes rewarding. Alternatively, to the extent that remorse takes the form of mere bitterness and disappointment, its contact with the past remains limited – the consolations of felt loyalty are denied it. Memory in its fullness, therefore, must be represented in such narratives as being exclusively benign.

Such patterns appear repeatedly in George Eliot's fictions. Both Arthur and Hetty, for example, have lost their parents, but neither remembers sorrow. Of Hetty in love George Eliot writes: 'Does any sweet or sad memory mingle with this dream of the future – any loving thought of her second parents – of the children she had helped to tend – of any youthful companion, any pet animal, any relic of her own childhood even? Not one.' (ch. 15). In her flight from Hayslope she thinks obsessively of 'the same small round of memories' (ch. 36). The poverty of Hetty's remembered life creates additional difficulties in the representation of her relationship with Arthur. In all George Eliot's fiction, strong feeling, including strong sexual feeling, invariably derives its strength from the past. But Hetty is virtually without a past. She must therefore desire and yet be passionless. Thus within days of Arthur's departure, she decides to marry Adam, even though he stirs 'no passion in her' (ch. 34). But the nature of her original feelings for Arthur is no less obscure. On the one hand his eyes seem 'to touch her', and he looks 'as dazzling as an Olympian god', on the other, thinking about him only produces 'a pleasant narcotic effect' (ch. 9), and meeting him, she is 'no more conscious of her limbs, than if her childish soul had passed into a water-lily, resting on a liquid bed, and warmed by the midsummer sunbeams' (ch. 12), a curious image, sensuously describing a loss of sensation. It is never clear whether passion enlivens or dulls her. She calculates the effect of her tears and values her ear-rings for their own sake, not Arthur's, her passion for him being 'a little less strong than her love of finery' (ch. 22). But Arthur also sets her own 'passion vibrating in return' (ch. 15), and his farewell letter brings 'a rush of remembered sensations' and memories of 'short poisonous delights' (ch. 31). Almost immediately after this, however, we are reminded that she had 'a luxurious and vain nature, not a passionate one'. She is thus morally compromised by marvellously suggested intoxications which we are repeatedly assured she is incapable of feeling.

A related difficulty arises in *The Mill on the Floss*. Because memory and passion are identical in George Eliot's ascetic morality, Maggie's relations with Philip and Stephen can never acquire the intensity or moral importance of her relations with Tom. For the same reason, Tom's guilt and punishment alike, even though in a sense determined by the biological and historical destiny imposed on the male sex, take the form of forgetfulness. To do his duty, Tom has to quench 'memory in the stronger light of purpose, losing the sense of dread and even of wounds in the hurrying ardour of action' (Bk V, ch. 2). The wounds are his own and other people's, and they are deep, but Tom cannot afford complexity in life. He has 'a very strong appetite for pleasure – would [like] to be a Tamer of horses' – hence his fear of Maggie's role of Hecuba to his Hector. Her talent for 'watching the world's combat from afar, filling . . . long empty days with memories and fears', her impractical commitment to emotion and memory, threaten his powers of self-repression and decision. The historically necessary activity in which his personality expands imposes its particular narrowness upon him almost as a duty. His fate is not, like his father's, to fear his own confusion, but to be ignorant of ignorance itself.

This creates difficulties. Tom embodies a compulsive forgetfulness, yet as the most important object in Maggie's memory he must not be shallow or passionless. It is necessary for the part he is to play in 'The Final Rescue' that he should be capable of a genuinely passionate love for Lucy. He must therefore be in touch with springs of affectivity in his relations with her which are closed to him in his relations with Maggie. In itself this is not an unusual situation for someone to be in, but it is a situation which George Eliot is not free to explore, for it would mean that Tom's self-control as an adult might be due, in whole or in part, to the influence of those 'long deep memories of early discipline and effort, of early claims on . . . love and pity' (Bk VI, ch. 9) which underlie Maggie's love for Stephen and her capacity in the end to resist him. But in that case Maggie's special role in the novel as the unique bearer of such values would be compromised. Tom's falling in love must therefore be kept at a distance. We are told about it indirectly in Bob Jakin's private talk with Maggie, whose reaction to it is unpleasantly off-hand. 'It was a totally new idea to her', the commentary runs, 'that Tom could have his love troubles. Poor fellow – and in love with Lucy too!' (Bk VI, ch. 6). This is Maggie's least sympathetic moment. Intellectually it is also the novel's weakest.

The logical identification of passion with past joy rather than with present pleasure which George Eliot's agnosticism imposes on her has equally disturbing effects on the narrative in *Romola*. Romola herself is constituted by the memories she inherits and accumulates. Initially memories are her only inheritance –

> memories of a dead mother, of a lost brother, of a blind father's happier time – memories of a far-off light, love, and beauty, that lay imbedded in dark mines of books, and could hardly give out their brightness again until they were kindled for her by the torch of some known joy (ch. 6).

But even known joys are finally valued more as memories than as experiences. Thus helping the villagers is important in the end for the perspective it helps Romola to take on a past which rises up 'with a fresh appeal to her' (ch. 69) and makes her realize that 'the grounds on which Savonarola had once taken her back were truer, deeper than the grounds she had had for her second flight.' Memory is thus the ultimate value in the novel, and George Eliot accordingly has to invent biographies for Tito and Tessa which will keep this beneficent status intact. The results are wholly unconvincing. Like Hetty and Arthur, both are alone in the world. Tessa has a step-father who beats her, a younger sister who is preferred to her, and a mother who dies an apparently painful death. As for Tito, 'he was only seven years old, [when] Baldassare . . . rescued him from blows' (ch. 9). But George Eliot does not allow the pain both have experienced in childhood to remain part of their felt lives as adults. This is not a failure of perception, however, but a direct consequence of the structure of thought informing the novel: sympathy for Tito and Tessa must be limited in order to protect the standing of Romola herself, as the embodiment of self-sacrifice ennobled and rewarded by her past.

Another consequence of the priority which asceticism must accord to the past in the context of the determinist principles espoused by George Eliot is a surrender to what Nietzsche called 'crass causality'. Among 'English' psychologists, he argued, this tendency led to an unseemly reliance on 'the inertia of habit . . . something that is purely passive, automatic, reflexive, molecular, and, moreover, profoundly stupid.' Such a tendency repeatedly makes its appearance in George Eliot's fiction, most obviously in those characters like Adam who embody the Comtist ideal of Submission, but more damagingly in apparently active, devoted heroines – Dinah, Maggie, and above all Romola – each of whom, as we have seen, is intended in a certain sense to embody the future. Again we are confronted with the inexorable logic of asceticism. In the first place, unconsciousness of the kind Nietzsche disliked is written into the Feuerbachian position: if religion projects a human ideal, and if that ideal is the human personality enriched by religion, then religion is necessarily narcissistic and therefore unconscious. The difficulty becomes especially acute if the religious object is made specific in terms of recognizable roles and personalities, as it is repeatedly in George Eliot's fiction.

Dinah Morris is an obvious example of this. She *is* religion in *Adam Bede*, and therefore the embodiment of the ideal she herself longs for. Of course she must herself be unconscious of her own status as an object of veneration, her own and other people's. A condition of her moral perfection is thus an organic incapacity for self-scrutiny: 'when religion – consciousness of God – is designated as . . . self-consciousness,' Feuerbach writes, '. . . this is not to be understood as affirming that the religious man is directly aware of this identity; for, on the contrary, ignorance of it is fundamental to the peculiar nature of religion.'[20] Consequently Dinah's thoughts have 'no connection with the present moment or with her own personality' (ch. 3); her mental life is remote from local pressures and personal needs. And the same logic which forbids her from analysing herself inhibits George Eliot from analysing her also. In a book so emphatically committed to theoretical perspectives, a mind under a moral necessity not to understand itself will not bear close scrutiny. The concept of the individual personality as the unconscious object of its own religious instincts, round which the novel is written, is clearly inconsistent with the values George Eliot properly assumes both as a rational moralist and as omniscient author.

A similar problem arises in *The Mill on the Floss*. Maggie's life is represented as the unfolding of potentialities inherent in her experience as a child. Moreover, the difficulties in which she finds herself, first as a child, then as a woman, can ultimately be attributed to circumstances rather than to her personality: always there is the sense that it is Tom, or the Dodsons, or St Ogg's, who are out of step, not Maggie herself – however much appearances may suggest the contrary. Certainly to the extent that Tom adapts well to circumstance, he becomes more remote from Maggie, and thereby puts himself, from the reader's point of view, in the wrong. The relation between them is thus not really one of mutual need, as the evolutionary assumptions in their characterization suggest. Maggie needs Tom conditionally. In the perfect situation, her mercurial vitalities would be revealed for what they are, and even Tom could respond to them with 'awe and humiliation' (Bk VIII, ch. 5). In brief, his virtues are useful on the journey, but hers give value to the journey's end. Unlike him she does not need transformation, only an epiphany.

Reliance on process and the unconscious rather than on choice and deliberate action is even more marked in *Romola*. The novel is in effect written to make history itself an unconscious process of mind, operating according to the mysterious but unworrying principles of Associationism. According to Bain, sensation and emotion were aspects of consciousness by definition; only thought and movement could be unconscious,[21] but this was the only opening George Eliot needed. Romola, as we have seen, incarnates the historical process, but repeatedly her bodily movements and her thoughts happen without deliberation. Her 'queenly step' is 'the simple action of her tall, finely-wrought frame, without the slightest conscious adjustment of herself' (ch. 5); she fails to react visibly to an insensitivity of Tito's because she is 'too unconscious of her body voluntarily to change her attitude' (ch. 32). She hardly thinks about doctrines; Savonarola gives her 'a reason for living, apart from personal enjoyment and personal affection' which can only be sustained by 'greater forces than she [possesses] within herself'; her 'submissive use of all the offices of the Church [is] simply a watching and waiting if by any means fresh strength might come' (ch. 44). Her mental state in prayer is one of 'expectant passivity' (ch. 47). The heart, Feuerbach noted, unlike the imagination or intelligence, 'has a passive, receptive relation to what it produces; all that proceeds from it seems to it given from without';[22] or as the dying Dino declares: 'in visions and dreams we are passive, and our souls are as an instrument in the Divine hand' (ch. 15). Romola's development has just such a quiet, receptive character. In her case, as in Maggie's, 'tenderness is passive . . . flourishing best in the quiescence of the moving members.' On the boat, will, movement and thought are suspended. The baby's cry finally stirs her into activity, yet even then, she never thinks about her actions but simply lives 'with so energetic an impulse to share the life around her . . . that the reason for living, enduring, labouring, never [take for her] the form of an argument' (ch. 69).

This quasi-ecstatic condition of passivity and spontaneity redeems

Romola from the tragic wilfulness which entangles Savonarola, but it also undermines the theme which is supposed to unite them, that of sacred rebellion. In her essay on the *Antigone*, George Eliot had declared that until 'the outer life of man . . . is brought into harmony with his inward needs . . . we shall never be able to attain a great right without also doing a great wrong.'²³ Tragedy involves choices, and so does history. The plot and characterizations of *Romola* are accordingly elaborated to make the heroine an Antigone-figure to Savonarola's Creon. But George Eliot's whole effort is nonetheless to relieve Romola of the need to choose, to make her spontaneous, unconscious, instinctive, to depict in and through her, a redemptive process rather than a tragic will. She thereby empties the saving process of all political and moral contradiction. Romola's transformation is passionate, organic, spontaneous, but only in an ecstatically self-denying sense, sexual, and her practical involvement in Florentine life is simply glamorized district visiting. The 'sacredness of rebellion' is thus not merely provisional but illusory. Our 'wonted life' must be allowed to resume its sway over 'the vision and the daring that [make] a sacred rebel' (ch. 64). Once Romola's second decision to return to Florence has been made, the elaborate play with the theme of rebellion becomes a charade.

Romola is the grossest example in George Eliot's work of the operations of 'purely passive, automatic reflexive' forces. The three novels written later all tackle the problem of choosing the greater seriousness and subtlety. Yet even in *Middlemarch* George Eliot tries to resolve certain semi-technical problems by giving her heroine's unconscious vitalities priority over her capacity to make responsible choices. This is especially obvious in the difficulties arising from Will's relations with Dorothea before Mr Casaubon's death. Such a relationship between a married woman and a bachelor was potentially very embarrassing, and George Eliot repeatedly assures the reader, often in painfully clumsy prose, that Dorothea's silence (about Will's presence at the Grange, for example) was due to the fact that she 'could not in the least make clear to herself the reasons for her husband's dislike of his presence' (ch. 34). No less clumsy and nebulous is the account of Will's reactions to her pain at Mr Casaubon's rudeness to him: Will, we are told, is convinced that she 'had not been visited by the idea that Mr Casaubon's dislike and jealousy of him turned upon herself' (ch. 39). Nor could it possibly do so, if only because neither the reader nor Mr Casaubon must ever suspect Dorothea of 'doubleness' or entertain 'any coarse interpretation' of her behaviour. Dorothea's purity must be protected at all costs. Unfortunately this clumsy defensive concern for the heroine's reputation takes no account of the more questionable aspect of her behaviour – her insensitive high-mindedness on the question of her husband's wealth. On this point, Dorothea's voice grows shrill. Oblivious of how common minds might interpret her words and actions, and of her husband's shrinking anxieties, Dorothea is carried 'safely by the side of precipices where vision would have been perilous with fear' (ch. 37). Like Romola, in fact, she becomes a blind automaton.

The explanation offered for this side of her character is the usual one. Dorothea is sensuous and tender, but conveniently unworldly and unselfconscious. As a child, for example, 'she believed in the gratitude of wasps and the honourable susceptibility of sparrows' (ch. 22). Such fetishism matures into 'sensuous force controlled by spiritual passion' (ch. 19) and this in turn can justify a kind of inattentiveness as when Dorothea absorbs 'into the intensity of her mood, the solemn glory of the afternoon' (ch. 3). Behaviour, therefore, which in others might be thoughtless and inconsiderate, is excused in Dorothea on the grounds of her intense and entirely spontaneous susceptibility. Will, too, is redeemed from the taint of ignoble motive by process rather than by choice. His thoughtlessness, like Dorothea's, is the consequence of an inability to control his nobler feelings. In Dorothea's presence he starts 'as from an electric shock'; his finger-ends tingle, and 'every molecule in his body' receives 'the message of a magic touch', but it is the subtlety of such touches, George Eliot assures us, which makes 'a man's passion for one woman differ from his passion for another', and Will's reaction to Dorothea is the moral equivalent of 'moving light over valley and river and white mountain top', while his feeling for Rosamond is the moral equivalent of 'Chinese lanterns and glass panels' (ch. 39). Once again an Associationist rhetoric speciously distinguishes between the tender and the erotic, the epigraph of the 39th chapter making quite explicit George Eliot's determination to 'forget the He and She'. Even in her maturest and most balanced novel, George Eliot's commitment to the altruistic ideal tends to soften sexuality into a merely moralistic reactivity.

'*Middlemarch*', Barbara Hardy rightly remarks, 'is only restrictedly truthful in its treatment of sexuality.'[24] This, I have argued, was in part a logical consequence of the asceticism inherent in the twin conceptions of retributive justice and self-rewarding altruism which dominated George Eliot's thought from the earliest years. The deepest satisfactions in such a perspective are necessarily non-satisfactions – memories of joys lost, of sacrifices sustained, of others given priority over the self. But as Nietzsche notes there is a selfish energy concealed in all such eager self-denial: 'We can no longer conceal from ourselves,' he writes at the end of *The Genealogy of Morals*,

> what exactly it is that this whole process of willing, inspired by the ascetic ideal signifies – this hatred of humanity, of animality, of inert matter; this loathing of the senses, of reason even; this fear of beauty and happiness; this longing to escape from illusion, change, becoming, death, and from longing itself. It signifies, let us have the courage to face it, a will to nothingness, a revulsion from life, a rebellion against the principal conditions of living. And yet, despite everything, it is and remains a *will*. Let me repeat, now that I have reached the end, what I said at the beginning; man would sooner have the void for his purpose than be void of purpose . . . [25]

Nietzsche thus brings us to a conception of concealment in human performances which is radically inconsistent with the repeated and naively optimistic assumption in George Eliot's work that the powers of the unconscious and of memory work exclusively in the interests of altruistic joy. This, of course, was precisely the problem that Nietzsche handed on to Freud, and we must now turn to Freud in order finally to define the unsatisfactoriness of George Eliot's teaching.

8 Lust and anger

The challenge of Freud's *Civilization and its Discontents*

THE traditions in which George Eliot, Feuerbach, Comte and Bain had worked were closely related to those of Freud and his successors. It is true that Freud's conception of the unconscious is radically innovatory, but the context in which this break was made included both Positivism and Associationism. For this reason *Civilization and its Discontents* is an exceptionally useful work with which to take bearings on George Eliot's position in European intellectual history, especially as she would herself have immediately recognized the direct and pressing relevance to her point of view of many of Freud's ideas. For example, Freud discusses the self-punishing character of Jewish theology which he contrasts with primitive man's tendency to punish his fetish for his misfortunes rather than himself;[1] it is on such a Jewish 'renunciation of instinct' that civilization, he suggests, depends.[2] The Tulliver family clearly exemplifies this principle. He also saw analogies between 'the process of civilization and the development of the individual', the aim of the first being to integrate the individual in a group and of the second 'the creation of a unified group out of many individuals.'[3] These are precisely the analogies and models with which Comte and Spencer had also worked.

There are, however, more specific and significant connexions than these between Freud's work and that of the Associationists. Freud, for example, describes the 'instinct of destruction' (i.e. innate aggression) as 'narcissistic' and, when directed on to external objects, as providing the ego with 'satisfaction of its vital needs' and with control over nature.[4] This conception is in important respects implicit in Bain's description of 'the sense of Power' as an 'exquisite and luxurious' experience, for some people 'the crowning experience of their life'.[5] 'Nothing', he notes, 'so specifically stimulates' the desire for power 'as resistance or obstruction',[6] and it enters, along with 'sensual excitement', into our physical reactions to 'the act, sight and imagination of inflicting bodily suffering.' The 'sensual passions', he observes, 'mingle strangely with the work of slaughter.'[7] These important insights into the operation of power-seeking and aggressive impulses indicate the considerable extent to which the Associationist account of instinct and response was capable of establishing connexions between apparently disparate areas of reactivity, and specifically, as here, between sexuality and therefore love on the one hand, and violence on the other. It was these connexions that Freud developed later in ways which proved fatal to the concept of innate altruistic responses upon which the evolutionary ethics of George Eliot's generation so heavily depended. Nietzsche was to expose this weakness by pressing the logic of atheism to the point at which logic itself was extinguished. It was Freud's task to press the logic of association beyond the limits of consciously discernible connexion into the anomalous areas of repression and the unconscious. Nevertheless, it remains the case that the preparatory work for both these developments was successfully undertaken by many of George Eliot's contemporaries and associates, including George Henry Lewes, and that she was herself led, not by the process of intuition but by conscious speculative endeavour, to ethical and psychological conclusions which seriously weakened her entire conception of human potentialities and prospects.

To amplify this point it is obviously necessary to examine more specifically how close she actually came to the terrain which psychoanalysis was later to occupy. This raises difficulties, however, because there is undoubtedly and inevitably an element of randomness in the anticipations which can be discerned in this area. But that does not justify our regarding them as the kind of anticipations which the mechanisms of mind proposed by psychoanalysis might be thought to explain away. They are not 'unconscious' anticipations. It is necessary yet again, therefore, to insist that they arise out of the deliberately developed theoretical positions discussed in earlier chapters, and that they lead directly, on the level of the history of ideas, to the thought of Freud and his successors. This does not, of course, exclude the possibility that powerful unconscious factors were also at work as these problems formed themselves in George Eliot's mind. As we shall have cause to note, they undoubtedly were. But it is to insist that many of the important anticipations of later theories and models in the novels were not exclusively the result of intuitive insights.

Tom Tulliver offers a particularly clear example of some specifically theoretical anticipations. As we have already seen, his personality is analysed in unambiguously Associationist and evolutionary terms. It also embodies a kind of egoism which a number of modern psychoanalysts might wish to regard as typical. Thus

Jacques Lacan writes that the 'pre-eminence of aggressivity in our. civilization' is 'usually confused in "normal" morality with the virtue of strength.' It is understood, he suggests, 'and quite rightly as significant of a development of the ego', its use being 'regarded as indispensable in society.' 'If necessary', he continues,

> the prestige of the idea of the struggle for life would be sufficiently attested by the success of a theory that could make our thinking accept a selection based only on the animal's conquest of space as a valid explanation of the developments of life. Indeed, Darwin's success seems to derive from the fact that he projected the predations of Victorian society and the economic euphoria that sanctioned for that society the social devastation that it initiated on a planetary scale, and to the fact that it justified its predations by the image of a laissez-faire of the strongest predators in competition for their natural prey.[8]

This judgment is in close theoretical agreement with the critique of the psychodynamics of Political Economy which we have seen to inform *The Mill on the Floss.* Tom Tulliver's fulfilment of the practical, male role converts the sadism of the child-savage into the civilized aggressivity of the property-obsessed entrepreneur, but though this is a process of which Herbert Spencer, the true father of Social Darwinism, would have approved, George Eliot clearly recognizes that it involves a kind of blindness which severely limits the personal life. Our experience, Lacan writes, 'teaches us not to regard the ego as centred on the *perception-consciousness system*, or as organised by the "reality principle" . . . we should start instead from the *function of méconnaissance* that characterizes the ego in all its structures.'[9] This is not far removed from George Eliot's representation of Tom as only apparently living in accordance with the reality principle 'by which Nature forces us to submit to the yoke, and change the face of the world', while, in fact, his entire life is grounded in specific *méconnaissances* which are the basis of his kind of ego-founded personality, notably that quenching of 'memory in the stronger light of purpose', and that loss of 'the sense of dread and even of wounds in the hurrying ardour of action' which make him so different from Maggie. The organization of the passions on which the ego is based, Lacan writes, crystallizes 'in the subject's internal conflictual tension, which determines the awakening of his desire for the object of the other's desire: here the primordial coming together *(concourse)* is precipitated into aggressive competitiveness *(concurr-ence)*, from which develops the triad of others, the ego and the object.'[10] Thus from both Associationist and psychoanalytical points of view the struggles between Tom and Bob for the wagered pocket-knife, and between Tom and Wakem for the Mill, are *typically* structured incidents. But, Lacan continues,

> if the ego appears to be marked from its very origin by this aggressive relativity . . . how can one not conceive that each great instinctual metamorphosis in the life of the individual will once again challenge its delimitation, composed as it is of a conjunction of the subject's history and the unthinkable innateness of his desire?

'That is why', he concludes, . . . 'man's ego can never be reduced to his experienced identity.' It is on just such a reduction of his personality to his experienced identity, however, that Tom tries to base his adult life, and it is equally just such a challenge to his egoistical delimitations which his discovery of the depths of life offers to his ego in the last great instinctual metamorphosis of his life, during the final moments on the boat with his sister.

But while it was relatively easy for George Eliot to recognize and condemn the resistances which issue in an ego-centred consciousness such as Tom's, it was very difficult indeed for her to contemplate other resistances in herself, resistances on which the 'consciousness' of Positivism itself was based, and which depended on the polarization of rationality and emotion, egoism and altruism, and the individual and society. In *Civilization and Its Discontents*, however, these are precisely the categories and distinctions which Freud calls into question. He suggests, for example, that egoism is the principal source of individual self-development, and that altruism is the principle source of social integration – a separation of individual and social process which would have been equally abhorrent to Comte and George Eliot. In any case he regards the level on which such distinctions have to be made as a superficial one, and thereby exposes the real gap between psychoanalysis and Positivism. Feuerbach and Comte were on the whole content to specify the social function of an activity or impulse; Freud, however, argues that a true analysis of, for example, the 'need of religion' must penetrate to its *'fons et origo'*[11] as well as its present function, and in exploring the *fons et origo* of altruism he moves decisively into the Nietzschean camp. Specifically he rejects Comte's notion of altruism as an innate capacity and argues that love of neighbour and love of enemy are defensive responses to innate aggression in oneself. Authentic love, for Freud, is libidinal not altruistic. The basic forces contending in his view for supremacy in man are not egoism and altruism but violence and desire. As we shall see, there are elaborate structural resistances throughout George Eliot's work to just these realignments in the mental life, indicating both the closeness of her thinking to Freud's and the anxieties which speculation in this area induced in her.

The first of the realignments which she resists is Freud's identification of fulfilled selfhood with genital self-realization rather than altruistic self-obliteration. This can be most clearly seen in the kinds of polarization she introduces into her narratives of young love. In *Adam Bede*, for example, the sensual shallow Arthur and Hetty are at the furthest possible remove from the self-sacrificing, passionate Adam and Dinah. This has predictably serious consequences for the effectiveness of the narrative when Adam and Dinah replace Arthur and Hetty as the novel's centrally representative lovers. A comparison between two carefully paralleled lovers' meetings is illuminating. Of Hetty and Arthur's encounter in the woods, George Eliot writes:

> Love is such a simple thing when we have only one-and-twenty summers and a sweet girl of seventeen trembles under our glance, as if she were a bud first opening her heart with wondering rapture to the morning. Such young unfurrowed souls roll to meet each other like two velvet peaches that touch softly and are at rest; they mingle as easily as two brooklets that ask for nothing but to entwine themselves and ripple with ever-interlacing curves in the leafiest hiding places. When Arthur gazed in Hetty's dark beseeching eyes, it made no difference to him what English she spoke; and even if hoops and powder had been in fashion, he would likely not have been sensible that Hetty wanted those signs of high-breeding (ch. 12).

There are blemishes here: 'brooklets' is awkward, 'entwines' visually unclear. But the suggestions of sensation, secrecy and fruitfulness succeed, and the discreet pastoral interchange between vegetable and animal images is truly erotic. Very different is the effect of the address to the reader about Adam and Dinah's similar meeting in the cottage:

> That is a simple scene, reader. But it is almost certain that you, too have been in love – perhaps, even, more than once, though you may not choose to say so to all your feminine friends. If so, you will no more think the slight words, the timid looks, the tremulous touches, which two human souls approach each other gradually, like two little quivering rain-streams, before they

mingle into one – you will no more think these things trivial than
you will think the first-detected signs of spring trivial, though
they be but a faint indescribable something in the air and in the
song of the birds, and the tiniest perceptible budding on the
hedgerow branches. Those slight words and looks and touches
are part of the soul's language; and the finest language, I believe,
is chiefly made up of unimposing words, such as 'light', 'sound',
'stars', 'music', – words really not worth looking at, or hearing, in
themselves, any more than 'chips' or 'sawdust': it is only that they
happen to be signs of something unspeakably great and beautiful
(ch. 5).

None of these images, except that of the rain-streams, suggests
feeling and sensation. Looks and touches are dematerialized into a
language of the soul which notably fails to speak for itself; and for all
the arch appeal to common experience, the unspeakable beauties
referred to seem at the furthest possible remove from the delights,
poisonous or otherwise, of ordinary lovers. Yet the parallels between
the two passages are evidently carefully worked, and one can only
conclude that the passion of the altruistic lovers has been deliberately emptied of erotic content.

Ostensibly the love-situations in *The Mill on the Floss* and *Romola*
are more complex than those in *Adam Bede*: Maggie in turn loves Philip
and Stephen; Tito, Romola and Tessa: in neither triangle are the moral
contrasts quite so stark as those in the earlier novel. The reader is
evidently invited to form some kind of judgment about the quality
and significance of each relationship and each participant, and in
principle this could have brought erotic and spiritual intensities into
closer, more intimate connexion. In Maggie's case, certainly, that
would appear to be the effect George Eliot is seeking. The many
references in the sixth book, for example, to Philip's 'poor crooked
little body' (Bk VI, ch. 5) seem to specify discreetly but precisely
why Maggie finds Stephen's 'strength' attractive. However, the
pressures on her are never specifically erotic; the manliness Philip
lacks and Stephen enjoys is social as well as physical – Stephen can
provide her with 'wealth, ease, refinement' (Bk VII, ch. 13) as well as
love, and in any case Maggie's relations with Stephen are subtly but
consistently de-eroticized, just as Dinah's and Adam's were: the
apparently erotic response is always interpreted as something else.
Thus Stephen's love appeals to Maggie's delight in admiration, in
effect to her vanity, while it is specifically passion which enables her
to resist him:

there were things in her stronger than vanity – passion, and affection, and long deep memories of early discipline and effort, of early claims on her love and pity; and the stream of vanity was soon swept along and mingled imperceptibly with that wider current (Bk VI, ch. 9).

Passion and vanity are thus polarized, and the form which passion takes is precisely renunciation. The procedure is the same as the denial of a passionate nature to Hetty Sorrel in *Adam Bede*. Both novels assert the moral value of passion, but both insist on its being distinguished from the intoxicating egoism of young love.

In *Romola* a comparably elusive but pervasive unease about passion and purity in a love relationship characterizes George Eliot's account of Tito's feelings towards the heroine. When they first meet, her reserve is compared to 'a snowy embankment hemming in the rush of admiring surprise' but attention soon shifts from Romola's to Tito's reactions; the following passage is indicative of how this manoeuvre is effected:

> The finished fascination of [Tito's] air . . . was that of a fleet, soft-coated, dark-eyed animal that delights you by not bounding away in indifference from you, and unexpectedly pillows its chin on your palm, and looks up at you desiring to be stroked – as if it loved you (ch. 6).

The comparison develops with characteristically razor-edged irony at Tito's expense and the problem it raises is the reverse of that raised by Adam's love for Hetty in *Adam Bede*, since it is one thing to identify a noble man's mistaken feelings for a worthless girl with the finest potentialities of his nature, quite another to find that the influence of a noble woman on a shallow sensualist may well be attributable to his appetite for pleasure. It is a problem to which the account of the marriage of Tito and Romola repeatedly returns but which it elaborately fails to resolve. Romola, we are told, could have become 'an image of . . . loving, pitying devotedness' (ch. 12) for Tito. What, then, is the actual nature of her influence upon him? It is certainly a 'delicious influence, as strong and inevitable as . . . musical vibrations', and since the same comparison is used later about the impact of Savonarola's preaching on Romola herself, which is said to be like that of 'vibrating harmonies' (ch. 27), Tito's 'musical' responsiveness may actually be a sign of authentic moral elevation. Significantly the analogy is used far more frequently in George Eliot's work about a woman's feelings for a man, which may account for Leslie Stephen's suggestion that the characterization of Tito is in fact essentially feminine.[12] This would be consistent with

the development of a distinction in Tito's make-up between high
passion (love, we recall, is essentially feminine) and trivial, merely
sensual desire (the prerogative of the shallow male seducer). Such a
distinction, however, is never decisively established. The lovers'
most physically intense moment is described in 'Under the Loggia'.
'My Romola! my goddess!' Tito murmurs, kissing the thick golden
ripples on her neck. At that moment he is 'in paradise', but he has
never had a 'real caress from her' and consequently the sensuality of
paradisal experience would seem to be limited. He is beginning to
wish, indeed, 'that she had been something lower', and when at last
they do kiss properly, he declares that he longs to see her 'subdued
into mere enjoyment', knowing the 'happiness of the nymphs' (ch.
17). The moral and sensual components of his feelings for her seem
to be at odds already, yet though it is clearly the decline of the
former rather than of the latter that the subsequent narrative
concentrates upon, it does so consistently in the language of physical
passion. Moral dramas, in other words, take place in the flesh
without being necessarily sensual. Eighteen months into their
marriage Tito's caresses are still 'tender' and he lingers 'about her
with . . . fond playfulness', but Romola is feeling 'a little heartache
in the midst of her love' (ch. 27): the impression is one of the ecstasy
missed, but not precisely of sexual ecstasy. Thus even though the
touch of Romola's hair seems to Tito to 'vibrate through the hours',
it does so apparently, because of his 'young ideal passion' and not his
'soft nature' (ch. 34). Later when Tito sells the library, the rupture
between them is carefully described in terms of lost sensations.
Romola, for example, is indifferent to, and so unconscious of, the
touch of his lips, or later the touch of his arm as he leads her to a
seat. Not long afterwards, her 'touch and glance' cease to stir 'any
fibre of tenderness' in him, and he complains that her 'impetuosity
about trifles . . . has a freezing influence that would cool the baths of
Nero' (ch. 48). It is not impetuosity, however, but her 'self-
sacrificing effort' which apparently hardens his nature 'by chilling it
with positive dislike' (ch. 50). The failure of the relationship is thus
physically tangible; it is even sexual in that it represents the rise and
fall of passion between a man and a woman; but whether that
passion was ever in its essence sensual, or merely associated with
eroticism as a concomitant of marriage, is left deliberately and
elaborately obscure.

This kind of ambiguity was inherent in the methodology of
Associationism. Bain, for example, regarded tenderness – the most
characteristic component of authentic passion in George Eliot's
novels – as a maternal rather than an erotic response. It was, he

believed, associated with 'the breast, neck, mouth, and the hand . . . in conjunction with the movements of the upper members'; 'sexual excitability', on the other hand, he located 'in the surfaces and movements of the inferior members.'[13] Of course he recognized that tenderness was 'too considerable' a response to be 'left out when joy [was] in the ascendant', since it was 'the nature of a great excitement to spread itself over all parts of one's being',[14] but tenderness and sexuality in the last analysis remained distinct. Their effects were separable if incalculably diffuse. Bain writes at great length and some subtlety about interactions and distinctions such as these, and in ways that continually illuminate George Eliot's characterizations in particular. Nevertheless it is precisely this fundamental commitment of Associationism to its own categories, and to the principle of mind-body cartography, which in the end vitiates much of his work, as it does much of hers.

Nor is it just uneasy distinctions between passion and lust which Associationism facilitates and Positivism insists on. Even more serious to our sense of George Eliot's willingness to confront the depths in life, however disturbing to 'consciousness', is her reductive treatment of good and evil. From the beginning of her career as a novelist she allowed the theoretical necessity of keeping them distinct to influence her presentation of character. In 'Janet's Repentance' Dempster and Mr Tryan are moral opposites of a disturbingly theoretical kind. Janet's moral union with the latter completes the programmatic isolation of evil from altruism which constitutes the essential movement of the narrative. This is particularly clear in the description of Dempster's illness and death, a description which is in every sense appalling. The writing characteristically evinces both disturbing excitement in the brutality and violence of his delirium and a kind of intoxication in the relief Janet finds in nursing him: 'Here is a duty about which all creeds and all philosophies are at one . . . where a human being lies prostrate, thrown on the tender mercies of his fellow, the moral relation of man to man is reduced to its utmost clearness and simplicity' (ch. 24). This admitted *reduction* of human relationships to their allegedly simplest form is especially revealing. It suggests the absolute ascendancy of altruistic devotion over egoistical brutality, and thus becomes the implicit measure of their polarization. A similarly naive and tendentious polarization is represented in the characterization of Lapidoth and his children in *Daniel Deronda*.

However, the brutalized characters in George Eliot's fiction who are comparable with Dempster and Lapidoth – Dunstan Cass, Dolfo Spini, Raffles – are insufficiently prominent to merit close psychological analysis, and consequently the threat they represent to her sense of the altruistic impulse as innate and uncontaminated is a remote one. They are all degenerates, brutalized by debauchery which is itself caused by the absence of morally positive 'associations' in their mental lives, and morally positive relationships in their domestic and social lives. They are thus examples of masculine aggressivity in decay, just as Tom Tulliver and Harold Transome are examples of the same tendencies achieving a degree of morally positive transformation. There is in fact no clear case, at least until *Felix Holt*, and possibly not until *Daniel Deronda*, of evil having anything but a negative presence in George Eliot's fiction. Her villains and seducers simply exhibit a more or less psychopathic deficiency in positive moral qualities. Such a view of human corruption is in fact almost logically entailed in the synthesis of Associationist analysis and Positivist ethics to which George Eliot was committed. Once she had accepted that there are stores laid up in our nature that our understandings can take no inventory of, she could only protect the purity of altruism by making the unconscious – that is (to use her own endlessly repeated analogy) the 'musical' potentialities of human nature – a source of good feelings only. As a result the majority of corrupt characters in the novels are not only denied a memory, as we have noted already, but also an unconscious.

This is true even of Arthur Donnithorne in *Adam Bede*, in spite of the celebrated explanation of his refusal to admit to Mr Irwine that their discussion of abstract moral principles has any immediate bearing on his own life: 'Was there a motive at work', George Eliot asks,

> under this strange reluctance of Arthur's which had a sort of backstairs influence, not admitted to himself? Our mental business is carried on much in the same way as the business of the State: a great deal of hard work is done by agents who are not acknowledged. In a piece of machinery, too, I believe there is often a small unnoticeable wheel which has a great deal to do with the motion of the large obvious ones. Possibly there was some such unrecognised agent secretly busy in Arthur's mind at this moment – possibly it was the fear lest he might hereafter find the fact of having made a confession to the Rector a serious annoyance, in case he should *not* be able to carry out his good resolutions? I dare not assert that it was not so. The human soul is a very complex thing (ch. 16).

The images of backstairs influence, the unnoticeable wheel and the unacknowledged and unrecognized agent do not on analysis suggest unconscious – that is, repressed mental activity – but rather that willed withholding of attention by which the minister of state ensures the effective operation of unscrupulous subordinates. Similarly the possible motive we are given for this reticence is just the kind of suppression about which self-scrutiny could inform us if we wished it to do so. We are dealing therefore with the reverse of the Freudian model of repressed material evading the supervision of the super-ego and manifesting itself in speech or action in disguised form. George Eliot remains faithful to a very traditional model of bad conscience, and she does so because she wants the terrain of the unconscious, where Adam's rather than Arthur's love for Hetty originates and where Dinah finds the resources to give unlimited sympathy to her rival in love, to be wholly uncontaminated by contradiction and violence.

The consequences of this approach to evil are noticeable even in as tactful a novel as *Silas Marner*. Godfrey Cass's struggles with his conscience, like Arthur's, are presented with impeccable logic and adroit irony, but they inevitably seem light-weight and convenient when set beside his subjection to the brutal Dunstan, a situation altogether too 'legendary' and psychologically deep-seated for logical scrutiny of conscious motives and inexorable consequences. However, the work which is most clearly and damagingly organized around a negative view of evil is *Romola*, and in particular the story of Tito. Like Arthur and Godfrey, Tito is elaborately trapped by the iron law of consequences, this being, according to the *Westminster Review*, 'the central idea to which all else is made subservient.'[15] His case, therefore, covers important theoretical ground, the interior act of self-decepttion, the consequent distortion of his relationship with external fact, and a nurturing within himself of 'a brood of guilty wishes'. But though they are 'cherished by the darkness', these desires are not in the modern sense repressed, since like Arthur's they are always available for confession. But they are not confessed, and the resulting habit of 'tacit falsity' soon compels Tito to externalize that falsity in 'an ingenious lie' (ch. 11). He then discovers how indestructible past deeds are, 'both in and out of our consciousness' (ch. 16). The result is a schematized, transparent characterization. Tito is a wholly negative figure, and a completely visible one. He has 'an innate love of reticence' (ch. 9); he is 'not passionate but impressible'; the 'strong, unmistakable expression in his whole air and person [is] a negative one' (ch. 10); his fear generates 'no active malignity' (ch. 23) – he is merely 'clever, unimpassioned' (ch. 32), the embodiment of an evil at once formidable and unmysterious.

There are admittedly points of view from which the lack of ambiguity and contradiction in Tito's character can be defended. It gives the moral drama in which he is involved an aesthetically satisfying clarity and directness. In general, however, the problem of egoism, of love of power and of the aggressive instincts associated with them requires ampler and more penetrating treatment than George Eliot gives it in *Romola* or any of the earlier novels. Its connexions with other aspects of the mental life are nonetheless evident in her work, apparently without her being aware of the fact. In order to see the extent and depth of these connexions, we may turn first of all to her treatment of what appears to be the obsessive interest which many of her characters exhibit in their own reflected images. The following appears in one of her earliest contributions to the *Coventry Herald*:

> Idione loved to look into the lake because she saw herself there; she would sit on the bank, weaving leaves and flowers in her silken hair, and smiling at her own image all day long, and if the pretty water-lilies or any other plants began to spread themselves on the surface below her, and spoil her mirror, she would tear them up in anger.[16]

Nearly thirty years later in *Daniel Deronda* George Eliot described Gwendolen Harleth, about to leave Leubronn after reading her mother's letter announcing the family's ruin, also looking at her own image and finding her spirits revive in the process:

> She had a *naïve* delight in her fortunate self, which any but the harshest saintliness will have some indulgence for in a girl who had every day seen a pleasant reflection of that self in her friends' flattery as well as in the looking-glass. And even in this beginning of troubles, while for lack of anything else to do she sat gazing at her image in the growing light, her face gathered a complacency gradual as the cheerfulness of morning. Her beautiful lips curled into a more and more decided smile, till at last she took off her hat, leaned forward and kissed the cold glass which had looked so warm. How could she believe in sorrow? If it attacked her, she felt the force to crush it, to defy it, or run away from it, as she had done already (ch. 2).

In both these passages a young woman, who is evidently meant to strike us as egoistical and immature, sees her identity in terms of her reflected image; in both she is ready to defend it, and the space in which it apparently flourishes, with violence. In the second passage this self-image is reflected back not only by the glass but also, 'kaleidoscopically', in the flattery of friends. As we shall see, this would suggest to the modern psychoanalytical theorist typical and significant psychological situations. It did so also to George Eliot, and the differences between her sense of this kind of situation and that of recent analytical theory precisely defines the grounds for the justified unease which many readers have felt about her work.

George Eliot's thinking about obsessive narcissism is most clearly in evidence in the elaborately argued characterization of Hetty Sorrel in *Adam Bede*. Hetty is forever looking at the pleasing reflection of herself in the polished surfaces of her aunt's furniture, and this habit assumes the importance and intensity of a religious rite when she is alone in her room in front of her mottled looking-glass. As we have seen, this moment represents for George Eliot the apotheosis of atheism, the worship of an absence, a ritualized solipsism. Lacan would see it in similar but more elaborately defined terms. Hetty's obsession with her own image would suggest to him a failure to negotiate everything that follows from what he calls 'the deflection of the specular I into the social I'.[17] There are two ways, he suggests, in which the I is precipitated. Through language the individual exists 'in the universal'[18] with the function of a subject, but before man learns to use language he thinks of himself as a body in space such as one sees in a glass, and to the extent that he continues to think of himself in this way, he 'situates the agency of the ego, before its social determination, in a fictional direction.' The mirror stage, then, locates the self in a fantasy world, and, while far from being anxiety-free, it has at least not yet arrived at that sense of a possible discordance between the perceived self and subjectivity in its entirety which maturity seeks constantly to resolve. All this can be paralleled in George Eliot's theoretical assessment of Hetty's mental development, notably in her indifference to the other (Feuerbach's 'Thou'), her solipsistic fantasy-life, and her lack of internal tension. Moreover the mirror stage, the stage of the 'specular I', is also fundamental to Lacan's acccount of 'the so-called "instinct of self-preservation"'[19] which is so powerfully operative in Hetty during her wanderings. In certain animals, he suggests, and especially in man, the individual's relation to the space in which it lives is 'mapped socially'[20] through its sense of 'subjective membership' of the group. If this sense of belonging is dominated by the mirror-stage, the individual thinks of himself and others in 'kaleidoscopic' terms. He envisages himself on the basis of what he sees in a glass, and this conditions his sense of others, and of how they see themselves and him. It is in such patterns, Lacan suggests, that 'the imagery of the ego develops' – and it is in just such subjective or 'imaginary' space that Hetty also floats.

Equally relevant to the analysis of Hetty's character is Lacan's suggestion that the mirror stage, which makes possible the projection of such 'imaginary' space, is marked by the infant's acute recognition of its own physical inadequacies. Man, Lacan argues, is born prematurely by the standards of other mammals: thus while 'the function of the mirror-stage . . . is to establish a relation between the organism and its reality',[21] in man 'this relation to nature is altered by . . . a primordial Discord betrayed by the signs of uneasiness and motor unco-ordination of the neo-natal months.' The fundamental anxiety of the mirror-stage arises out of this lack of physical co-ordination, and the narcissistic fear it induces of damage to the body's surfaces. This, Lacan suggests, rather than the fear of death as such, lies at the heart of 'the so-called "instinct of self-preservation"'. This is strikingly consistent with that intense moment of self-love in *Adam Bede* when Hetty suddenly grasps the fact that she has not drowned herself:

> It was an ill-smelling close place, but warm, and there was straw on the ground: Hetty sank down on the straw with a sense of escape. Tears came – she had never shed tears before since she left Windsor – tears and sobs of hysterical joy that she had still hold of life, that she was still on the familiar earth, with the sheep near her. The very consciousness of her own limbs was a delight to her: she turned up her sleeves, and kissed her arms with the passionate love of life (ch. 37).

Hetty's narcissistic sense of being an integral body in shared space constitutes the whole of her self-identity at this point, and at the same time precisely registers her immaturity. In addition her dominant sense of shame suggests just that structure of feeling which Lacan sees as arising out of the ego's passionate interest in itself – 'a passion whose nature', he suggests,

> was already glimpsed by the traditional moralists, who called it *amour-propre* . . . This passion brings to every relation with this image . . . a signification that interests me so much, that is to say, which places me in such a dependence on this image that it links all the objects of my desires more closely to the desire of the other than to the desire that they arouse in me.[22]

In other words, if for me the other takes the narcissistic form of a mirror image of myself, I will think myself into the relation which the other has to the object of my desire, and that relation will then become more real for me than the feelings which the object arouses in me directly. Thus Hetty's desire 'to be back in her safe home again' is countered by thoughts from which she shrinks

> as she might have shrunk from scorching metal: she could never endure that shame before her uncle and aunt, before Mary Burge, and the servants at the Chase, and the people at Broxton, and everybody who knew her. They should never know what had happened to her (ch. 37).

In isolation this is simply a vivid description of shame. In the context of Hetty's lack of memories, her insensitivity to symbol, and her intense preoccupation with her own image and with the satisfactory wholeness of her body, it indicates the proximity of the tradition in which George Eliot was working to that of Lacan. These correspondences, however, also suggest important ways in which George Eliot's engagement with the mental lives of her characters failed to take adequate account of the problem of violence. Specifically, at the heart of the Feuerbachian concept of the Thou and the Comtist concept of altruism, there is a simple and morally loaded polarization of love of self and love of others which Bain's analysis of the love of power and its relation to sadism should have led George Eliot to question as psychoanalysis was later to question it, but on which she resolutely turned her back.

Where psychoanalytical questioning led is again illustrated by Lacan. He envisages a moment which the mirror stage comes to an end and the individual identifies with 'the *imago* of the counterpart'.[23] But he does not see this coming into awareness of the other as ever being pure in the way that recognizing the Feuerbachian Thou is pure. He sees it rather as a 'drama of primordial jealousy', this being 'the dialectic that will henceforth link the I to socially elaborated situations.' As a result of this moment, he suggests, 'the whole of human knowledge' is mediated 'through the desire of the other'; the objects of knowledge are constituted in 'an abstract equivalence' through 'the co-operation of others'; and the I becomes an 'apparatus for which every instinctual thrust constitutes a danger.'[24] (The relevance of this to Tom Tulliver's case has already been considered.) As a result normal maturation is dependent on cultural mediation (as in the case of the Oedipus complex). Hence the important distinction in psychoanalytical theory between the narcissistic libido (love of the self as an image) and the sexual libido, since (according to Lacan) the former is connected with 'the alienating function of the I', that is, with the aggression which is *invariably* directed towards the other 'even in a relation invoking the most

Samaritan of aid.' In other words, love of neighbour is necessarily contaminated by narcissism and violence. This recognition more than anything else in the work of Freud and his successors most seriously calls into question major structural contrasts in George Eliot's work, notably that between Hetty Sorrel and Dinah Morris in *Adam Bede*.

The key to our understanding of this contrast is the celebrated fifteenth chapter of the novel, 'The Two Bedchambers'. In principle, the contrast developed in this chapter might be thought to anticipate the distinction made by Lacan between the 'social I' and the 'specular I'. However, in attempting to conceal and deny the presence of aggression in the 'social I', that is in Dinah Morris, George Eliot introduces a dangerously uncontrolled ambivalence into her writing. This comes sharply into focus in her references to the embryonic sexual rivalry between the two women. Dinah, we are told, feels particular concern over 'the coldness of [Hetty's] behaviour towards Adam' (ch. 15). But Adam has already given Dinah (for the first time in her life) an experience of 'painful self-consciousness' (ch. 11). One might expect, therefore, some slight consciousness in Dinah of Hetty as a rival, but this is laboriously denied. Hetty's 'lovely face and form', George Eliot assures us, affected her only 'as beauty always affects a pure and tender mind, free from selfish jealousies: it was an excellent divine gift, that gave a deeper pathos to the need, the sin, the sorrow with which it was mingled.' The word 'always' is suspiciously over-confident, especially since this pure and tender mind promptly imagines 'a thorny thicket of sin and sorrow' in which Hetty struggles 'torn and bleeding, looking with tears for rescue and finding none.' George Eliot ignores the cruelty in this image. 'It was in this way', she insists, 'that Dinah's imagination and sympathy acted and reacted habitually, each heightening the other.' In effect, she illicitly and illogically assumes the existence of a 'pre-established harmony' by which, according to Lacan, the suppressions demanded by social conformity are freed 'of all aggressive inductions.'[25]

Lacan believes that the dream of such a harmony has its basis in 'imaginary' post-specular fantasy. It would follow that Dinah in fact occupies the same mental and moral terrain as Hetty. She too floats in the kaleidoscopic world of a subjective space void of internal contradiction, and not exclusively in the life of symbols. But the latter (at least according to Lacan) is 'the only life that endures and is true.'[26] Admittedly he also believes that we find 'what is primordial to the birth of symbols . . . is death,'[27] but that does not align the symbolic order with aggressivity, for, as we have noted, aggressivity is associated for Lacan with a narcissistic fear of bodily injury, rather than with the will towards pure extinction. The experience on which aggressivity draws is that of the mirror stage: 'in experience [it] is given to us as intended aggression and as an image of corporal dislocation.'[28] It is 'the correlative tendency of a mode of identification that we call narcissistic, and which determines the formal structure of man's ego and of the register of entities characteristic of his world.'[29] Finally it is this 'notion of aggressivity as one of the intentional co-ordinates of the human ego, especially relative to the category of space, [which] allows us to conceive of its role in modern neurosis and in the "discontents" of civilization.'[30] From this point of view, Dinah's 'altruistic' meditation on Hetty's future in 'The Two Bedchambers' is both individually specific and broadly representative. It is individual because a highly developed, symbolically enriched 'social I', becomes entangled with a more primitive, unacknowledged 'specular I', and as a result the symbolic and 'imaginary' become confused. Thus Dinah imagines her rival not just as a lost lamb who is liable to the possibility at least of that extinction which is inherent in the mere act of seeing her symbolically, but also to all those possibilities of corporal dislocation inherent in the act of visualizing and identifying with a body in space. But the meditation is also representative because just such ambivalence is written into the structure of all human development, though this cannot be recognized by either a Feuerbachian or a Positivist morality, so that even when she records it, George Eliot is compelled at the same time to ignore it.

Thus the heart of the case against her fiction – at least in psychoanalytical terms – is that by not acknowledging the essential connexions between the sympathetic and aggressive instincts she effectively (if maladroitly) illustrates them – in Dinah Morris's thoughts about the torn and bleeding Hetty, in Maggie Tulliver's violence towards her doll, in Savonarola's self-immolation, even in Felix Holt's desire to cut off Esther Lyon's hair. The result is a streak of ugliness in George Eliot's work which serves strikingly and persistently to confirm Nietzsche's diagnosis of her case. In particular her concentration on the individual subject which we saw to be inherent in the logic of her aesthetic is vitiated by a distorted, heavily rationalized version of subjectivity itself. 'Rationalized' seems to me to be the appropriate word, though one might also use the word 'overdetermined' since her version of subjectivity is simultaneously the product of false ethics, a false epistemology and a false psychology. The epistemology, as we have seen, is fundamentally political – its function is to give personality superiority

over the secular foundations of human life. Her ethics in turn
require her to structure this personality in such a way that priority is
given to memory and unconscious process over conscious freedom;
and this in turn compels her to find ways of protecting the
unconscious from those very associative processes on which her
entire thinking about the human personality is based, but which
threaten the cornerstone of the whole structure, the Positivist
concept of pure altruism. 'Overdetermined' is consequently a thoroughly appropriate word to use of George Eliot's massive dependence on the myth of evolving subjectivity around which all her
works are organized. But it also suggests too high a degree of repression and ideological determination in her reliance on this myth. A
better model, it seems to me, is suggested by the image of backstairs
influence used of Arthur Donnithorne. In other words, the point to
return to is the one on which I was so insistent at the beginning of
this chapter, and which is implicit in the word 'rationalization'. The
discomfort experienced in reading George Eliot is a moral discomfort. If there are failures in her work, they are, first and foremost if
not exclusively, failures of intellectual integrity, so that if a case for
the defence is to be mounted it must be made out on terms of what
George Eliot consciously chose to teach, rather than in terms of any
'work' her novels may do in the world independently of her
intentions as she wrote them.

Part Three: Affirmations

9 Contexts of Uncertainty

MY DEFENCE of George Eliot's teaching, and particularly of its political, ethical, and psychological content, will not take the form of a complete rebuttal of the kind of charges which Marx, Nietzsche and Freud enable us to make against her, nor in principle could it do so. This would be to make her thought reductively compatible, even identical, with theirs. The function of Part Two, therefore, has been to specify the difficulties her didacticism has to negotiate, so that her own distinctive contribution to the humanist dilemma can be defined in and through the fissures, inconsistencies and tensions which her fiction exposes in the largely derivative view of history, morality and psychology from which she worked.

At the heart of this dilemma is Nietzsche's aphorism: 'Nothing is true: everything is permitted' – an assertion which every atheist must at some point examine to see if it is logically entailed in his position. The death of God, and so of the soul and of acccountability in any ultimate sense, constitutes a particularly pressing challenge to a novelist as intensely didactic as George Eliot. It implies a principle of perspectival relativity ('All seeing is essentially perspective,' Nietzsche insists, 'and so is all knowing')[1] which must considerably complicate the very notion of teaching itself. Besides, in proclaiming that the goal of history is 'the sovereign individual, equal only to himself', Nietzsche specifically locates the artist in a non-didactic role. The artist, he writes, should stand 'proudly and independently in (or against) the world', wholly uncommitted to 'the service of . . . ethics, or philosophy or religion', or for that matter of 'vested interests'.[2] He should be no less detached from the humanity he depicts: 'Homer would not have created Achilles, nor Goethe Faust, if Homer had been an Achilles or Goethe a Faust. An artist worth his salt is permanently separated from ordinary reality.'[3] Finally, there is the 'problem' of morality, which in his attack on George Eliot, Nietzsche specifically asserted that the English had not learned to recognize, and by which he meant all that arises from a radical uncertainty about values in a world where 'evil' can certainly be said to exist but where God does not.

It is possible to argue, however, that it was Nietzsche for whom morality was not a problem, so completely was he able to sweep it from sight, and that it was George Eliot, needing strong, simple affirmations of value, yet aware, throughout her writing career that such affirmations were barely sustainable, for whom the problem remained a real and pressing one. This crucially important tension is evident even in her early criticism. On the one hand she looked to literature for assured simplicities. Typically, for example, she wrote of Elizabeth Barrett Browning's *Aurora Leigh:*

> Its melody, fancy, and imagination – what we may call its
> poetical body – is everywhere informed by a *soul*, namely by
> genuine thought and feeling . . . there is simply a full mind
> pouring itself out in song as its natural and easiest medium. The
> mind has its far-stretching thoughts, its abundant treasure of
> well-digested learning, its acute observation of life, its yearning
> sympathy for multiform human sorrow, its store of personal and
> domestic love and joy.[4]

The suggestion in the word 'simply' of an unconstrained flow of feeling from the poet through the poem to the reader assumes all that Marx condemned in sensuous contemplation. But George Eliot also showed an early interest in contradiction as a necessary condition of art. She points out in 'The Antigone and its Moral', for example, that 'two principles, both having their validity' can be at war with each other,[5] and that Creon's stand against Antigone, at least from a purely aesthetic point of view, must have its own kind of legitimacy, since coarse 'contrasts . . . are not the materials handled by great dramatists.'[6] The implications of this acceptance of contradiction only become apparent in the various articles she wrote on Heine. Twice she compares Heine and Voltaire. The latter plainly confuses her, but she admires his 'distinct moral conviction'[7] and regrets Heine's lack of it. However, she finds that 'the sense of the ludicrous' in *Candide* 'is continually defeated by disgust, and [that] the scenes, instead of presenting us with an amusing or agreeable picture, are only the frame for a witticism.'[8] Similar confusions characterize her judgment of Heine. On the one hand there are specific issues on which he and George Eliot were in apparent sympathy. His contempt for the spiritual superficiality of English life expressed sentiments she was to echo in the essay on Young, and his quarrel with the patriotic party made his political views relatively easy to accept. But she felt his 'magnificent powers . . . often served only to give electric force to the expression of debased feeling'; he shows a 'Mephistophelean contempt for the reverent feelings of other men';[9] his irony 'repels our sympathy and baffles our psychology.'[10] Yet in spite of these difficulties, which for George Eliot were very serious, she finds she cannot resist his 'bewildering double-edged sarcasms'.[11] It is true that her pleasure in his work is cautious, even timid: 'the paradoxical irreverence with which [he] professes his theoretical reverence' she finds 'pathological . . . the diseased exhibition of a predominant tendency urged into anomalous action by the pressure of pain and mental privation'.[12] But this very anxiety makes her pleasure in Heine especially significant, for verbal anarchy of the kind she detected and welcomed in his work represents a far more serious threat to her views of life and art than the purely situational contradiction in the *Antigone*.

This can be shown from the claims made for language in the Riehl review, also written in 1856. Language lies at the heart of the essay's political argument. It is a sign of the organic nature of the human world, and a proof of its resistance to effective intellectual scrutiny and political decision. The 'historical conditions of . . . language', its elements of uncertainty, idiomatic whim, cumbrous form and 'many-hued significance', enable it to express not 'science, but . . . *life.*' Characteristically enlarging one 'organic' analogy with another, George Eliot continues: 'The sensory and motor nerves that run in the same sheath, are scarcely bound together by a more necessary and delicate union than that which binds men's affection, imagination, wit, and humour, with the subtle ramifications of historical language.' It follows that language cannot be 'reformed'; it must be left to work out the laws of its own development, 'to grow in precision, completeness and unity' just as minds 'grow in clearness, comprehensiveness, and sympathy. And there is an analogous relation,' George Eliot maintains, 'between the moral tendencies of men and the social conditions they have inherited.' The nature of European men has its roots intertwined with the past, and can only be developed by allowing those roots to remain undisturbed.[13] Significantly, this elaborately organized argument is itself dependent on these very qualities of tentativeness or unreliability in language which it so effectively describes. Because language and mind, social conditions and moral tendencies, are all related and alike, they can in utterance be treated as one amorphous whole; laws for one can be silently made into laws for all, and social disturbance, as against disturbance in principle, need never be subjected to precise scrutiny. By implication, all political interventions in society are prohibited while the abrupt and radical nature of commercial and economic change can be disguised as natural law. The whole argument is carefully designed to limit political discussion by locating analysis and decision, science and action, understanding and will, morally below language and life. But in the Heine essay George Eliot recognizes a principle radically disruptive of this comfortable arrangement, for the linguistic strategies by which she and her circle justified organicist complacency are precisely those used by Heine to subvert complacency in all its forms. Language, the effective sign and instrument of prudential conservatism, is also the effective sign and instrument of daemonical freedom. Hence the acute embarrassment and real significance of George Eliot's writing on Heine.

Matthew Arnold, Heine's other great champion among the Victorians, had, of course, none of these difficulties. For him Heine's claim to be a liberator of humanity could be safely composed into a war against Philistinism. George Eliot, however, had roots among the Philistines; she could distinguish between Dr Cumming and 'the Rev. Amos Barton' and she knew, as Arnold seemed not to have known, that the distinction mattered. Thus she had sound, 'English' reasons as well as weaker ideological and personal ones for feeling anxious about what Arnold describes as Heine's 'absolute freedom, his utter rejection of stock classicism and stock romanticism' and his 'intrepid application of the modern spirit to literature.'[14] But that is why her reaction to Heine in particular and literature in general in the essays, although infinitely more naive than Arnold's, is potentially far more creative and in the end intellectually more testing. It encompasses ideological disingenuousness, moralistic asceticism, enclaves of immaturity, and unwieldy, lymphatic humanism, on the one hand; but it also takes in astringency, integrity, contradiction and doubt, on the other – all that is suggested by Heine's 'wonderful clearness, lightness, and freedom'.[15] The important fact, moreover, is George Eliot's unwillingness to opt for one against the other. The tension is only obscurely and tentatively expressed at this stage; the essays veer unsteadily between delightfully incisive and authoritative judgment and emotional or intellectual double-dealing in the interests of sympathy and simplicity. Moreover, George Eliot's position between these extremes seems to have been only partly a chosen one. Nevertheless her enthusiasm for Heine, and her refusal to condemn absolutely either Voltaire or Balzac, are major and significant achievements for a woman of her background and experience in the 1850s. They establish the true level of her mental life at that time: when George Eliot began writing 'The Sad Misfortunes of the Rev. Amos Barton', morality was already a problem for her.

Even so, the differences between her first stories and everything she had written before them are striking, notably in their

Nietzschean sense of perspective. In her very first sentence – 'Shepperton Church was a very different-looking building five-and-twenty years ago' – the mere fact of her specifying a rememberable past, not as part of an argument, but with the concrete immediacy of fiction, a past involved in its own experiences and its own memories, none of which is wholly communicable to an outsider, establishes an effect of receding temporal horizons and alternative points of view, through which the prose has to manoeuvre with a new kind of caution and flexibility. In the essays her task had been to communicate as clearly as she could what she understood to be the case, to question, inform and discuss with as much authority as she could command. Now, that very understanding, which remains the informal, modern Victorian intelligence of the essays even when it is relaxing into the privacies of nostalgia, has to place itself in its very knowledge at a specific geographical and historical distance from the world it is remembering. It has also to relocate itself in its own times. In presenting her fictional world as memory George Eliot assumes a proprietorial relationship with her material, and therefore a position of authority vis-à-vis her readers, which she did not have when she was writing about public matters as a journalist. Those readers, however, are of a new kind, and she has also to make specific adjustments with respect to them. Writing for the *Westminster Review* or the *Leader* put her more or less on a level with her audience, since reviewers and review-readers are mutually self-selecting. But the readership of a novel is vastly more varied, including men like Charles Hennell and Herbert Spencer, but also including people like her mother's relations and her old neighbours in Nuneaton, whose perspectives were now so different from her own. She has to cope, therefore, with distances between herself and those for whom she is writing as great as, but different from, those between herself and her characters. The varied points of view which her writing must take into account not only differentiate the past from the present but the present from itself.

The results are immediately obvious in the relatively complicated movement from the authorial present, in the opening sentence of 'Amos Barton', through the choric minor characters, first to Amos himself, who seems initially to be hardly more than a 'character' like the others, and then to the somewhat intimidating figure of the Madonna-like Milly, whose unexpected appearance in the role of Amos's wife forces a quick backward revision of attitude towards her husband. This typically measured and circuitous introduction exemplifies a cardinal principle of all George Eliot's subsequent literary practice: the terms on which the reader becomes acquainted with character and incident in her narrative almost always imply an adjustment of ethical perspectives. Thus, quite apart from her overtly ethical interventions, George Eliot's aesthetic performance in the narrative itself, and therefore her relations with the reader at every level, become inherently didactic. But this does not preclude writing of the greatest subtlety. The richest and most effective passage in 'Amos Barton', for example – the account of Amos's morning-service in the workhouse – beautifully exemplifies this point. Here in painfully negative terms (and so all the more effectively) George Eliot treats the very problem which was central to her own practice as a writer – the relation of the teacher and his message to those he is addressing:

> the university-taught clergyman, whose office it is to bring home the gospel to a handful of such souls, has a sufficiently hard task. For, to have any chance of success, short of miraculous intervention, he must bring his geographical, chronological, exegetical mind pretty nearly to the pauper point of view, or of no view; he must have some approximate conception of the mode in which the doctrines that have so much vitality in the plenum of his own brain will comport themselves *in vacuo* – that is to say, in a brain that is neither geographical, chronological, nor exegetical. It is a flexible imagination that can take such a leap as that, and an adroit tongue that can adapt its speech to so unfamiliar a position (ch. 2).

This passage specifies simultaneously both Amos's difficulties and those of the author and her readers in teaching and being taught. Its transitions from the humorous to the serious leave the reader free to feel his own way through the prose towards an appropriately discriminating and yet sympathetic response. The touches of facetiousness – 'geographical, chronological and exegetical' – in parts of the passage, in effect repeat and exemplify Amos's own clumsiness. The prose has therefore to dissociate itself from itself, to disentangle itself from its own mimetic moral clumsiness in its efforts to place Amos's. It is successful to the extent that his subsequent failure to offer Mrs Birch her snuff, and to enlighten the wet-nosed young Fodge about being beaten by Mr Spratt and either burnt or loved by God, do not elicit simple responses, of laughter, indignation, or contempt. The mutuality of confusion and helplessness between the characters bears significantly on the complex experience both of writing and of reading about them which author and readers share.

George Eliot seems to have had an immediate awareness of this kind of complexity in her fictional prose. Even the sometimes unjustly condemned address to the reader on the subject of tea in the first chapter, for all its technical naiveties, has a representative elaborateness and freedom of movement. The last sentence – 'If I am right in my conjecture, you are unacquainted with the highest possibilities of tea; and Mr Pilgrim, who is holding that cup in his hands, has an idea beyond you' – with its faintly Hegelian and evolutionary implications, is clearly designed to amuse the intellectual reader without confusing Mr Pilgrim himself, were he to read it. The main effect of this sensitivity to different points of view in the writing of 'Amos Barton' is of a new kind of freedom notably in the humorous deployment of intellectually weighty allusions. The humour is not always successful, but it is humour – a faint reflection of the implicit anarchy which George Eliot found so attractive in the works of Heine. It tactfully suggests that intelligence does not always have to be detached, neutral, earnestly theoretical and consecutive. On the contrary, the free play between the precisely differentiated perspectives of author, characters and readers adds an extra dimension to literary space for George Eliot, in which for the first time she is able to reveal in something like its fullness what Virginia Woolf described as her 'large mature mind spreading itself with a luxurious sense of freedom in the world of her "remotest past" and filtering down all its experiences through layer after layer of perception and reflection.'[16]

This is not to suggest, however, that the distances between the author, her characters and her readers are all successfully negotiated in *Scenes of Clerical Life*. On the contrary, all three of the stories leave us with a painful sense of strain in this respect. But the important fact is still that in each of them perspective is didactically crucial – the problem, at least, is continually felt. Even in 'Janet's Repentance', the least poised and controlled narrative of the three, George Eliot insists on the uncertainty of all seeing and therefore of all knowing. The first words of the story – 'No!' said Lawyer Dempster – and the whole of the first chapter (so unlike the first chapter of 'Mr Gilfil's Love-story') are strongly negative, but this unpleasantness is then adroitly distanced. Nowadays Milby has 'a handsome railway station', at which 'perfectly sober papas and husbands' may be seen (presumably by the enlightened London-based reader) 'alighting with their leather bags' (ch. 2). However, George Eliot's irony attaches itself also to 'the refined and fashionable ideas associated with this advanced state of things'; the prose adroitly manoeuvres the reader into a condition of relative moral confusion which is well sustained in the following chapters, with their broad comedy which disconcertingly confronts us with moral and physical ugliness, and their satirical descriptions of foolish and ignorantly religious ladies, who invite laughter and command respect. George Eliot thus sets her scene in 'Janet's Repentance' with impressive fullness, and in doing so establishes a clear imperative, at once moral and aesthetic, against premature judgment. But she then introduces Janet Dempster herself in a climax which is embarrassingly bathetic. Through a series of jerky shifts in viewpoint, the narrative moves from Dempster laying violent hands on Janet to the portrait of her mother over the mantlepiece, and thence to the real Mrs Raynor who also has a picture over the mantlepiece, drawn years before by Janet herself. 'It is a head bowed beneath a cross, and wearing a crown of thorns' (ch. 4). All the finely orchestrated manipulation of mood and perspective in the preceding narrative is thus apparently discounted by a conclusion designed to compel reverence and exclude thought. Without such a discrepancy, of course, there would be no need for a subsequent narrative and it also highlights the very problem which Nietzsche was so confident the English were incapable of acknowledging. But whatever the degree of acknowledgment this problem receives at this moment in 'Janet's Repentance', no one, I think, would claim that the subsequent narrative successfully engages with it.

The acknowledgment, however, remains important and is rarely lost sight of in George Eliot's later works. Admittedly *Adam Bede*, originally conceived as a continuation of *Scenes of Clerical Life*, is of all George Eliot's works the least informed by a sense of agnosticism in tension with an uncompromisingly emotional appeal to high moral feeling as a common base for author and reader. Possibly because it grew into a much larger work than was at first intended, it is the most insistently explanatory of her fictions. But in *The Mill on the Floss*, which is not just a narrative set in the past, like *Adam Bede*, but a truly historical novel about representative if obscure developments in the history of English culture, George Eliot registers her full awareness of the fact that reading about such a past will require of different readers very different acts of intellectual, moral and historical self-location, if only because of the variety of intellectual, moral and historical forces already acting on them. The resulting technical difficulties were those she had already attempted to solve in writing about Milby in 'Janet's Repentance'. 'You could not live among such people', a celebrated passage informs her notional metropolitan readers; 'you are stifled for want of an outlet towards something beautiful, great, or noble' (Bk IV, ch. 1). E. S. Dallas, in his review of the novel, certainly expressed feelings of this kind.

George Eliot undoubtedly adopted her famous sociological approach to her characters in *The Mill on the Floss* partly to appease readers like him. However, by describing the Dodsons in particular as a human sub-species bizarrely but successfullly adapted to their provincial rock-pool, she places herself in a position from which her irony can strike equally at her characters and her readers, even as she appears to flatter and reassure the latter. At the same time she implies the possibility of a serious approach to the Dodsons precisely in the natural historian's terms she seems to parody. To do so, however, she must create the right conditions for the reader to think about her characters for himself, and this makes *The Mill on the Floss* a very different book from *Adam Bede*. It continually recognizes that the conditions under which it is both written and read are inseparable from the history which its characters simultaneously experience and embody.

The chapters about Tom's education are especially relevant in this respect. As a teacher, Mr Stelling seems a far better prospect than Amos Barton. However, his worldliness, his ignorance of modern educational theory, and his wife's selfishness quickly become oppressive. One prefers their provincial neighbours. But then the crash comes, and the Stellings prove unexpectedly decent. For all their airs and education. it becomes apparent that after all they belong to the world of sloth, self-love, ignorance, and good-heartedness which the half-educated Tullivers and their friends have occcupied since the novel's opening pages. They too live 'from hand to mouth, [like] most of us . . . with a small family of immediate desires', and a haze of 'pleasant little dim ideas and complacencies' (Bk I, ch. 3). Self-confidence like Mr Stelling's or like Mr Tulliver's and Mr Deane's when they talk politics, or, for that matter, like the reader's when he judges them, is so innocent and dangerous that the whole question of responsibility has to be reviewed. Blaming the Stellings would itself be a complacency, indistinguishable from the mass of minutely documented ignorance and ordinariness which the novel records.

The theme of ignorance takes us simultaneously to the heart of the novel's didactic method and to one of its major theoretical assumptions. If social change is an evolutionary process, it must generally go forward independently of the consciousness of those involved in it. Ignorance of what is 'really' happening is built into the human condition. Logically, of course, this applies to George Eliot and her readers as well as to her characters, and her recognition of this in *The Mill on the Floss* ensures its superiority over *Adam Bede*. In the earlier novel she had been compelled virtually to abandon that sensitivity to other people's perspectives which characterizes the best parts of *Scenes of Clerical Life*. Now by giving her own views equality of status with those of her characters, she places all theory, her own and the Dodsons', in the light of the same infinite uncertainty. A common condition of ignorance has thus become the basis of her relations with the reader, replacing that combination of directly communicable feeling and tendentiously objective analysis which characterizes *Adam Bede*.

Irony applied equally to character and idea is one mark of this relationship. When we are told, for instance, that 'Tom was very fond of his sister and meant always to take care of her, make her his housekeeper, and punish her when she did wrong' (Bk i, ch. 5), the satire is as much against easy sociological assumptions about feminine domesticity and masculine authority as against Tom himself. Not that George Eliot wanted to challenge the ideas themselves, only the bland assurance with which Comte, Tom, and the informed reader, in their different ways, could assume them. Her stance is more sharply seen during the visit to the Pullets. When Tom is left alone with his uncle, his embarrassment is the subject of an elaborate comment which blends the two figures of Aristotle and Uncle Pullet, and while enforcing the view that a boy's savagery is natural and functional also succeeds in mocking the complacency of development theorists who, not being neighbours' dogs or small sisters, tend to forget what savagery involves in practice as they contemplate its positive function in the onward tendency of human things. A similar irony characterizes the procession to view Aunt Deane's bonnet and the description of her as 'a striking example of the complexity introduced into the emotions by a high state of civilisation – the sight of a fashionably-dressed female in grief' (Bk I, ch. 7). In both instances the natural historian's intellectual and verbal manners are folded so neatly into Dodson customs and eccentricities that it becomes impossible to distinguish between them. The Dodson mentality, and the sort of understanding Spencer would have brought to bear on it, are equally placed. The theoretical is not the only genuinely human attitude.

The range of George Eliot's sympathies expands with and in this irony. Mrs Tulliver, for instance, provides her with an irresistible opportunity for cuttingly clever prose which is by no means undeserved. When Mr Tulliver has his stroke, after all, Mrs Tulliver apparently thinks 'more of her boy even than of her husband' (Bk III, ch. 1), and more of her 'household goods' than either. The novel avoids the easy moral reflex, however, and the patronizing stance which almost spoils the portrait of Lisbeth Bede. Humour has replaced earnestness in *The Mill on the Floss* as the medium for George Eliot's ideas and sympathies. Thus Mrs Tulliver's blundering in Mr Wakem's office suggests the pain as well as the comedy attaching to stupidity. Implicit in it is a recognition – which only an intellectual may make – that confusions like Mrs Tulliver's are not so very different from those of the wise and clever. This carefully unsentimental assessment in *The Mill on the Floss* of the common ground between author and character ensures that Mrs Tulliver is as representative and therefore as fully human a personality as both her children are.

What this mode of writing recognizes, in short, as Nietzsche apparently could not, is the paradox that the principle of infinitely varying perspective, which isolates the sovereign individual in general and the artist in particular, can also be seen as the true basis of unity between men and women, that is between characters in their fictional worlds, and authors and their readers in real ones. This is undoubtedly one of the most important insights informing *Silas Marner*. Ostensibly *Silas Marner* is a safe book to read. However, it is not quite the stolid, comfortable bucolic story that it seems. A small but significant sign of this is the presentation of the Lammeter sisters. Mrs Leavis suggested that one of Dolly Winthrop's 'many functions is to incite us to decide in what ways the code she lives by differs from Nancy Lammeter's, for Nancy's', Mrs Leavis believed, 'is seen to be inferior to Dolly's as the Lantern Yard's is to Raveloe's. Nancy actually reminds us of Lantern Yard, in the narrowness of her outlook and her arbitrary moral laws'.[17] Joan Bennett, however, maintains that 'Nancy's instinctive moral certitudes and her narrowness of judgement are counterbalanced by a warmth of heart and quickness of sympathy'.[18] This is surely right. Nancy has her small vanities, and her moral principles, though brave, are hopelessly muddled. But as Lilian Haddakin points out, she is 'vitally important in the rendering of "feeling and form" on the realistic level' precisely because her 'feeling is incorporated in various traditional forms'.[19] And it is also quite clear that Nancy has a modest theoretical importance as the wife who, in accordance with Positivist norms, is an 'image of purity, order, and calm' (ch. 3) in Godfrey's life. When she at last becomes the 'new presiding spirit' (ch. 17) in the Red House, she is careful to preserve 'sacredly in a place of honour . . . [as] relics of her husband's departed father', the guns and whips and walking-sticks of the old Squire. Hers is a shy kind of fetishism, but quite as important in its way as Silas's. This exemplary status of Nancy's, however, makes her sister's personality all the more remarkable. Priscilla's hyperactive, cheerful awkwardness disturbingly unbalances the discreet idealization of womanly purity, order and calm which Nancy embodies:

> '. . . For I *am* ugly – there's no denying that: I feature my father's family. But, law! I don't mind, do you? . . . the pretty uns do for fly-catchers – they keep the men off us . . . And as for fretting and stewing about what *they*'ll think of you from morning till night . . . leave it to them as have got no fortin, and can't help themselves. As I say, Mr Have-your-own-way is the best husband, and the only one I'd ever promise to obey . . .' (ch. 11).

This is an intelligently witty speech, but it also has a neurotic wildness about it, and a brutal cutting-edge, which are not comfortable because they are only half-intentional. The comic toughness of Priscilla's adjustment to life's limitations comes near to subverting the gentle Comtist ideal of femininity implicit in Nancy's conduct if not in her principles. Mrs Leavis may have been mistaken, therefore, in suggesting that we are meant to compare Nancy unfavourably with Dolly, but we are clearly meant to see that even in the safe and stable world of Raveloe the Positivist ideal of womanliness only has limited application.

Recognitions of this kind are characteristic of the whole novel. Both its optimistic didacticism and its legendary idealizations are continually counterpointed by a strain of satirical tough-mindedness, which is often amusing but which is also disruptive of didactic assurance. Thus the fairy-tale opening is far from striking 'the note of legend'[20] as Walter Allen suggests; instead it gives precedence, unsettlingly, to a real, hard-working pastoralism. There is a similar emphasis at the beginning of the third chapter – 'It was still that glorious war-time which was felt to be a peculiar Providence towards the landed interest' – while the evocative account of Christmas celebrations in Raveloe is astringently qualified by Betty Jay's reveries concerning the 'unctuous liquor' which is all she will taste of the Squire's fine hams: seasonal merry-makings, George Eliot explains tartly, 'were regarded on all hands as a fine thing for the poor' (ch. 3). Later we see 'Fleet, the deer-hound . . . [consume] enough bits of beef to make a poor man's holiday dinner' (ch. 9). The unexpectedness of phrases such as these give them a special significance. They demand a freshness of attention to the world of the novel which, if we are like Dallas or James, we believed we

understood. And in being thus shaken, in thoroughly Wordswor-
thian fashion, out of the lethargy of custom into acknowledging our
ignorance of peasant life we can acquire a new kind of unity and
even familiarity with it. Raveloe's ignorance of the great world and
the great world's ignorance of Raveloe paradoxically unite them. If
humanity is in the dark, at least it is a darkness shared.

The range of implication in perspectival atheism of this kind,
however, could not be adequately displayed in so modest a work as
Silas Marner. Hence the importance of Romola, which raises the
problem of perspective through its treatment of history in a particularly testing manner. In this connexion the treatment of Savonarola
is crucially important. Robert Browning felt that Savonarola 'dwin-
dled strangely'[21] at the end of the novel, but he is surely meant to do
so. He functions in its organization as a sign of doubtful meaning, as
the personification of his own desperate question (the same question
confronts Silas when the lots go against him): has the world 'ceased
to have a righteous ruler?' This, of course, is a question about
history, not theology. Properly understood, Savonarola's uncertainties about God are identical with George Eliot's about Savonarola.
What, she implicitly asks, is the standing vision, value and hope in
our world? – or, more precisely, what is the standing of those
Catholic and Protestant principles which, in their Feuerbachian,
that is their human, essence Savonarola represents? But these are
unanswerable questions, as the novel itself teaches us to recognize.
Browning's expectations had to be frustrated. To have dramatized
the final stages of Savonarola's life, to have shown him as saint,
martyr, or fraud, or even as a mixture of all three, would have been
to obscure the fact that merely to ask questions is sufficient to make
the world a moral place, irrespective of the answers available at any
one time. The prophet and historian, precisely as questioners, are
part of that life in which they seek direction and purpose, and are
themselves evidence that the world is not morally inert. Admittedly
it is not morally secure either. Men are at best given only glimpses,
momentary insights, visions, icons, metaphors – all of which are
potentially as deceptive as they are prophetic. But all such attempts
at understanding – the prophet's, the historian's and even the novel
reader's – have objectively transforming implications nonetheless.
The night student of the Proem may be only a personified metaphor
of man's search for answers to questions which he can only put to
himself metaphorically, but he is a deeply significant fact to the
historian for that very reason.

Making sense of Romola itself, therefore, involves the reader in
adjusting to imponderables rather than discovering irrefutable or

even probable historical truth. It is thus very much a work for its own time, as reviewers readily recognized when it was published. R.H. Hutton, for example, argued that the 'great artistic purpose of the story is to trace out the conflict between liberal culture and the more passionate form of the Christian faith in that strange era, which has so many points of resemblance with the present.'[22] Not surprisingly, therefore, the characters in *Romola* have been frequently dismissed as mere Victorians in fancy-dress. Didactically, however, there were real advantages in their being so, in a cultured nineteenth-century entrepreneur, for example, being able to feel, as he read the novel, that precise 'sense of familiarity . . . stronger than the perception of change' which is attributed to his ghostly counterpart in the Proem. The reader is encouraged by such means, not just to escape the limiting perspective of his own time, but also to descend from the abstracted, 'omniscient' viewpoint of the night student or the ghost, and to enter experimentally but sympathetically into a world, which is alien, antipathetic and yet not after all so different in its ignorance and its folly from his own. Approaching Florence intelligently and generously from Victorian, Protestant Britain thereby becomes a paradigm of social submission generally, of accepting one's place in history, and with it all the confusion and error which in one way or another are inevitable in human affairs. For once the price of this localized folly and ignorance has been paid, the rewards of accepting life in a human community are immeasurably great. The real virtue of the ghost's inner life, for example, is precisely his localized sense of the unknown, as exemplified by his very Florentine feeling that the 'crucified Image' over the altar of San Giovanni is 'disturbing to perfect complacency in one's self and the world'. The most important result of attachment to a particular cultural community, Victorian or Florentine, is the development of a capacity to transcend by means of the symbolic language that it makes available those very limitations of perspective and feeling that it also imposes.

Thus even though *Romola* is George Eliot's least successful and least enjoyable novel it remains a work of major intellectual significance as possibly the most complex formalization of the problems of varying and uncertain perspective in the whole of nineteenth-century English fiction. Like its predecessors it looks to the reader's acceptance of a specific teaching – in this case the reality principle of Positivism, the ideal of Submission. But to grasp that teaching it is initially necessary to lose confidence in the possibility of grasping anything, to join the author, and the public at large with whom the reading of a text like this is a shared experience, in the radical uncertainty of serious historical study. The novel consists of a precise documentation of widely different modes of ignorance. The ignorance of Florence is not modern ignorance. The ignorance of the author is not that of her readers. The ignorance of one reader – Browning for example – is necessarily different from the ignorance of another. Each of us is thus locked into an ignorance so specific as to be virtually incommunicable. Yet as the sense of this solipsistic darkness is borne in on us, a sense also of our common humanity becomes possible, and therefore of our sharing moral ideas. But a willingness to share a lot with others is itself authentic Submission, an infinitely complex act of self-adjustment by which even the act of writing or of reading a fiction acquires the character of a duty. This strong and subtle sense of the implications of uncertainty also makes it possible for George Eliot to explore the problem of morality at a far deeper and more troubling level than that of mere agnosticism. These explorations we must now consider.

10 The problem of evil

ONE of the most serious deficiencies which Nietzschean and Freudian insights expose in George Eliot's fiction is the shallowness of her sense of evil, a shallowness which Nietzsche forthrightly attributed to timidity. This judgment, however, applies only to her earlier novels. In the last dozen years of her writing life, she encountered this problem with a new openness and subtlety, and though the poems must figure fairly prominently in any acount of her achievement in this field, and they are the least Jamesian of all her works, it remains the case – perhaps ironically in view of her earlier conservatism in this matter – that she addresses the problem of evil in both *Felix Holt* and *Daniel Deronda* with an attention to the subtleties of nuance, ambiguity and implication unrivalled in nineteenth-century English fiction.

Perhaps the new level of her engagement with evil can be related to the darkening of her political outlook in the 1860s. In both the essays of this period, and in *Felix Holt*, there is what Raymond Williams has called 'the petty cynicism of a mind that has lost, albeit only temporarily, its capacity for human respect'.[1] The bleakly stupid behaviour of some of the minor characters – the trick played on Christian by Scales and 'the fair Cherry' for example – is indicative of this cynicism. Chorus-figures like Wace, Nolan, Rose and Joyce are noticeably less sympathetic than their counterparts in *Romola*, and even little Job Tudge is condemned to a future in which his tongue will 'get large and thick, wag out of season, do mischief, brag and cant for greed and vanity, and cut as cruelly for all its clumsiness as if it were a sharp-edged blade' (ch. 22). This mood, however, was not of as short duration as Williams suggests. It can be found in works as early as 'Janet's Repentance' and as late as *Impressions of Theophrastus Such*. Moreover, its importance in *Felix Holt* is that it is not incidental to George Eliot's purposes but is given a deliberately articulated presence in the novel in the person of Mrs Transome. Thus one of the novel's least attractive characteristics is inextricably connected with what is universally acknowledged to be

its greatest success. It remains to be seen whether this relationship
has precisely definable didactic or theoretical implications.

The social problem most emphatically associated with the figure
of Mrs Transome is what John Morley described as 'the evil usage
which women receive at the hands of men'.[2] On this question
George Eliot herself was far from being an orthodox Positivist. In
fact she puts some very Comtist thoughts into the glib mind of
Harold Transome. Harold talks of the 'things that don't properly
belong to a woman' (ch. 1), of women not being 'called upon to judge
or to act' (ch. 2), and of 'the general futility' of women's attempts to
transact men's business. But this apparent if only implicit repudiation of Positivist ideas on women is less decisive than it seems.
Harold proposes that his mother will henceforth 'have nothing to do
. . . but to be grandmamma on satin cushions' (ch. 1), that it 'doesn't
signify what [women] think' (ch. 2), and that 'a woman ought to be a
Tory, . . . graceful and handsome' and indifferent to her husband's
opinions (ch. 8). He emphasizes only what is comfortable and
conventional in his views about women; he has no sense of a
challenging and idealistic role for them; and in this he is decidedly
not a Positivist.

George Eliot undoubtedly accepted the practical subordination of
women as at any rate inevitable, but she did not see that subordination as an easy condition for women to endure, or something men
should be complacent about. In *Felix Holt* womanhood is a trap. Mrs
Transome feels 'her powerlessness' (ch. 1) the moment Harold
returns. However, with typical perversity, she then weakens her
position still further by wilfully irritating him. 'In this way', George
Eliot remarks, 'poor women, whose power lies solely in their
influence, make themselves like music out of tune, and only move
men to run away' (ch. 36). Esther, too, feels trapped. Most women,
she reminds Felix, unlike St Theresa or Elizabeth Fry, 'are
dependent on what happens to [them. They] must take meaner
things, because only meaner things are within [their] reach' (ch. 27).
However, as the remarkable Denner observes, though it 'mayn't be
good luck to be a woman . . . one begins with it from a baby: one
gets used to it' (ch. 39). The problem of what it means to be a woman
from a baby is obviously one of the novel's principal concerns.

A crucial question is whether woman's ill luck is social or organic.
Power is the key issue. Mrs Transome is innately capable of being
'an empress in her own right,' of daring like Maria-Theresa or
Catherine the Great, 'the violation of treaties and dread retributive
invasions'. Yet even if she had been given such imperial scope, she
would still have been left, it seems, with a 'woman's hunger of the

heart . . . unsatisfied' (ch. 1). Her problem is a recurring one in George Eliot's work, the conflict between wishing 'to have her hand kissed and be the object of chivalry' (ch. 9), and the need also to surrender to a lover and depend upon him. Esther learns to balance these two tendencies in her nature. At first she is 'Queen Esther' to Mrs Transome's Empress, with a 'woman's love of conquest' (ch. 10) strong within her. Felix irritates her for this reason; but later, when she notes 'signs of her power' over him, she becomes 'generous, not chary' (ch. 32). She learns that there 'is a sort of subjection which is the peculiar heritage of largeness and love', and that strength can be nothing but 'a blind wilfulness that sees no terrors' (ch. 6). This reconciliation of conflicting instincts is more or less a Positivist one. Like every other question in *Felix Holt*, the problems of women are finally resolved in psychological rather than social terms.

What distinguishes *Felix Holt* from the earlier novels, however, is the lower aesthetic status accorded to this solution. Henry James complained of the lack of 'genuine *passion* in George Eliot's men and women';[3] but at least in *Adam Bede*, *The Mill on the Floss*, and *Romola*, she discoursed elaborately if tendentiously on the psychopathologies of love and religion. In *Felix Holt* there is not even that. When Esther declares that she never appreciated her father until taught to do so by Felix, Harold thinks to himself, 'This is not like love' (ch. 43). He is right. It is not much like religion either, even if Felix's fervour does allegedly give Esther the 'first religious experience of her life' (ch. 27). The result is a love-story in which all important opportunities are missed. Felix's solemn anxiety about 'foolish women who spoil men's lives' (ch. 10), for example, points to a naivety about his own feelings that could have been both touching and gently amusing. In the event it is neither. More serious is the denial of adulthood to the lovers. A hint of this is given in Esther's challenge to Felix to remember when he was 'foolish or naughty' (ch. 27); it is confirmed in the last scene when they hold each other's arms 'like girl and boy' (ch. 51). George Eliot's unwillingness to enter as fully into Esther's feelings as she had into Maggie's and Romola's is significant. The marriage of Felix and Esther enshrines her commitment to social unconventionality, but the possibility of a radically new emotional basis for a sexual relationship was something she was apparently unwilling or unable to explore.

This does not explain, however, the cursoriness of so much else in *Felix Holt*. The usually important theme of memory and continuity, for instance, is very superficially attended to. Esther, has no more than 'a broken vision of the time before she was five years old' (ch. 6), nor is much made of her subsequent memories. It is as if George

Eliot were relying on our recalling *The Mill on the Floss* and *Silas Marner* to make the meaning of such allusions clear. Equally routine are references to 'the unwonted spirit of tenderness' (ch. 25) which Esther shows towards Mr Lyon under Felix's influence, the 'vision of passion and struggle, of delight and renunciation' (ch. 26) which Mr Lyon's confession gives her, and her growing sense of 'what it would be to abandon her past' (ch. 40). For the first time in a novel by George Eliot, tender memories are cursorily presented. The novel's purported optimism fails to arouse George Eliot's interest.

This thinness in the treatment of Esther's mental progress is in notable contrast to the study of Mrs Transome. Mrs Transome's useless embroidery, for instance – 'the resource of many a well-born and unhappy woman' (ch. 7) – is entirely convincing as a symbol of the triviality of women's lives. Esther's fussing about her 'naughty' father's twisted collar and wrongly buttoned waistcoat (ch. 18), is inadequate as an alternative. The problem is a social, not just a personal, one. The fine description of Mrs Transome's education in the first chapter shows her to be a victim of society's complacencies. School-room trivializations of how the world is ordered and civilization advanced – George Eliot knows exactly how cant can dehumanize and degrade – leave Mrs Transome ignorant of the purposes of womanhood, and for all her vigour and intelligence, without either the gifts or the scope to live maturely. George Eliot knows that women are denied adequately diverse and fulfilling lives. She has little confidence in motherhood in this connexion, an issue on which she emphatically disagrees with Comte. The more advanced a civilization, Comte argued, the more a woman is set apart for the offices of wife and mother.[4] On the contrary, George Eliot insists, 'mothers have a self larger than their maternity' (ch. 8). Even Harold admits that he would not like 'to be an elderly woman' himself (ch. 34), and George Eliot obviously feels the restrictions imposed on Mrs Transome more intensely and truly than the confidence she expresses in Esther's emancipation. Formally we are assured that socially imposed limitations can be advantageous to a woman: her ardour can break 'through formulas too rigorously urged on men by daily practical needs', and her 'inspired ignorance' can give 'a sublimity to actions so incongruously simple, that otherwise they would make men smile' (ch. 46). Unfortunately George Eliot herself tries to make the reader smile when Mrs Holt acts on her 'feminine conviction that if she could "get to speak" in the right quarter, things might be different' for Felix (ch. 43). Belief in womanly influence carries little conviction in *Felix Holt*. Far more vivid is the negative vision of 'a silken bondage that [arrests] all motive and [is] nothing better than a well-cushioned despair' (ch. 49).

But memory and instinct as well as external circumstance have also gone terribly wrong in Mrs Transome's world. Indeed for the first time in George Eliot's fiction memory becomes a destructive force. In the Introduction she writes of wrongdoing which carries

> with it . . . some hard entail of suffering, some quickly satiated desire that survives, with the life in death of old paralytic vice, to see itself cursed by its woeful progeny – some tragic mark of kinship in one brief life to the far-stretching life that went before, and to the life that is to come after, such as has raised the pity and terror of men ever since they began to discern between will and destiny.

The allusions to inherited disease, to Nemesis and to catharsis in this passage are reflections of George Eliot's well-known preoccupation with Greek tragedy at this period as well as her darkening sense of the human condition. The quotation also indicates and unifies most of the novel's themes in a succinct anticipatory summary of the narrative. A powerful sense of the past as a merciless threat to the present is thus a governing factor in the organization of *Felix Holt*. A comparison with *Romola* is illuminating. In Tito's case, the law of consequences works only through symbol and external circumstance. In Mrs Transome's tragedy, Nemesis is internalized and inexpressibly intensified. The hard entail of suffering is at work in her long before chance confirms and publicizes it. The shift in emphasis is well illustrated in the silence which she and Jermyn maintain about the past – 'on her side because she remembered; on his, because he more and more forgot' (ch. 9). Memory is thus a force of intimate and organic retribution and its private, corporeal intensity is superbly captured in an exchange between Mrs Transome and Denner:

> 'Denner,' she said, in a low tone, 'if I could choose at this moment, I would choose that Harold should never have been born.'
>
> 'Nay, my dear' (Denner had only once before in her life said 'my dear' to her mistress), 'it was a happiness to you then.'
>
> 'I don't believe I felt the happiness then as I feel the misery now. It is foolish to say people can't feel much when they are getting old. Not pleasure, perhaps – little comes. But they can feel they are forsaken – why, every fibre in me seems to be a memory that makes a pang' (ch. 39).

In the earlier novels the bodies into which George Eliot entered imaginatively vibrated with ennobling passions. In Mrs Transome she examines evil and suffering not as mere deficiencies and absences but as malignant and apparently invincible presences in life and mind.

And more than memory is malignant. Formal pre-eminence may be given to the triumph of tenderness and Submission in the marriage of Felix and Esther, but the narrative concentrates imaginatively on the will to power and its proximity to sexual and sadistic instinct. (The connexion, as we have seen, had been noted by Bain in the first edition of *The Emotions and the Will*.) Mrs Transome is physically almost nothing but will – the antithesis of the 'sort of subjection which is the peculiar heritage of largeness and love'. Unable 'to ward off the great evils of life', she finds 'the opiate for her discontent in the exertion of her will about smaller things'. She likes 'every little sign of power her lot [has] left to her'. She is not cruel, but images of cruelty surround her: her tongue is 'a whip upon occasion'; having advanced in life 'without any activity of tenderness or any large sympathy', she has 'contracted small rigid habits of thinking and acting'; she likes giving 'small orders to tenants' and replying to the ill-natured remarks of Lady Deberry with 'lancet-edged epigrams' (ch. 1). When Jermyn addresses her, every sentence is 'as pleasant to her as if it had been cut in her bared arm'; she longs in reply 'to lash him with indignation, to scorch him with the words that were just the fit name for his doings'. She bears his 'brand', but for all her love of power, is 'as powerless with him as . . . with her son' (ch. 9). The physical basis of her wilfulness is as vivid as that of Romola's or Maggie's tenderness. Her rising temper is

> turned into a horrible sensation, as painful as a sudden concussion from something hard and immovable when we have struck out with our fist, intending to hit something warm, soft, and breathing, like ourselves. Poor Mrs Transome's strokes were sent jarring back on her by a hard, unalterable past (ch. 36).

In the important conversation in which Denner discusses the ill-luck of being born a woman, all these images come into disturbing focus. Esther, Mrs Transome says, will never master Harold:

> 'No woman ever will. He will make her fond of him, and afraid of him. That's one of the things you have never gone through, Denner. A woman's love is always freezing into fear. She wants everything, she is secure in nothing. This girl has a fine spirit – plenty of fire and pride and wit. Men like such captives, as they like horses that champ the bit and paw the ground: they feel more

triumph in their mastery. What is the use of a woman's will? – if she tries, she doesn't get it, and she ceases to be loved. God was cruel when he made women' (ch. 39).

George Eliot knows this is not the whole truth, but it is a major part of human experience nonetheless. The problem of the subjection of women thus resists easy solution. It is not ultimately a question of law, or custom, but of a sadistic malignancy in love itself; will and sensation are capable of essential corruption; there is cruelty in God. In this troubling sense, Mrs Transome, for all her smallness and selfishness, evokes our pity as well as our terror. In writing *Felix Holt* George Eliot has accepted an element of positive evil in the human condition, something that neither art, nor passion, nor religion, nor sympathy can soothe or dissolve away, something as persistent and irreducible as the 'small, neat, exquisitely clean . . . and godless little woman', Denner, whose character is 'to be reckoned on as you reckon on the qualities of iron' (ch. 1).

Yet for the very reason that it undercuts the novel's Comtist optimism (which, though it expresses a genuinely progressive intention, is finally defensive and insecure), this pessimism is the opposite of conservative, because it disrupts orthodox complacencies as Felix Holt's young heartiness does not. The dark elements in Mrs Transome's story introduce a new openness into George Eliot's writing. Ideological and personal tensions which revealed themselves in earlier fictions merely passively as failures in literary effectiveness, now receive explicit and overt attention. The fact that this happens in a text which is also extensively and tendentiously ideological, exactly as the earlier novels were, makes *Felix Holt* in some respects the most unsettled of George Eliot's works. But however uneven the achievement, what she has chosen to see and say in the story of Mrs Transome is new. For the first time she effectively touches on the Nietzschean theme of man's capacity to turn against himself whenever 'the more natural outlet of his cruelty'[5] becomes blocked. This in its turn strikingly anticipates Freud's conception of Thanatos, the will to violence and death. But the social and sexual violence which thus so deeply penetrates and darkens the world of *Felix Holt*, and which George Eliot, notably in the passages Williams finds so ungenerous, seems herself barely able to control, has more than the importance of a major theme. It puts the reader and author in a condition of equality. A theoretical attitude, essentially superior to society, is helpless before the workings of Nemesis in Mrs Transome's heart.

However, it was not just in the heart that George Eliot discovered at this time the workings of an actively malignant principle. *Felix Holt* is an important work not least because it initiates an exploration into the problem of evil which is sustained in all George Eliot's later works and which embraces the processes of history as well as those of mind. When *The Spanish Gypsy* was published, for example, Richard Congreve called it 'a mass of Positivism',[6] but Frederic Harrison, a fellow Positivist, judged it to be 'treason to human life'.[7] Both judgments make sense. The poem is a Comtist work about contradiction and defeat. Inspiration came from an Annunciation by Titian. George Eliot regarded the Virgin's call to divine motherhood as 'a terribly different experience from that of ordinary womanhood . . . a subject grander than that of Iphigenia'.[8] This is entirely consistent with her argument in the essay on the *Antigone* that tragedy is concerned with incompatible but legitimate claims. The poem's title is inherently expressive of such incompatibilities. There are in fact a number of 'Spanish Gypsies' in the narrative. Fidalma is a Gypsy by birth but Spanish by upbringing; Zarca, her father, a Gypsy in Spain; Silva a Spaniard who becomes a Gypsy; and Juan an artist who can be both and neither virtually at will. All these hybrid states are intrinsically tragic, for they involve the literal incorporation of social contradictions in individual lives so that any attempt to resolve them, such as Silva's when he opts out of his responsibilities as a duke, necessarily involves self-mutilation. Sephardo, the Jewish astrologer, warns Silva that 'there's no such thing As naked manhood' (p.195), and the young nobleman quickly discovers that even among the Gypsies he remains an embodiment not only of Spain but of a broader principle also, of wider scope and deriving from darker sources than any merely national characteristic or institution, the principle of death underlying the Inquisition itself. This is a strikingly Nietzschean conception. The Inquisitor in the poem, Isidor, is actually described as 'pure incarnate Will' (p.30), and his ultimately heroic death suggests that, as Nietzsche was to imply, George Eliot was indeed inclined to sanction fanatical asceticism. She was certainly anxious to place 'Death' in a larger conceptual framework. In 'Jubal', for example, Cain's children are impelled into positively creative activity when they experience death for the first time. Admittedly Silva's vision is darker; for him,

> Death is the king of this world; 'tis his park
> Where he breeds life to feed him (p. 193);

but in the poem as a whole death is a seed-bed. The image of the seed, long a favourite, comes in *The Spanish Gypsy* to symbolize the reconciliation of science and prophecy. Sephardo's elaborate justification of astrology as

> The constant action of celestial powers
> Mixed into waywardness of mortal men (p. 208)

is made consistent with scientific determinism in such images. Silva bitterly condemns this 'Certain uncertainty', but the astrologer insists that his doubtful predictions are

> Fruitful as seeded earth, where certainty
> Would be as barren as a globe of gold.

But to grow, a seed must fall and die. Zarca's vision, and Fidalma's devotion to it, are examples of this. As Zarca declares:

> Let men condemn us: 'tis such blind contempt
> That leaves the winged broods to thrive in warmth
> Unheeded, till they fill the air like storms . . .
> Huge oaks are dying, forests yet to come
> Lie in the twigs and rotten-seeming seeds (p. 268).

Death, which for Nietzsche perversely conceals within itself the redemptive will to power, for George Eliot is the tragic but enriching condition of life. She does not justify this faith, however, by showing glorious results. On the contrary, Zarca's heroic dream is obliterated. By centring her poem on the Gypsies, George Eliot denies us even the tentative promise offered by the marriage of Felix and Esther. For her contemporaries, Gypsies were undoubtedly rotten-seeming: the conception of a Gypsy girl with a conscience struck Henry James, for example, as 'a signal error'.[9] *The Spanish Gypsy* is George Eliot's first explicitly anti-racialist literary work, but its meaning inevitably depends on the racialist responses in its readers which it is challenging. We watch values literally disappearing into a wandering race of thieves and vagabonds, with no clear indication of when or how their resurgence might be effected. This is undoubtedly what upset Harrison. George Eliot seemed ready to abandon the fundamentally optimistic stance of Positivism.

There was even more to alarm him, if less obviously, in *Daniel Deronda*, a novel in which the problem of evil is treated with a fullness, complexity and honesty which goes far beyond the question of historical optimism or pessimism. The novel's key character in this respect is Grandcourt. One's initial impression of Grandcourt is of a personality whose vice, like Tito's, is mere negation, the absence of feeling, energy and distinctness. However, in the celebrated description in the 20th chapter of his meditations on his forthcoming marriage, it becomes clear that these negations are only a matter of appearance. The passage I have in mind begins 'He spent the evening in the solitude of the smaller sitting-room', and ends with Grandcourt thinking with pleasure of Gwendolen as a woman to be mastered though she would perhaps have been 'capable of mastering another man'. The first paragraph of this remarkable description concentrates on Grandcourt's apparent negations and absences. His style and status as a gentleman, we are told, are grounded in abstentions – from literature, from politics, from thought and from feeling, while even the most positive thing about him, his wealth, merely subserves his freedom to abstain from everything else. Grandcourt as a rich man is compelled neither to consume nor to act: impulse 'is born and dies in a phantasmal world'. At the conclusion of this paragraph, however, a strikingly new image is introduced. Grandcourt, we are told, is like an old man; but old age can involve a stripping down to essentials, and specifically to an 'intense obstinacy and tenacity of rule, like the main trunk of an exorbitant egoism'. In effect, the composure and indifference of the English gentleman conceal a will to power as brutal and corrupt as overt violence. The imagery from the chemistry of explosives in the next paragraph and that of the murderous navvy justify this reading. Evil is thus explicitly accorded a new ontological status in *Daniel Deronda*. Grandcourt in his very indolence embodies a principle of violent brutality which would seem to be genuinely comparable with Freud's instinct of destruction. But the latter, Freud suggests, is a particularly difficult instinct to grasp 'unless its presence is betrayed by its being alloyed with Eros',[10] and this is precisely the view George Eliot also offers us in the next paragraph – organic corruption stepping out of apparent negation and revealing its positive character in and through sexuality. The implications of the history of Mrs Transome have thus been decisively developed.

But if the study of Grandcourt is impressive for so exactly anticipating the movement of Freud's thought, that of Gwendolen is even more so because it takes account, as it were, of Freud's insights and moves beyond them. In the early stages of the novel Gwendolen, like Grandcourt (or Rosamond Vincy), is an almost entirely negative figure, 'busy with her small inferences of the way in which she could make her life pleasant' and confidently indifferent to that greater world where ideas make 'armies for themselves, and universal kinship . . . [declares] itself fiercely', and 'the soul of man' awakens to long-buried impulses 'until the full sum [makes] a new life of terror or of joy' (ch. 11). Encapsulated in her 'fierceness of maidenhood', she is inhibited from actualizing the potentialities of her nature. She is a huntress who avoids being in at the death, and whose 'grace and power' at archery are happily without 'associations of bloodshed' (ch.10). Her life, it is true, has not been without its inexplicable moments of violence and terror, but their significance only becomes apparent when she and Grandcourt come together in a plainly sado-masochistic relationship. The interactions of joy and terror in Gwendolen's marriage reveal what Freud was to call the struggle 'between Eros and Death', a struggle in which he claimed to discover 'the meaning of the evolution of civilization'.[11]

Gwendolen's complicity in the sado-masochism of her relations with Grandcourt is initially signalled in the images of horses connected with it. In day-dreaming about marriage, Gwendolen sees herself always as a rider. Others, however, particularly Mr Gascoigne, reverse the image and in the narrative itself she is referred to as 'a young race-horse' (ch.3). She comes near to accepting this image herself for the first time when she looks out delightedly at 'the two horses being taken slowly round the sweep' (ch. 27) after Grandcourt's proposal. Symbols of 'command and luxury', the horses also represent the instincts she and her future husband share, and the exact nature of those instincts is made subtly apparent in the description of her wedding day, with its hideous chorus of gossips exchanging stories about horse-whipped wives, and Gwendolen herself caught up in 'the brilliancy of strong excitement, which will sometimes come even from pain' (ch.31). Admittedly she does not feel pain at the wedding itself, but the excitement of a gambler able to suppress the pangs of conscience 'amidst the gratification of that ambitious vanity and desire for luxury . . . which it would take a great deal of slow poisoning to kill'. But the risk which she chooses to take in 'the game of life . . . daring everything to win much – or if to lose, still with *éclat* and a sense of importance' is at once vague, in a dangerous sense virginal, and yet horribly precise: she feels that 'a punishment might be hanging over her . . . that the cord which united her with this lover and which she had hitherto held by the hand, was now being flung over her neck'. (In this sentence she virtually assents to her own absorption into the equine imagery.) As her excitement increases on the journey to Rylands and the consummation of her marriage, the question of why she is so alive becomes more pressing: is it 'the novelty simply, or the almost incredible fulfilment about to be given to her girlish dreams of being "somebody" . . . or . . . some dim forecast, the insistent penetration of suppressed experience, mixing the expectation of a triumph with the dread of a crisis?' The specific and disturbing implications of words like 'penetration', 'triumph', and 'crisis' when applied to the consummation of this particular

marriage are not accidental. Gwendolen's expectations about the loss
of her fiercely defended virginity have been formed after all in the
company of a man who accepted her reluctance to be touched as a
'new kind of love-making' which would serve to introduce marriage
'by the finest contrast' (ch.29). Thus, although Jerome Thale is
probably right to suggest that the sadism in their subsequent
relations is not overt,[12] that does not make it any less real. When
Grandcourt talks to Gwendolen about Daniel, for example, he is
'conscious of using pincers on that white creature' (ch.48); he is
indirectly compared to Governor Eyre; his speech is 'a sharp
knife-edge drawn across her skin' and she herself feels branded in
the minds of her husband and Lush.

The implied perversion in this relationship, however, would have
little intrinsic interest if it were not for the astonishing involvement
of Daniel himself, precisely as the centre of value in the novel and
Gwendolen's spiritual director, in the imagery associated with it.
Thus in one chapter Gwendolen recognizes the inevitability of
'submission' to Grandcourt, in the manner of one of his dogs and
horses, in the next she 'submissively' asks Daniel to arrange for her
to have singing lessons, listens patiently to his praise of Mirah's
submission, and finally looks up at him 'with pain in her long eyes,
like a wounded animal asking help' (ch. 36). Later, when he speaks
to her a change comes over her face, 'that subtle change in nerve and
muscle which . . . is the subsidence of self-assertion', a response
which exactly matches her subsequent feeling that to defy Grandcourt would be 'to defy the texture of her nerves and the palpitation
of her heart'. Later we are told that Daniel is the only person who
can impress Gwendolen 'with the feeling of submission' (ch.44), yet
in fact Grandcourt can just as easily apply 'the spiritual pressure
which made submission inevitable'. Daniel, however, is 'always
among the images' that drive Gwendolen 'back to submission' to
Grandcourt and he is as responsible as the latter for making Mrs
Glasher's jewels physically painful to her.

This drawing of Daniel into the same psychological and symbolic
terrain as Grandcourt makes his relationship with Gwendolen
virtually a marital one. When Grandcourt first sees Daniel at Genoa,
for example, his initial reaction is to suspect some collusion between
him and Gwendolen. (He knows the idea is absurd, but it makes him
sadistically furious nonetheless.) He then correctly assumes that
Gwendolen will try to see Daniel, and at the same time notices in
her 'something he felt sure was the effect of a secret delight' (ch.54).
She is more beautiful than ever, 'her grace and expression' being
'informed by a greater variety of inward experience, giving new play

to the facial muscles, new attitudes in movement and repose'. A young wife, we are told, is often 'more interesting' after marriage than before, less narrowly self-confident, less prone to 'deer-like shyness – more fully a human being'. Gwendolen's 'elasticity of motion', however, her 'joyous expectation which makes the present more bearable than usual', and which also so movingly recalls her manner as a bride, was not apparent when she was alone with Grandcourt on the yacht. It must therefore be due to Daniel's presence. The guardian of Gwendolen's conscience is thus in a sense her spiritual bridegroom, just as in one way or another he is a partner of the sadistic oppressor of her spirit.

Such a partnership of conscience and oppression was of course to be enunciated by Freud as a general principle and to provide him with a decisive argument against that identification of duty with happiness which George Eliot had committed herself to discovering and exemplifying in all her fiction. Freud believed that an 'ever-increasing reinforcement in our sense of guilt'[13] was a necessary condition of civilization since civilized living depended on repression of externally directed violence, and this could only be achieved if violent impulses were redirected against the self. One consequence of this, he argued, was to dissociate the sense of guilt from remorse for sins actually committed. Once conscience (the super-ego) becomes internalized as an omniscient judge, he suggested, 'the distinction . . . between doing something bad and wishing to do it disappears entirely'.[14] And this is precisely the point made about Gwendolen's murderous feeling towards Grandcourt: 'a question as to the outward effectiveness of a criminal desire dominant enough to impel a momentary act, cannot,' we are told, 'alter our judgment of the desire' (ch. 56). In insisting on this point, Daniel becomes in effect Gwendolen's ominiscient super-ego. 'Your feeling', he tells her, '. . . urges you to some self-punishment – some scourging of the self that disobeyed your better will – the will that struggled against temptation' (ch. 65). She is therefore right, in his view, to punish herself for her feelings, irrespective both of how effectively or otherwise she resisted them, and of whether or not they had practical consequences. The 'need for punishment', according to Freud, 'is an instinctual manifestation on the part of the ego, which has become masochistic under the influence of a sadistic super-ego; it is a portion . . . of the instinct towards internal destruction present in the ego, employed for forming an erotic attachment to the super-ego'.[15] Taken together, the 'erotic' attachments formed by Gwendolen with Grandcourt, her sadistic husband, and Deronda, her omniscient super-ego, are unnervingly close to the Freudian model.

Such a specific anticipation in a novel published in 1876 of a psychoanalytical essay published 54 years later is less remarkable than it may appear. The coincidence of the terms employed by George Eliot and Freud, and of the thought they seem to share is a consequence of their both being involved in the same long-standing debate about duty, desire, morality, evolution, altruism and love of power, a debate to which they and so many others have devoted a great deal of hard thinking. What is surprising, however, is the relentlessness with which George Eliot pursues the logic of the Grandcourt-Gwendolen-Deronda triangle, her capacity to see Comte's concept of Submission being radically compromised by an instinct – the love of power – which Bain regarded as related to 'the most repulsive side of humanity and the deepest fountain of general corruption',[16] and which as we have seen he explicitly linked with sadism. In this respect, George Eliot effectively locates herself with Nietzsche and Freud against Comte: 'An enforced submission', Comte wrote,

> tends indirectly to the sway of altruism by the mere fact of its compressing egoism. But the moral reaction is specially efficacious when the obedience becomes involuntary [i.e. spontaneous], for then sympathy is directly fostered, and no murmur arises to prevent the tasting submission.
>
> Till the scientific discovery of the existence in our nature of the altruistic instincts, submission usually seemed degrading.[17]

Comte's diagnosis of the difficulty is acute, but his solution to it – the 'discovery' of those innate altruistic impulses which Freud was to call in question – disposes of the problem too conveniently. Notice, for example, the uncomplicated model of mind implicit in the notion that coercion simply 'compresses' egoism. George Eliot, however, grasps the implications for man's instinctual life of the word 'enforced': the entire Gwendolen narrative brings out the tensions and difficulties implicit in the words Comte uses so freely – 'sway', 'compressing', 'obedience', 'involuntary', 'murmur', 'tasting', and 'degrading' – and the truly remarkable fact about *Daniel Deronda* is that having seen these difficulties in such depth, having scrutinized all the implications of the emphasis which Associationist psychologists put upon the relevance to human moral evolution of the capacity of animals to submit to training,[18] George Eliot is nonetheless able to endorse enforced as well as spontaneous submissions, to make, in other words, the Will of Isidor the Inquisitor, or sado-masochism itself, a value. No one would question, I think, Klesmer's positive standing in the novel, yet when Gwendolen goes to him with her pathetic belief in her own talent – a belief which is like 'a bit of her flesh . . . not to be peeled off readily, but must come with blood and pain' (ch.23) – he has no hesitation in doing precisely that, and in insisting that she must submit to training in her art 'as a horse, however beautiful, must be trained for the circus'. Similarly the Princess Halm-Eberstein finds Kalonymos's words like 'lion's teeth' upon her (ch.51) and her duty as a Jewess like being 'put in a frame and tortured' (ch.53). Art and Judaism, in other words the strongest and most hopeful energies at work in the world of the novel, have their own kind of intimacy with Thanatos, with the malignant sado-masochistic principle embodied in Grandcourt, Tamer of Horses.

These are astonishing conjunctions. They run absolutely counter to the fundamental distinction between egoistic and altruistic instincts on which Positivism was based. They show that George Eliot not only recognized the epistemological atheism logically entailed in her rejection of Christianity, but in the final phase of her career deliberately and self-consciously invaded the territory of violence, ambiguity and radical doubt into which Nietzsche and Freud were later to make their own pioneering expeditions. Her world was thus every bit as dangerous and amorally structured as theirs. Unlike Freud, however (though perhaps more like Marx and Nietzsche than many of their followers would care to admit), she was not content simply to observe, record and accept the certainties of death and the uncertainties of perspective with which she found herself encompassed. From the beginning she entertained a basically optimistic commitment to resolution and hope. For this, of course, she has been censured. But in spite of her attachment to the ideals of Positivism, Social Darwinism, and the religion of humanity, the affirmations she made, especially in her mature works, were not, and could not have been, the mere reiterations of second-hand pieties which her critics have taken them to be. The reasons for this have been the subject of this chapter and the last: George Eliot's entire teaching was addressed to a world which she perceived to be without a centre. Her relevance as a teacher in our world may well consist in her willingness to make affirmations about human nature in the context of an atheism that is so truly uncompromising.

11 *Judgment and rapture*

THE 'judgment *good*,' Nietzsche declares, 'does not originate with those to whom the good has been done. Rather it was the 'good' themselves . . . who decreed themselves and their actions to be good'.[1] This we have already found to be Dolly Winthrop's view of the matter in *Silas Marner*. Dolly, however, is untypical of the altruists in George Eliot's fiction. She is comfortable in her trusting, earnest, self-effacing and wise. Her fellow altruists, tend to be rapturous, self-denying and socially inept. Thus Dolly effectively embodies what Martin Green has called George Eliot's 'broad and understanding and forgiving wisdom . . . itself so much a matter of synthesis and compromise',[2] while characters such as Janet Dempster and Maggie Tulliver remind us of the lack of 'animal heat and animal grace'[3] in George Eliot's attitude to life. There has been a strong and natural tendency among critics to represent the former tendency as the profoundest and most important in George Eliot's work. The difficulty with such an evaluation, however, is its agnostic conservatism. In representing maturity in terms of resignation, self-containment and social conformity, and in dismissing the embarrassingly intense asceticism in the novels, it extinguishes the will which Nietzsche finally discerned in ascetic morality. Liberal critics thereby deny value to rapture and rebellion. Thus in spite of Nietzsche's contemptuous dismissal of altruism as utilitarian we are faced with the possibility that the most intensely altruistic and ascetic of George Eliot's characters are also the most Nietzschean – but this is a paradox, after all, on which the entire argument in *The Genealogy of Morals* is founded.

The extent to which, from the beginning, the good define themselves in George Eliot's fiction is evident from the following passage in 'Janet's Repentance':

It was probably a hard saying to the Pharisees, that 'there is more joy in heaven over one sinner that repenteth, than over ninety and nine just persons that need no repentance'. And certain ingenious philosophers of our own day must surely take offence at a joy so entirely out of correspondence with arithmetical proportion. But a heart that has been taught by its own sore struggles to bleed for the woes of another – that has 'learned pity through suffering' – is likely to find very imperfect satisfaction in the 'balance of happiness,' 'doctrine of compensations,' and other short and easy methods of obtaining thorough complacency in the presence of pain . . . The emotions, I have observed, are but slightly influenced by arithmetical considerations: the mother, when her sweet lisping little ones have all been taken from her one after another, and she is hanging over her last dead babe, finds small consolation in the fact that the tiny dimpled corpse is but one of a necessary average . . .

Doubtless a complacency resting on that basis is highly rational; but emotion I fear, is obstinately irrational . . . it absolutely refuses to adopt the quantitative view of human anguish . . . And so it comes to pass that for the man who knows sympathy because he has known sorrow, that old, old saying about the joy of the angels . . . has a meaning which does not jar with the language of his own heart. It only tells him, that for angels too there is a transcendent value in human pain . . . that for angels too the misery of one casts so tremendous a shadow as to eclipse the bliss of ninety-nine (ch.22).

The argument in this passage develops curiously. In the gospels, after all, the angels do not learn through their own sore struggle to bleed for another; nor is their compassion for human suffering a logical gound for their rejoicing more in the repentant sinner than in the ninety-nine righteous who, if they have never suffered, have by definition never caused any suffering either. The passage in effect fails to distinguish between moral evil and suffering – but then so does the utilitarian felicific calculus which it attacks. The utilitarian, however, seeks to offset evil-as-suffering by identifying a greater good co-existing alongside it. George Eliot, though, insists that suffering cannot be comfortably disposed of in a book-keeping exercise of this kind. If values are to survive in a world in which pain exists at all, they must be found in the pain itself, and not in any co-existent 'happiness', however calculated. But real pain, certainly at its most acute, obliterates a sense of values in the sufferer. George Eliot responds to this by citing the capacity of 'angels' to match even such a depth of pain through their powers of sympathy, to have their own happiness blighted by the unresolved horror of the mere existence of suffering. Paradoxically, sympathy actually increases the sum of suffering in the universe, but it is sympathy nonetheless which gives suffering its transcendent value. 'As we bend over the sick-bed', George Eliot writes, 'all the forces of our nature rush towards the channels of pity, of patience, and of love, and sweep down the miserable choking drift of our quarrels, our debates, our would-be wisdom and our clamorous selfish desires' (ch. 24). A central aspect of this claim is that its validity does not depend on the reader's being included in the moral revolution it describes, still less on the sufferer's being relieved by another's pity. Even when Janet persuades herself that her efforts at her husband's sick-bed will make his 'harshness and cruelty . . . melt away under the heart-sunshine she would pour around him', her feelings acquire value through their effect on her, not their effect on him: 'Her bosom heaved at the thought, and delicious tears fell'. This is undoubtedly distasteful, yet in a sense everything that is 'wrong' in this passage is intentionally wrong. George Eliot's point is that the transcendent joy to be found in evil is the joy which the angels experience in feeling compassion for its consequences: altruism is in itself a greater good than the deeds it motivates or their effects. The tough-mindedness of this conception may appear to be compromised by the broader theme of charity in 'Janet's Repentance'. Janet, Mr Tryan and the Cheeryble-like Mr Jerome are all involved in relieving the sufferings of the poor. The question of outdoor relief of this kind, in the context of prevailing *laissez-faire* economic doctrine and current Poor Law practice, was a major theme of the fiction of the 1850s.[4] George Eliot, however, refuses to calculate the 'happiness' resulting from such good works in terms of their effect on those given relief. On the contrary, like Nietzsche, she rejects the 'lukewarmness which every scheming prudence, every utilitarian calculus' presupposes in favour of that 'quick jetting forth of supreme value judgements'[5] which he was to celebrate. Even in such intensely 'English' a town as Milby, 'the "good" themselves' – Janet and Mr Tryan – 'the noble, mighty, highly-placed and high-minded . . . [decree] themselves to be good', though admittedly they do so in ways that would have seemed disgusting to Nietzsche, and still seem so to us.

This emphasis on autonomous, self-justifying judgment in 'Janet's Repentance' is actually less surprising than it may seem, since it is entailed in George Eliot's Feuerbachian convictions. For Feuerbach, the act of making up one's own mind was at the heart of religion. 'Religion', he wrote, 'is a *judgment* . . . the discrimination of the praiseworthy from the blameworthy, of the perfect from the imperfect'; even cultic practices, he thought, were no more than 'a solemnising of the critical discrimination between the divine and the non-divine'.[6] The nature of this discriminating judgment inherent in religion is most clearly to be seen in his comments on the Protestant mystic Jacob Böhme. Feuerbach is unsympathetic towards Böhme. He objects in particular to Böhme's central concept of 'nature' as being in a sense prior to 'God' – that is to man's self-awareness – so that 'God' is thought of as wrestling 'himself out of the obscurity of confused feelings and impulses into the clearness of knowledge'.[7] This, Feuerbach argues, illicitly turns a human event into a cosmogenic one, since to describe the context of the divine struggle with such abstract words as 'nature' and 'ground' is necessarily to obscure the fact that the true 'ground' of all human self-definition (which that of God, of course, in Feuerbachian terms, merely reflects) is the flesh, in which sexuality in particular is 'essential'.[8] But though this religious struggle must therefore be seen taking place quite literally in sexuality, it is also for Feuerbach a struggle against the flesh. The gravest faults of mystics like Böhme, he suggests, is their failure to distinguish 'God' from 'Nature', that is true man from 'his fleshly nature',[9] or the 'intelligent from the non-intelligent'.[10] Hence the importance for Feuerbach of the anti-mystical doctrine of Creation, which for him is the sign and expression of 'absolute personality' standing over and against Nature as such. On similar grounds he condemns the Ancients for allowing themselves 'to be merged with the whole' and for considering the individual only 'in conjunction with other men, as a member of the commonwealth'.[11] For Feuerbach the religious man makes a critical discrimination between his 'divine self' on the one hand, and both the flesh and the commonwealth on the other.

After Janet Dempster, the character in George Eliot's fictions who is most clearly seen to make a choice of this kind is Maggie Tulliver, Dinah Morris having made hers before the action of *Adam Bede* begins. Moreover, Maggie's obedience to the divine voice within not only discounts her own and Stephen's happiness, as we have seen, but Lucy's, Philip's and Tom's also. Her commitment is to her own values, precisely as her own. It does not derive its validity from objective evaluations of public or private good. Tom, the utilitarian, stresses the importance of public respect for principle, Stephen defies public good in pursuit of authentic love. Maggie does not meet the arguments of either. She just asserts her own sense of the sacred. She may well tell Stephen that she cannot marry him because he does not have her whole soul, but she does not finally rely on his well-being, or Lucy's, or Philip's, to justify her actions. Joan Bennett is mistaken, therefore, in suggesting that 'the right solution will depend on the consequences of the choice'.[12] Maggie's rejection of a good that has been wrung out of Lucy and Philip's misery is not defended in terms of its effect on them, but because it 'would rend' Maggie herself 'away from all that [her] past . . . made dear and holy' to her. Thus the assertion that altruism is justified as an experience and not in its effects, first made in 'Janet's Repentance', is emphatically reaffirmed in *The Mill on the Floss*. Terry Eagleton is right, therefore, to suggest that Maggie rejects 'liberal individualism', but he oversimplifies when he maintains that she does so simply out of 'commitment to the traditionalist social milieu of her childhood'.[13] She certainly rejects liberalism, but her stance is fiercely individualistic: it is based, not on objective criteria of any kind, but on her *own* sense of the good, on her *own* feeling for nobility.

Thus the tension between what have been regarded as conformist maturity and immature rebellion in George Eliot's novels is more explicit and theoretically more significant than critics have generally taken it to be. The full implications of the tension, however, do not seem to have manifested themselves clearly in George Eliot's consciousness until relatively late in her career. She appears to have assumed in all her fictions, up to and including *Felix Holt*, that while personal self-definition and social integration were frequently and tragically incompatible with each other, they were not necessarily so. This certainly would seem to be the implication of the study of Dolly Winthrop, and of the reconciliations with the worlds of Florence and North Loamshire apparently effected by Romola and Felix Holt in their maturity. Their disappearance is the measure of their success. With *Middlemarch*, however, the case is different. The Prelude announces the tension between rebellion and conformity as a major theme – in words that are clearly meant to seem relevant to both of the main narratives, that of Lydgate as well as that of Dorothea: 'With dim lights and tangled circumstances they tried to shape their thought and deed in noble agreement, but after all to common eyes their struggles seemed mere inconsistency and formlessness.' The themes of nobility and commonness here introduced are carefully developed through the novel as a whole. *Middlemarch* may be properly read as a complex and deliberate meditation on a hitherto unresolved contradiction in the structure of George Eliot's teaching. A full analysis of both its major narratives will be necessary in order to establish how this meditation is developed and concluded.

The act of Feuerbachian judgment on which Lydgate bases his life and which involves him in an intensely personal struggle for self-definition in both the flesh and the commonwealth is his decision to become a medical man. Contemptuous of that 'wordy ignorance supposed to be knowledge' prevalent in his family and class, and of the muddled 'metaphysics' of provincial practice, he rejects ordinary, socially acceptable ways of thinking and feeling, and commits himself instead to a 'philosophy of medical evidence' based on 'a scientific culture' (ch. 13). 'Every man,' Feuerbach writes, '. . . must place before himself a God, *i.e.*, an aim, a purpose . . . the focus of self-knowledge'.[14] For the man of science, he adds, the understanding is such a god, 'that part of our nature' – Feuerbach's description has a cruelly ironic relevance to Lydgate's history – 'which is neutral, impassible, not to be bribed, not subject to illusions'.[15] But Feuerbach also writes of the 'joys and passions'[16] of the intellect, what George Eliot calls in *Middlemarch* the 'makdom and fairnesse' (ch. 15) of intellectual experience, and as we have seen, passion in her work is invariably corporeal. Lydgate's struggle to achieve intellectual and professional eminence is literally a matter of flesh and blood. He is hot from play when he first reads about the valves of the heart, and the most intimate description of his physique occurs as he meditates on the body's 'minute processes' and that 'delicate poise and transition which determines the growth of happy or unhappy consciousness' (ch. 16). The prose of this celebrated description accumulates and penetrates. There is indeed a sense of almost sexual release when at last Lydgate's mind seems, as it were, 'to throw itself on its back after vigorous swimming and float with the repose of unexhausted strength'. As Henry James noted, Lydgate is in every way a 'portrait of a *man*'.[17] He is athletic even in his intellectual life. His goal is distinction; his enemy is therefore commonness.

This does not, however, mean that the moral discriminations he needs to make and which ought to be made about him are at all clear-cut. George Eliot's celebrated use of the term 'commonness' in this connexion is very complicated. She notes, for instance, that many apparently uncommon men of Lydgate's age come in the end 'to be shapen after the average' (ch. 15). Distinctiveness is not the same as distinction, for the 'self-confident and disdainful' are often 'spotted with commonness' too. The word also strikes her as dangerously periphrastic and inclusive. Quite commonplace person-alities 'have distinguishable physiognomies, diction, accent and grimaces'. There is thus a kind of individuality which comes not from authentic acts of critical discrimination, but from the mere shaping of personality by body, milieu and opportunity. Yet paradoxically such passivity towards circumstance can be a sign of nobility: Lydgate, for example, is casually determined in 'his feeling and judgement about furniture [and] women', and he walks by hereditary habit in insisting on 'green glasses for hock'. This, it is true, is partly a consequence of 'that personal pride and unreflecting egoism . . . called commonness', but it is also a result of that *naïveté* which [belongs] to preoccupation with favourite ideas' (ch. 36). Even his energetic virility can trap him in ordinariness. It is 'the massiveness in [his] manner and tone, corresponding with his physique' (ch. 63) which makes it impossible for Mr Farebrother to press him to accept help when he needs it.

Lydgate's great weakness, however, is that his sense of the sacred is too narrow. It excludes music and books (he is as undiscriminating about Scott as Ned Plymdale) and it also excludes women. If he could have regarded women as he regarded medicine he would have been less rude to Mary Garth and less drawn to Rosamond's 'adorable kindness to Mary' (ch. 12). Yet his greatest pre-marital folly, the affair of Laure, is not really a consequence of this shallowness but of 'the chivalrous kindess which helped to make him morally loveable' (ch. 15), and he proposes to Rosamond, not as a result of trivial or vulgar impulses, but because an 'outrush of tenderness' towards her apparent vulnerability raises 'the power of passionate love lying buried there in no sealed sepulchre' (ch. 31). Shallow self-indulgence allows Lydgate to flirt with Rosamond, moral loveableness makes him propose to her. He is thus a man who is frequently a victim of his own virtues, and this makes *judgment* of his case far from easy.

In one respect only is his situation free from ambiguity. In marrying Rosamond, he marries commonness incarnate. Rosamond's vulgarity is appalling. She envies Dorothea's position as 'mistress of Lowick Manor with a husband likely to die soon' (ch. 31); she assumes that it is normal for married women to 'enslave men' (ch. 43) and faced with the prospect of social loss of face, she demoralizes her husband with insensitive allusions to their dead baby. The innate vulgarity of her constitution has been reinforced by education. This is evident even in her finely controlled manner. The suppression of ungainly movements, Bain suggests, and the superaddition of graceful ones, 'in the Fine Art of theatrical . . . display, and in the graceful accompaniments of everyday converse', are 'the work of education'.[18] Rosamond's 'controlled self-consciousness of manner . . . the expensive substitute of simplicity' (ch. 43) is the product of such an education. Even more dangerously, she is 'by *nature* an actress of parts that [enter] into her *physique*' (ch. 12 – my emphasis), and she always has an audience in her own consciousness. Performing artists, Bain notes, such as actors, musicians and, he adds, those accomplished in social graces, 'often have a very low order of intellect'.[19] For Rosamond, thus perpetually and consciously on display, the only valid criteria are common ones. 'It cannot answer to be eccentric,' she insists: 'you should think what will be generally liked' (ch. 64). Rosamond's education and her physique thus incorporate and synthesize a formidable anti-religious principle, an unyielding opposition to private judgment.

The domestic scenes in the Lydgate household which so impressed Henry James are notable for their application of a mature treatment of sexuality to this theme of commonness. As a lover, Lydgate is skilful and urgent. His way of kissing Rosamond's 'ear and a little bit of the neck under it' (ch. 36), his ease of body as she plays the piano (ch. 45), his responsiveness to 'the exquisite nape' of her neck (ch. 58) – such moments prepare us for the fine fusing of lover and doctor when at the greatest crisis in their relationship he takes hold of 'her waist with one hand' and lays 'the other gently on both of hers' in a way that appropriately expresses what for the Victorians was his expert knowledge of women, 'the weakness of their frames and the delicate poise of their health both in body and mind' (ch. 64). But Rosamond is frigid; flirtation merely flatters her 'vanity' (ch. 75), and Lydgate's sexual energies are consequently brutally frustrated. She tells him about the house, for example, shortly after he has been talking to her in 'the "little language" of affection . . . With such fibres astir in him, the shock' of her confession is one of 'confused pain' (ch. 64). But he is passionate about medicine as well as about women and this sexual coldness is therefore a rebuff also to 'the medical man' in him. The failure of their marriage is not due to any one cause, money, immaturity, social pressures, class differences, or sexual incompatibility, but to the interaction of them all. Each problem is a devastatingly bitter expression of their whole case, of vulgarity and distinction in tragic union.

Their tragedy, moreover, is a representative one in a very particular way. Herbert Spencer described society's high valuation on the ornamental particularly in the education of middle-class girls, as fortifying the 'ramified network of restraints by which society is kept in order'. It thereby constitutes, he argued, one of the most formidable of obstacles to the pursuit of personal independence.[20] He would surely have been justified in seeing Rosamond as the community's way of keeping Lydgate's critical discrimination between the divine and the non-divine under merciless control. Lydgate's marriage is thus a concentrated version of his more diffuse struggle with the institutionalized philistinism of provincial life. It is true that George Eliot's attitude to this philistinism is subtle and sometimes even forgiving. She can enjoy Mr Trumbull while sharing Ladislaw's distaste for sale-room humour, and she knows of a musician in Middlemarch, 'worthy to compare with many a noted Kappellmeister' (ch. 16). But provincial life absorbs and neuters greatness. The musician's 'noble music' is coldly appropriated by Rosamond Vincy, and Science itself is reduced to trivial communications in the *Twaddler's Magazine*. However, it is the moral rather than the intellectual condition of Middlemarch which finally frustrates Lydgate's efforts to break out of the obscurity of confused feelings and impulses into the clearness of knowledge, and here again his marriage is a wholly effective sign of his difficulties, since the most striking moral philistines in the novel are the Vincys and their relations.

Superficially the Vincys are a lively and successful family. Walter is sociable and free-spending, countering the gloom of Evangelicalism with 'the belief in life as a merry lot' (ch. 16), while Lucy is innocently agreeable. But Walter's relations with Fred, Rosamond and Bulstrode are degrading, and Lucy is culpably myopic. 'Rosamond', she boasts, blind to the difficulties in her daughter's marriage, '. . . was never the girl to show temper; from a baby she was as good as good, and with a complexion beyond anything' (ch. 63). The word 'show' is chillingly accurate: it evokes precisely that superficial appearance of well-being, the 'gossip, protracted good cheer, whist-playing, and general futility' (ch. 36) which characterizes the Vincy household, and in the midst of which the governess, Miss Morgan, withers silently away. And behind the good cheer there is something uglier than thoughtlessness and superficiality. The funeral of the 'unloved, unvenerated' Peter Featherstone (ch. 12) is not really comic. Its incipient Dickensian humour is undercut by Mary's anxiety and Fred's greed. There is no more than harsh satisfaction for the reader in Joshua Rigg's acquisition of Stone Court. Not surprisingly, it is in Stone Court that the poison which will destroy Lydgate later accumulates before bursting out into the community at large. The tradesmen who spread the gossip are good-natured enough, but they lack the ample humanity of the villagers of Raveloe. The viciousness of the climactic meeting of the Sanitation Board is even more unpleasant. Hawley's charges may be true, but Bulstrode is right to insist that they 'are dictated by virulent hatred' (ch. 71). The real victim, of course, is Lydgate. Like Rosamond, the vulgar provincial world is utterly estranged from 'the medical man' in him.

It would seem, then, that the society of Middlemarch in which

Rosamond and her family flourish is the enemy of distinction; but the problem is not that simple. As Henry James observed, the novel depicts Middlemarch as 'a deeply human little world',[21] nor does George Eliot in any direct way take Lydgate's part against it. Her position and his, in relation to the world of Middlemarch, can only be understood in the light of the alternative to provincial philistinism offered by the text. This is not metropolitan life – Paris, Rome and London have no moral standing in the novel – but 'Culture' in a broad, almost unlocated sense. James complained that in *Middlemarch* George Eliot tried too hard 'to recommend herself to a scientific audience'.[22] He should have included scholars as well, for the text is dense with allusions to ancient history, medieval hagiography, and Tudor and modern literature.[23] But these allusions are not superfluous. They take the measure of Middlemarch's provinciality, and they also form a strong and movingly intimate bond between George Eliot and Lydgate. In the course of the action, Lydgate admittedly receives the generous support of Mr Farebrother and Dorothea, but the one who loves him best, whose mind is truly attuned to his, is George Eliot herself, for only in her abundant capacity to link Bichat's great *Gestalt* 'conception that living bodies, fundamentally considered, are not [mere] associations of organs' (ch. 15) with that broader 'Romanticism, which has helped to fill some dull blanks with love and knowledge' (ch. 19) can his struggle for independence and distinction be adequately placed. Yet at the same time George Eliot is herself one of those 'midland-bred souls' who learned to love the Warwickshire landscape 'standing between [her] father's knee while he drove leisurely' (ch. 12), and who are in a sense Lydgate's enemies. She understands his struggles, therefore, not only because she loves him, but also because she loves the world which defeats him. The perspectives of Culture and Memory unite as a medium for her compassion; hence the range of implication in the novel's title. The name 'Middlemarch' is strongly suggestive of mediocrity; it implies that provincial life is peripheral to, or on the marches of, 'the great world . . . of science, the arts, and of history',[24] but it is also a reminder of the central place of provincial life in the moral progress of the author and many of her readers.

These positive aspects of provinciality are concretely established in various ways, in the courage with which Mr Farebrother defers to younger men both in science and love, for example, and above all in the Garth family. Hence the moral centrality claimed for the love-story of Mary and Fred,[25] a story which teaches the simple lesson that maturity consists in learning, as Freud later suggested, to love and to work. Like all George Eliot's young men, Fred has to transform his glamorized notions of manliness ('riding across country, and doing as other men do' – ch. 52) into the responsible prudence of adulthood. His success modestly affirms ordinariness as an indispensable value. It is a generous, not an ironic touch that his little book on cattle-feeding is probably more valuable than Lydgate's on gout. Mary is admittedly less ordinary than Fred. She and her mother, however, effectively suggest that women as well as men have the need and right in the ordinary course of things to work as well as to love. Each marries an apparently 'weak' man but each knows his real strength.

The positive evaluation of provincial life suggested by the success of Fred and Mary is no less implicit, at least by way of contrast, in the representation of the one important Londoner to appear in the novel, Nicholas Bulstrode. In conception and the manner of his presentation, Bulstrode is also closely associated with Lydgate. Each is a flawed but earnest stranger in Middlemarch, seeking to impose his sense of the sacred on an unreceptive world, and each finds this unreceptiveness embodied in another person, Lydgate in Rosamond, Bulstrode in Raffles. Raffles's greedy subservience, David Carroll notes, was initially instrumental in encouraging Bulstrode to think that the world was providentially subject to his will.[26] Rosamond similarly confirms Lydgate's sense that after medicine there is nothing in life but flowers and music. Like Rosamond, Raffles expresses and strengthens his partner's deficient sense of the sacred. Then, in Carroll's words, he gains recognition for his independent existence 'by asserting actively those sleazy qualities which made him an instrument in the first place'.[27] Rosamond's torpedo-like power over Lydgate after their marriage is similarly the active version of negative capacities. Moreover, just as Nemesis follows similar patterns for Lydgate and Bulstrode, similar technical means are deployed to indicate their intimate experience. In the image of Lydgate as a resting swimmer, mental and physical states are compared in such detail that the distinction between them is finally lost. Similarly, Bulstrode's 'indirect misdeeds' are compared with 'subtle muscular movements' which consciousness can ignore (ch. 68); psychologically, of course, the Associationists saw no distinction between muscular movements and the will; vehicle and tenor therefore merge. 'Nerve' is another key word in the representation of Bulstrode. At the Sanitation Committee, the 'sense of exposure' affects 'not . . . the coarse organization of a criminal but – . . . the susceptible nerve of a man whose interest lay in . . . mastery and predominance'. Bulstrode's other 'nerve', however, is less socially functional than his love of power; it is that of a 'self-preserving will, which [leaps] out like a flame, scattering all doctrinal fears' (ch. 71). Both 'nerves' enliven his religious experience. Evangelicalism encourages him to 'gain as much power as possible . . . for the glory of God' (ch. 16); and the shifts in his doctrinal thinking conceal egoistic terrors 'of disgrace in the presence of his neighbours and of his own wife' (ch. 53). Bulstrode's commitment to religion, like Lydgate's to medicine, is thus morally, psychologically and corporeally the man himself. Like Lydgate, too, he finds in the end that the provincial world which he sought to illuminate has in fact the power utterly to extinguish his values and his hopes. Both are overwhelmed by the flesh and the commonwealth.

Bulstrode's defeat is, of course, different from Lydgate's: it is in no sense a defeat for the kind of authentic discriminations of value which Lydgate was trying to achieve. Middlemarch's victory over Bulstrode, however, reflects little credit on the town, for both men go down together, both victims, though not equally deserving ones, of the same combination of small-town gossip, malice and muddled thinking. Provincial life, however, does not come out of the affair altogether badly, because the humiliation of Bulstrode makes possible the moving epiphany of his wife, whose whole experience of life is confined to the philistine world which destroys the reputations of her husband and of Lydgate, but who, precisely because she is capable of integrating herself with the world around her, is also capable of rising above it. Her relation to Middlemarch, in other words, is Dolly Winthrop's to Raveloe. For most of the novel, Mrs Bulstrode is as indistinguishable from her neighbours as Dolly is. Her naive reconciliations of 'piety and worldliness' in 'the consciousness at once of filthy rags and the best damask' (ch. 27), and her friendship with Mrs Plymdale, based as it is on shared tastes in silks on the one hand and clergymen on the other, look like material for comedy or satire, and have often been interpreted as such. Mrs Bulstrode has been called 'a worthy, common place woman, as limited in her mental equipment as is her agreeable sister [sic], Mrs Vincy',[28] and 'a rather silly and stupid woman' who rises 'for a brief moment . . . to heights of acceptance'.[29] But is she ever really silly? Her judgments about Rosamond may be attributed either to mild malice or to something like wisdom, but they are always acute. Her conversation is invariably worth attending to; nor is her act of fidelity to her husband limited to a brief moment. It is based on years of conscious moral effort and entails years of bitter exile. For Mrs Bulstode, who is as authentic an incarnation of provinciality as ever Rosamond was, has secretly developed her own 'independent,

long-range will, which dares to make promises'. Her discriminations
are exact and heroic.

She also enables us to reassess Lydgate's defeat. His marriage is
'an unmitigated disaster', a 'soul-wasting struggle', a grief comprehensible only to those who know 'the supremacy of the intellectual
life' (ch. 73), bringing ruin to his sense of the sacred. In 'the debasing
company of money obligation and selfish respects' even his conviction that science 'is a contest with the mistaken, and must keep
conscience alive' finally collapses. Not surprisingly this struck the
early reviewers of *Middlemarch* as painfully depressing. Edith Sim-
cox found a 'grim distinctness' in its 'unrelenting' moral teaching.[30]
Blackwood's noted that 'the worthy life and the true life' advocated in
the novel is not always the life that attains its object or wins
content'.[31] George Eliot was even accused of despising the world for
its credulous idealism.[32] But if the disillusionment which undercuts the
professed optimism of *Felix Holt* is given structural as well as tonal
force in *Middlemarch*, there is still much hopefulness in its conclusion. Lydgate's situation and personality are comparable in various
ways with those of Caleb Garth, Fred Vincy, Nicholas Bulstrode
and Rev. Mr Farebrother, and in each case the comparison tells
against him. But he is also comparable with Mrs Bulstrode in a way
that tells in his favour. Both finally go into exile. Lydgate cuts
himself off from distinction as decisively as she denies herself the
happy commonness of Middlemarch life. Both do so, however, out
of a clearly understood sense of duty. Lydgate accepts a 'narrower
lot with sad resignation. He had chosen the fragile creature, and had
taken the burden of her life upon his arms. He must walk as he
could, carrying that burthen pitifully' (ch. 81). This is a real, though
only a partial victory, for it effectively reduces his earlier sense of the
sacred to the status of confused feelings and impulses. But this does
not mean that culture has capitulated to the commonplace. Lydgate
has simply accepted the priority of one duty over others exactly as
Mrs Bulstrode does. The fact that both are 'expelled' from the town
suggests that there are serious limitations in Middlemarch's sense of
priorities. Nevertheless their resolved submissions convincingly
affirm that authentic greatness is not antithetical to ordinary, even
ignoble experience but concealed within it.

It would seem, then, at least on the basis of the Lydgate-Vincy-
Bulstrode narrative, that George Eliot is principally concerned in
Middlemarch to reconcile the claims of the ordinary and the exceptional, the apparent incompatibility of which had struck her so
forcibly when she was looking at Titian's Annunciation and while
she was writing *The Spanish Gypsy*. A number of modern critics have

argued that the history of Dorothea reveals a similar pattern of the heroic assimilated into the ordinary and matured by it.[33] Related to such readings are strongly positive evaluations of Celia, Mr Brooke, Sir James Chettam and Mrs Cadwallader, and generally negative ones of Will Ladislaw. Mr Brooke in particular has often had a surprisingly good press. We are told, for example that we 'should always pay attention to Mr Brooke',[34] that he is the source on occasion [of] an essential wisdom',[35] and a man humanely aware of 'the oddity of things'.[36] Similarly Celia's vigorous defence of 'the commonest minds' as 'rather useful' (ch.1) apparently suggests that she is wiser than Dorothea, especially since the irony deployed at Dorothea's expense so often takes Celia's point of view. But Celia and Mr Brooke are themselves subjected to ironic scrutiny. What needs to be considered, therefore, is whether, in Henry James's phrase, there is 'a deliberate plan'[37] in the Dorothea narrative which dictates the shape and disposition of the novel's evaluations of Dorothea, her family and friends.

The cases of Mr Brooke and Celia are more complicated than their defenders might suggest. Mr Brooke has 'benevolent intentions' (ch. 1) but he is also culpably parsimonious about them. He is compassionate towards criminals, but dismisses Caleb Garth and votes supinely for Tyke. Objectively, his behaviour might even be called dishonourable and cruel. He consents to the Casaubon match because 'Casaubon stands well' socially (ch. 5) but when Dorothea marries Ladislaw he has to be persuaded out of snobbishly disinheriting her son. But he also invited Ladislaw to return to the district and failed to consult Mr Casaubon before doing so. Later, having learned about the codicil, he resorted to making shifty excuses to keep Ladislaw in the neighbourhood. Of course we forgive Mr Brooke; but it would be dishonourable and cruel in us if doing so involved any connivance in his shortcomings. His likeableness, in other words, seems to be a carefully laid trap for the morally unwary reader.

A similar pattern is discernible in the presentation of Celia. We are initially encouraged to feel safe with her. Her reactions to Mr Casaubon and Sir James seem unaffected, and her 'carnally minded prose' healthy. Far from being 'a great pet' (ch. 22), she is in fact an astute ironist, notably when she reports seeing someone 'quite young' (ch. 9) in the grounds of Lowick. But she is ominously compared to Queen Henrietta-Maria, and when she disobeys Sir James and tells Dorothea about the codicil, her remarks are almost as insensitive and her motives as dubious as Rosamond's when she tells Will about the gossip concerning Dorothea. Celia secretly despises Dorothea's high-mindedness, but she exploits it nonetheless. At the division of the jewels this trait suggests charming illogicality, but a similar lack of logic lies behind her assumption that for Baby's sake Dorothea ought not to mind the bleak prospects of widowed childlessness. Like Mr Brooke's charming confusions Celia's astute guilelessness is clearly calculated, possibly by Celia herself and certainly by George Eliot, to be seriously misleading.

The irony attaching to Dorothea misleads in the opposite way. Its development can be measured by allusions to her enthusiasm for good works. During her first visit to her future home, we are told that she feels 'some disappointment, of which she was yet ashamed, that there was nothing for her to do in Lowick' (ch. 9). There is irony here but it is muted. Later the point is raised rather more sharply when 'in her quite unemphatic way' Celia shoots 'a needle-arrow of sarcasm' at Dorothea's proposal to live alone in Lowick. 'What will you do . . . Dodo?' she asks, '. . . there is nothing to be done there: everybody is so clean and well-off, it makes you quite melancholy' (ch. 54). This is to deny Dorothea personal as distinct from philanthropic impulses; it is also plainly selfish; yet it is so adroitly put that we are inclined to sanction it. The problem is raised a third time, however, when Dorothea is living through her greatest crisis: 'What was there to be done in the village? Oh dear! nothing. Everybody was well and had flannel; nobody's pig had died' (ch.83). The tone here is overtly ironic, even ludicrous. But the sentence has the ambiguous status of *erlebte Rede*: in whole or in part the thought could either be Dorothea's or the narrator's. In any case, immediately after the great scene with Rosamond, no response towards Dorothea is conceivable except a compassionate one. The irony, like that surrounding the Garths, has thus become protective, and readers who have connived at Celia's sarcasms, stand, deservedly I think, rebuked.

This pattern of irony provisionally adopting the perspectives of common minds but finally sanctioning Dorothea's, is perhaps less easily accommodated to the attitudes and standing of two other characters, Mrs Cadwallader and Will Ladislaw. Mrs Cadwallader's remarks that religious enthusiasms 'wear out of girls' (ch.6), that marrying Casaubon is 'going to a nunnery', and that if Dorothea were to live alone in Lowick she would 'see visions' (ch.54) have apparently much to recommend them. When the novel opens Dorothea is clearly suppressing ordinary sexual awareness. She feels guilty about the pagan sensuousness of horse-riding and has 'very childlike ideas about marriage' (ch.1). Mr Casaubon enables her to fall in love with the part of herself she is most eager to acknowledge. It is also possible that her ignorance is matched on his side by impotence. Mrs Cadwallader and Sir James imply as much, and recent critics have argued the case to some effect.[38] But is the sexual problem quite as important in this case as common sense would have us believe? After all, Mrs Cadwallader's is a notably inglorious view of the personal lives of women. In her eyes marriage is a lightning conductor by which unruly feelings in young girls are brought safely down to earth. Yet taken as a group the young women in the novel hardly need marriage as a 'cure'. The virginal Mary Garth, for example, may not know what the word 'unsteady' might imply in a young man (ch. 12), but her delight in Fred's youth and her conviction that the needs marriage satisfies have to do with wholeness, work, and self-esteem, are equally healthy and mature. Celia, on the other hand, is as agreeable and limited before marriage as after it, while Rosamond does not require marriage as a defence against feelings of any kind. Her married life indeed reveals the danger of assuming that youthful vivacity has any emotional basis at all.

A similar view may be taken of Mrs Cadwallader's notions about Dorothea and Mr Casaubon, amusing as they may be, if only because they are too direct, forceful and simple, and so ignore the possibility of ambiguity and deceptive appearances in the relationship. Mr Casaubon makes a painfully self-revealing remark when he insists that motives 'are apt to become feeble in the utterance' and that 'the germinating grain' should be kept 'away from the light' (ch. 2). The phrasing calls both his scholarship and his manhood into question; but it also contains an important and more elusive truth, which Dorothea recognizes, and which George Eliot herself puts into practice in the ambiguous manner with which she describes the Casaubon marriage. For even though the sexual issue implicit in Mrs Cadwallader's strictures is undoubtedly raised, it is far from certain whether it operates as vehicle or tenor in the elaborately metaphorical account we are given of the marriage. Uncertainty, in fact, is at once a theme and a technique in the story of Dorothea's marriage. We are assured that there was 'nothing external' by which Mr Casaubon could account for 'a certain blankness of sensibility' (ch. 10) in his feelings as an engaged man; in sexual terms the two phrases cancel each other out. Again, six weeks after her marriage, Dorothea has 'no distinctly shapen grievance, that she could state even to herself' (ch. 20). In other words her honeymoon may have been sexually tolerable; alternatively she may still be completely ignorant about marriage; or again it could be that her problem is too appalling to be articulated. In any case her experiences have been undramatic, her relationship with Mr Casaubon having changed 'with the secret motion of a watch-hand from what it had been in her maiden dream'. This could mean, of course, that the marriage is indeed unconsummated; on the other hand Dorothea's specifically maiden dream is over. Clearly the facts are unknowable, but one thing is certain: the sensitive caution of George Eliot's account is at variance with Mrs Cadwallader's opinionated plain-speaking.

And precisely because the Casaubon marriage cannot, therefore, be directly compared with the scandalous failure of John Ruskin's marriage to Effie Gray, there emerges from the germinating dark-ness of the narrative the possibility of a scandal which exactly reverses the terms of the Ruskin affair. In place of a large-souled but impotent husband and a commonplace, sexually normal wife, we may have a sexually fairly competent but spiritually inert husband married to a woman of altogether exceptional spiritual potential, a woman for whom feelings of 'anger and repulsion, or else forlorn weariness' (ch.20) are a far more painful experience than a sense of sexual neglect, and for whom 'the seeds of joy are for ever wasted', not in moments of intimate disaster, but rather in the 'horrible' sensation of 'unresponsive hardness' (ch.42) which greets all her efforts to comfort an unhappy husband. For such a woman, George Eliot appears to be suggesting, a 'resolved submission' to wait at the head of the stairs after a quarrel, and to spend 'days and months and years . . . sorting . . . shattered mummies, and fragments' of aborted thought (ch.48) may well be acts of self-giving more truly intimate and impassioned than anything Mrs Cadwallader's world-liness and robust decency could envisage. Thus the happily pre-empted decision to continue Mr Casaubon's work after his death can be read as a tragic but intensely *personal* attempt by Dorothea to wrestle herself out of the obscurity of confused feelings into a clear sense of a unique vocation, to which she is called not by 'law', nor by 'the world's opinion', but rather by 'the ideal . . . yoke of marriage'. Only if that is 'weakness', George Eliot insists, is Dorothea weak. Thus the key question raised by the Casaubon marriage is whether or not it is ever legitimate for the inexperienced idealist to opt for a life of scandalous self-sacrifice.

George Eliot's answer to this question is to be found not in Dorothea's behaviour as a wife but in her behaviour as a widow. Everything, therefore, depends on the standing of Will Ladislaw. The *Saturday Review* sarcastically complained that Dorothea's choice of him was indistinguishable 'from the ball-room choice of any ordinary girl'.[39] For some modern critics, however, Will's function is precisely to introduce Dorothea to imperfect reality, by being imperfect himself. He is the kind of man, after all, who intrudes insensitively on the Casaubons at church, and has later bitterly to upbraid himself over the meagre rewards of 'worshipping the sight of a woman' (ch. 47). 'In a novel which . . . tries to deal plainly with an unideal existence', Barbara Hardy argues, 'this rejection of worship is an important strand in the pattern of feeling'.[40] Will's marriage to Dorothea may accordingly represent an encouraging victory for 'unideal existence' over an idealistic and destructive asceticism.

The difficulty with such readings is that they ignore the extent to which George Eliot at least tries to make Will an altogether extraordinary character. He is a synthesis of key elements in the characters of Piero di Cosimo and Tito Milema. On the one hand he is a rootless, and therefore a potentially amoral man, on the other so sensitive to others that he can take 'the pressure of [their] thoughts instead of urging his own' (ch. 50). In effect, he exemplifies Bain's principle that, while conscience is formed by, and on the model of, social authority, the sympathies can operate independently of both.[41] His rootlessness, however, brings him very close to George Eliot's own point of view since it makes him an embodiment of that unlocated cosmopolitan culture which lies at the heart of her feeling for Lydgate. Hence the intimacy between the two men. Will's task as far as Dorothea is concerned is similarly to bring the spirit of culture into her life. Before meeting him she is bewildered (not, one notes, shocked – rather puzzled) by the 'severe classical nudities and smirking Renaissance-Corregiosities' (ch.1) of her uncle's pictures. Art, she discovers in Rome, is in a language which she does not understand. What Will gives her is the Romanticism which he learned in Naumann's company, a sense of the relationship between Idealism and Joy. His function is not to bring her down to earth, but to open up her English- and Swiss-educated mind to the uncensorious but heroic humanism of the South. This is far from being the part played by the average 'ball-room choice'.

And the lesson he learns from Dorothea is no less idealistic. By 'desiring what is perfectly good', she tells him, 'even when we don't quite know what it is . . . we are part of the divine power against evil' (ch.9). In other words, goodness, like enjoyment, radiates. Each, then, enlarges the other's capacity for idealism by giving it 'European' rather than provincial scope. Dorothea does this for Will by spontaneously incorporating in herself all that is best in the classical, medieval, renaissance, and modern conception of womanhood. She is Quaker and Madonna, a Christian Antigone, Catholic and Protestant. As a type of the Virgin Mary she thus becomes a legitimate object for Naumann, Lydgate and Ladislaw to worship. The latter, incidentally, condemns himself for worshipping the *sight* of his beloved, not for having her as a poem in his consciousness.

But Dorothea is not just an icon. She is above all a woman who makes up her mind, whose life is willed, and her willing is presented far more precisely than Esther Lyons's had been. All internal feelings, Bain suggested, all sensations and thoughts, 'form so many beginnings of trains of association passing far away in the remotest regions of recollection and thought; and we have it in our power to stop and change the direction as often as we please'.[42] Dorothea's moments of deliberate action fit this description exactly. Hers is a nature that is not only 'ardent' but 'theoretic, and intellectually consequent' and she longs for 'the freedom of voluntary submission' (ch.1). Her decision to wait for Mr Casaubon is a 'resolved submission' (ch. 22), and she deliberately dwells 'on every detail' of the scene between Rosamond and Will (ch. 80). Maggie Tulliver was revealed to Tom; Romola emerged transformed from the plague-stricken village; but the emphasis in Dorothea's history is on willing, and this considerably enriches the novel's feminism. The Prelude refers to the indefiniteness of women's natures and so of their social lot. The novel is never specific about the latter. But over and above their right to love and work *Middlemarch* asserts the right of women to make judgments, to choose something better than a husband or a father would choose for them. Thus Dorothea, far from being 'satisfied with having a wise husband' wishes, 'poor child, to be wise herself' (ch.7). The implications of this ironic comment are initially unclear. Her second love-story, however, is an emphatic demonstration of the rightness of her marrying Will Ladislaw *contra mundum*. The question 'will she or will [she] not marry Will Ladislaw' is thus far from being the 'slightly factitious' one[43] which Henry James found it. On the contrary, in dramatizing the choices which bring that union about, George Eliot makes important affirmations about the moral life.

The story she tells is that of two exceptional people struggling against the intrusions of ordinariness into their lives. The crucial embodiment of this ordinariness, for both of them, and for Lydgate, is Rosamond. It is only when Dorothea sees Will and Rosamond together, for example, that she appreciates for the first time at how poor a level intercourse between men and women can take place. Will's image is accordingly 'mysteriously spoiled' (ch. 43) for her. Will for his part thoroughly understands where his behaviour is leading him, and feels diminished to the extent that he has been thrust 'to a new distance' from Dorothea's unworldliness. It may be, of course, that in reacting in this way Dorothea is really rationalizing unacknowledged jealousy and Will half-acknowledged pride. But

Dorothea's maturity must be uncertain, and Will's moral condition must be dubious if George Eliot's task of demonstrating the true distinction of her lovers is to be *identical* with their task of discovering and demonstrating their true feelings for each other. Seen in this light the love-story of Dorothea and Will becomes a technical triumph: its means are its ends.

Another barrier between the lovers besides Rosamond is the codicil and all the vulgar secrecy and gossip surrounding it. The codicil accounts for the apparently inexplicable confusion they both feel when Will first calls to tell Dorothea of his imminent departure; it accounts for Lydgate's thoughtless assumption that an understanding exists between them, and consequently for Rosamond's remarks on the matter to Will. Aware of the codicil, at last, Will finally has no choice but to leave Middlemarch if only to escape 'the bitter sneers' (ch. 62) which his staying might arouse. Mrs Cadwallader has gleefully reported the gossip about Will and Rosamond to Dorothea – a further instance of the codicil making decent people behave badly – and their second farewell is thus almost irretrievably damaged; for even though their shared fineness of temper ensures that Will's parting words communicate his real feelings to Dorothea, the vulgar order of class distinction is brutally victorious when she finds herself compelled to pass him in her carriage. Before it can be overcome they each have to endure absolute humiliation, Will when he contemplates how 'his life might come to be enslaved' by Rosamond (ch.78), through 'the small solicitations of circumstance, which is a commoner history of perdition than any single momentous bargain' (ch.79), and Dorothea during her night alone, after seeing Will and Rosamond together yet again. Out of these two experiences of despair, however, they finally meet and recognize, not in words but in an openness of accent and gesture, their right to stay together in defiance of the shallow, mean-hearted spirit of the world.

Nor is it just in relation to love that they stand above the world, but in relation also to work and money. For Caleb, Lydgate and eventually Fred, only intrinsically worthwhile work is honest. Ladislaw, however, engages in politics simply to remain close to Dorothea. His support for the injured through morally dubious agents – 'crying up men who are a part of the very disease that wants curing' Lydgate calls it (ch. 46), thus echoing the complaint against politicians most strongly urged in *Felix Holt* – is almost shockingly defended simply as a manifestation of his love for a woman. (E.M. Forster, incidentally, never dared claim as much for passion.) But this love is also a manifestation of Will's all-embracing idealistic tendency and thus justifies his otherwise dubious confusion of means and ends. The same idealism, moreover, characterizes his and Dorothea's attitude to money. Will repudiates a sensible accommodation with dubiously inherited good. His childishness and Dorothea's in their final love-scene is thus as much a consequence of their naivety about money as their naivety about love. They refuse to regard either with the mature common-sense perspectives of ordinary worldly adults.

Childishness of a similar kind characterizes Dorothea's response to the Lydgate-Bulstrode scandal. She plays no part in the Seventh Book until briefly in its closing paragraphs she cuts through Mr Brooke's cowardice and Mr Farebrother's despair to assert her determination to 'find out the truth and clear' Lydgate's name (ch.71). This dramatic reassertion of vitality, innocence and truth against lies, failure and corruption is very moving; and even though Dorothea can do little to help Lydgate recover his lost reputation, she is able to help him in a way that neither could have anticipated. Beset with troubles he finds he lacks the energy to work on Rosamond's 'vision and will' (ch. 73); Dorothea, however, though equally distraught, does not. The excellently titled 'Sunset and Sunrise' emphasizes the differences in determination and destiny which distinguish the novel's two central characters and which are therefore essential to its meaning.

That meaning is implicit in the structure of *Middlemarch*. The histories of all the characters in both narratives, Dorothea excepted, form an intricate pattern of simple curves, either rising like Fred's or falling like Lydgate's. But for Dorothea the curve falls and rises twice. Like Lydgate she marries into the Middlemarch world; unlike him she marries out of it again. Yet the world which rejects him seeks reconciliation with her in the end. The Finale does not of course register the unqualified triumph of idealism. Dorothea continues to feel that 'there was always something better which she might have done', and 'insignificant people', like the reader and George Eliot, continue to frustrate her energies. But her life does have 'its fine issues', and Jerome Beaty is therefore mistaken in emphasizing as he does the alteration in draft of the novel's closing words from 'life nobly' to 'unvisited tombs'. Against that change, after all, can be set the earlier one which he also records but ignores, of 'the growing life of the world' to 'the growing good of the world'.[44] It is the latter which the idealism of Ladislaw and Dorothea enriches and serves.

And that idealism also enables us to reassess the much discussed comparison of Dorothea and St Teresa of Avila with which George

Eliot introduces the theme of conformity and rebellion in the Prelude. This has been the subject of some debate. The traditional and obvious interpretation of the Prelude represents Dorothea's frustrations as essentially tragic; she is potentially a woman of gifts and graces comparable with those enjoyed by Teresa, but historical circumstance frustrates and deflects them; Protestant, provincial England in the 1830s is simply not the setting in which such a soul can flourish, and were it not for the romantic intervention of an outsider, Will Ladislaw, the embodiment of the new spirituality, her life would be utterly blighted. It is also felt by those reading the Prelude in this way that George Eliot's evaluations of Dorothea's powers and Will's promise are misjudged, that there is an inappropriate element of fantasy, probably of a personal kind, informing this aspect of the novel. David Daiches, on the other hand (and he is not alone) has argued that George Eliot keeps the Teresan theme and her assessment of Dorothea and Will under careful control. The moral centre of the novel for him is Mary Garth. In the light of Mary's capacity not to make unreasonable claims, he suggests, 'the Saint Theresa concept . . . is . . . seen as a form of unreasonable claim on life, which it is the part of moral maturity to forego.'[45] As Laurence Lerner has so amply demonstrated, however,[46] both approaches miss the point in failing to take account of Teresa of Avila's personality and her achievements. She is after all among the most important of writers in the Spanish language, a politically astute and effective reformer of her Order, and a very great mystic. She is Julian of Norwich, Elizabeth Fry and George Eliot herself, in a single person. Consequently while it may be unreasonable for most of us to make great claims on life, it was not for Teresa herself to do so, and it may not have been for Dorothea either. In any case Dorothea makes no such claims on her own behalf: they are made by others, and specifically by George Eliot, for her. The question is are they justified?

The answer to this question is to be found in Teresa's *Life*, the connexions between which and *Middlemarch* are more detailed than is generally realized. In particular, Teresa's experiences as a young woman are remarkably like Dorothea's. Dorothea's attitude to 'the crowd' in her night of agony, for example, (she asks nothing from them, and prays only 'that they might be less contemptible' – ch.83) exactly matches Teresa's 'contempt . . . for the things of this world'[47] after her soul has been 'crucified between heaven and earth, suffering and receiving no help from either'.[48] Dorothea emerges from her agony 'in the narrow cell of her calamity', but forces herself to consider others, opening a window and seeing a man 'with a bundle on his back and a woman carrying her baby'. For her part, Teresa describes the soul, 'purified by . . . pain', being raised 'to a height from which it looks down on everything . . . is not enmeshed in it . . . and feels pity for those who are still blind . . . It longs', she writes, 'to cry aloud and call attention to their delusions, and sometimes it actually does so, only to bring down a storm of persecution on its head [particularly] if the person is a woman'; she then remarks how weary she is 'with points of honour'.⁴⁹ Detachment, humiliation, compassion, the constraints of being a woman, impulsive benevolence, fierce unconventionality – all these things and more the young Teresa and the young Dorothea have in common. Teresa was 40 before she made progress in prayer, 45 when she founded St Joseph's. She was 54 when the *Life* was completed, and even then her *epos*, founding the daughter-houses of St Joseph's, had not begun. Like Dorothea she had been frightened of marriage and in need of spiritual direction. Apart from books, she writes, 'I found no other guide . . . I mean who understood me'.⁵⁰ She too had unrealistic ambitions; she wished to speak to kings, to be martyred – 'since there is no real living once we see . . . the great illusion in which we walk'. Like Dorothea also, she was afflicted with a sense of uselessness. Some women, she complained, had 'done heroic deeds', but she herself was 'only fit to talk'; her will to serve God leaked away.⁵¹ She was lonely in the midst of 'calumny and persecution', though those who blamed her were 'innocent' and showed her truths about herself which she needed to learn.⁵² She knew also that those who distrusted her were 'great servants of God' and 'men of learning',⁵³ yet she could not accept their opinions. Even when she had Peter of Alcántara to advise her, she was warned that she must suffer 'the opposition of good people'.⁵⁴ 'There was so much chatter and fuss' about the founding of St Joseph's, she reports, that the Provincial withdrew his support on the grounds that the funds were insufficient and the opposition too strong.⁵⁵ Like Dorothea, Teresa found all her plans were dismissed as 'absurd feminine whimsy'; the gossip at her expense increased, and her fellow nuns felt she had insulted them. Avila and its convents, in fact, were remarkably similar to 'the unfriendly mediums of Tipton and Freshitt' (ch.4).

Middlemarch and *The Life of Saint Teresa* have thus a great deal in common, and the point George Eliot makes in highlighting the connexion in the Prelude and the Finale is that Dorothea and Teresa, similarly placed, similarly will themselves into nobility, in spite of their provincial obscurity and the frustrations of womanhood. They both make judgments; neither is determined by the world and neither is assimilated by it. The claims which are advanced on behalf of Dorothea, therefore, must be distinguished from those advanced on behalf of Mary Garth. Dorothea is committed to a discrimination between the divine and the non-divine as absolute as that made by the Spanish saint. In Nietzsche's terms she places herself in 'the highest rank in contra-distinction to all that [is] base, low-minded and plebeian'.[56] The good woman in *Middlemarch* is good by no other standards but her own and those of the one she chooses to love. *Middlemarch* is thus a deeply anti-liberal, anti-utilitarian, anti-determinist book. But it is also anti-Nietzschean. It defines the noble over and against the plebeian, but it does not empty the latter of value. In this respect, at least, George Eliot is closer in spirit to her great Spanish predecessor than to her younger German contemporary. But from either point of view, whether she is read as asserting the supreme value of mystical charity or that of atheistic moral autonomy, she undoubtedly affirms in *Middlemarch* her deep convictions about the importance of judgment and rapture, which are radically at variance with the norms of common sense. Yet if she steps outside those norms she does so in full knowledge of the legitimacy of the claims they make upon us. The teaching of *Middlemarch* is that Mary Garth and Dorothea Brooke do not invalidate each other; both demand scrupulous and courageous evaluation.

12 Discernment and resolve

WITH a scrupulous attention to the need for qualification, and a recognition of alternative priorities, *Middlemarch* affirms the legitimacy of the highest, the most exultant spiritual ambition. One is nonetheless left with the clear sense that the qualification and scrupulousness underlie the novel's aesthetic wholeness, not its high spirituality, and·this, from a didactic point of view, raises a fundamental difficulty. To what extent are the coherence and flexibility in the writing of *Middlemarch* devices to conceal the problems of moral impotence and political quietism which may be inherent in determinism? Is there a sense in which it can be described as a Paterian novel? Modern art, Walter Pater argued, should react to the 'magic web' of necessity by representing 'men and women in these bewildering toils so as to give the spirit at least the equivalent for the sense of freedom'.[1] Do the subtlety and flexibility of the web of cause and effect comprehensively determining the lives of the characters in *Middlemarch* preserve for us and for them the sense – or, to be more accurate, the illusion – of personal autonomy?

In fact George Eliot loathed Pater's principles. Her commitment to didacticism was completely incompatible with his famous description of the modern consciousness 'for ever testing new opinions and courting new impressions, [but] never acquiescing in a facile orthodoxy of Comte, or of Hegel, or of one's own'.[2] The reason for her dislike was not that Pater rejected all forms of orthodoxy, facile or not, but that he represented stability and coherence as if they were merely the confidence tricks of art. Nevertheless she seems to have recognized a seductive strength in Pater's thought.

Her thinking on the whole range of issues raised by aestheticism and materialism is most explicitly in evidence in her late poem, 'A College Breakfast Party'. It consists of an informal debate in Horatio's rooms at university between a priest and five students - Hamlet, Osric, Laertes, Rosencranz *(sic)* and Guildenstern – each of whom seems to have an important truth laced with a significant error to communicate to the others. It begins with Osric, who is obviously the spokesman for Pater himself, attacking Philosophy as 'tasteless squabbling', utterly at odds with the 'butterfly existence' which he thinks is appropriate to them all. The manly and enthusiastic Laertes resents being called a butterfly and asserts the seriousness of life's dilemmas. The priest then makes his one intervention – he evidently brings together the Catholic and modernist tendencies in Anglicanism. His universe is sacramental, the invisible being manifested through the visible. The materialist, he maintains, may argue that values are subjective, but the pressure to distinguish values may in fact come from without, from some kind of immanent will. The Church accepts a determined universe, but insists on the soul's capacity to veto or consent, making 'arbitrament that we call faith' (p.227). On this point George Eliot probably agreed with him. At Hamlet's urging, the priest then discusses obedience. The Church, he says, makes a unique claim to authority; the will requires discipline; therefore the Church's 'promise of a high communion' (p.229) through that obedience should at least be tested, especially as this promise (which, being immaterial, cannot be disproved on material grounds) answers a need not met elsewhere.

The priest then leaves, and Guildenstern at once attacks the idea of an order of being not subject to normal scrutiny. On such premises, he argues, any tyranny or superstition could be justified. He then outlines the standard opinions of the serious Victorian rationalist. In particular, he denies that the Church meets authentic needs since the doctrine of eternal rewards and punishments is irrational and immoral. (This was a favourite theme of George Eliot's early essays.) Religion, Guildenstern concludes, cannot satisfy the ideal man, a point that Laertes enthusiastically endorses. Laertes declares that he will obey his own conscience if necessary against God. But that, Osric points out, is exactly his own view, only what Laertes calls conscience or Will, he calls Taste. Rosencranz is even more sceptical than Osric. Those who believe in values, he argues, must define them in such a way that it will be impossible for a majority of the population to reject them. He points out that the Good can be known only by way of contrast with the Ill; a wholly perfect world would be uniformly fixed and dead. Nor is it legitimate, he claims, to think of the Good in relative terms, for a relative system of values would inevitably be socially determined, in other words it would be the 'transient reflex of a prejudice' (p.240). He concedes that a certain law and inevitable sanctions would obviously command obedience, but short of that there is only custom which is inevitably and inertly backward-looking. There is thus nothing beyond the perception of each individual. Meanwhile 'Art and Poesy struggle like poor ghosts / To hinder cock-crow' (p.242); nor is the vaunted Religion of Progress any less illusory, if only because there is no way of affirming with any certainty that change is for the better. Rosencranz, therefore, contents himself with cigars.

But, declares Laertes (the social altruist) that disproves Rosencranz's argument. If life is valueless he should kill himself. If, however, cigars at least have value, then a better world, as a kind of seed in the present, becomes a possibility for the future, and in any case Rosencranz owes something to that seed-sifting in the past which has made him more comfortable than 20 million fellow-citizens. Laertes naturally does not wish to justify pain on the ground that it arouses those who pity it to virtue. Nevertheless he believes that a man is condemned to complete sterility if he accepts the social good, yet denies the value of social goals.

Guildenstern next proposes to specify that binding law the legitimacy of which Rosencranz has already conceded in principle. His position is again essentially that of Bray, Spencer and Greg. We are compelled, he says, to submit physically to the external world. Moreover, as Rosencranz has correctly maintained, this experience of reality bears down in the first instance on the individual soul. But though our conceptions of God, duty, love, submission and fellowship originate, therefore, in the constitutions and experiences of individual men and women, they are also objectified in society in a kind of outward reason, which makes good the deficiencies of the inner, and ensures that the rich are not left sole inheritors of the earth. (This was a favourite theme of Lewes's in the 1870s.³) Those incorporated values, Guildenstern continues, are such that even if the human race were in decline, mourning the dying good would in itself constitute a valid religion.

Rosencranz at once declares this last point to be mere elitism, and even Laertes dislikes admitting the possibility of social degeneration. The real degenerates, in his opinion, are the pessimists who are incapable of valuing the human struggle as a whole. Osric, however, agrees with Rosencranz. Schemes to flog men of taste into conformity are contemptible; he is indifferent to poverty, the imminence of socialism, or anything else for that matter. However, he does feel that Rosencranz has blasphemed against Art which is able to make Evil an aspect of the sublime. Art's votaries, he insists, are life's Olympians, and finer being – virtue included – is simply accepted privilege. Art, taking 'no account of modern or antique / In morals, science or philosophy' (p.254), is its own measure, a view which infuriates Laertes and elicits from Guildenstern the reply that since there is undoubtedly such a thing as cultural progress (the horrors of Chinese music and Hindoo sculpture prove this point) the aesthete owes as much to society as anybody. With this Hamlet agrees, but he also unexpectedly announces agreement with Osric, at any rate to the claims he has made for Art's moral autonomy. 'The ideal has discoveries' Hamlet says, 'which ask /No test, no faith, save that we joy in them', and by such discoveries virtue, rank, right and truth 'have but one name, Delight' (p.258). With this the conversation ends. Later Hamlet has a dream in which all contradictions are resolved, but it turns out to be incommunicable.

There are two important developments in this discussion. The first is the implicit alliance between the materialistic scepticism of Rosencranz and the aestheticism which Osric bases so frankly on social privilege. George Eliot clearly despises both – yet she concludes her poem with an endorsement of Osric's concept of art as a separate and autonomous realm of value. In the light of *Daniel Deronda* this is of particular interest since it helps to explain the novel's notoriously problematical structure. On the one hand the Daniel-Mordecai narrative in *Daniel Deronda* is overtly and insistently didactic, and therefore fundamentally at odds with the views advanced by Osric; on the other it seems to be largely symbolic rather than realistic, which suggests that it belongs to the autonomous realm of art defended by Osric with Hamlet's support. The tensions in George Eliot's work between the ideal and the real have already been discussed. The difference between the Deronda narrative and her other idealistic or symbolic narratives, however, is that its doctrine – its orthodoxy, to use Pater's word – is radically new. The basic teaching of *Romola*, for example, does not really require proof; the novel's reliance on symbol and coincidence is simply meant to bring the 'known' operations of retributive justice and altruistic devotion more vividly before us. In *Daniel Deronda*, however, George Eliot seems to be proposing new and possibly unscientific conceptions of human relationships and connexions and yet to be doing so in terms which rely on symbol and image rather than likelihood and verisimilitude, and therefore seem indifferent to questions of proof. This surely is to raise art to an altogether new level of autonomy. It suggests that the unexpected emphasis given to this particular conception in 'A College Breakfast Party' is not accidental. George Eliot, it seems, is not so much adjudicating between the opposed claims of positivistic science and hedonistic aestheticism as adopting a third position in overt opposition to them both.

The differences between Positivists and Aesthetes were in any case less significant than both sides imagined. The social and ethical integration of values anticipated by the first generation of Victorian rationalists becomes in effect an experiential integration of conflicting tensions in later aesthetic theory. Comte and Pater are thus both organicists, Comte socially, Pater subjectively. Both, if in different ways, sanction a principle of *assimilation* in art and in life, and it is this which *Daniel Deronda* resists. It repudiates, both structurally and thematically, those notions of social and aesthetic order on which Positivism and Aestheticism were equally based. Not surprisingly, therefore, George Eliot's contemporaries found it a difficult novel to accept. James was able to respond to its aesthetic unevenness with elaborate tact, but the reactions of other critics to its social and political themes were less gracious. To a certain extent this must be attributed simply to anti-semitism. The *Tablet* review is notorious, but anti-semitism was not exclusive to Christians. Feuerbach asserted that the Jewish religion had been based on 'the principle of . . . egoism',[4] and that the Jewish world had had 'no art, no science'.[5] 'Utilism', he wrote, 'is the essential theory of Judaism'.[6] But something more fundamental than prejudice is at stake in *Daniel Deronda*, if only because the novel is at least as interested in Judaism as in Jews. It thereby not only offends against the Paterian principles of non-didactic art, and the universalist claims of Positivism, but it also radically transforms our sense of George Eliot's political vision, particularly on the issue of Nationalism.

For most of her life George Eliot's attitude to Nationalism as an idea and in practice does not seem to have been very different from that of most of the more progressive-minded of her countrymen. Like many people she was briefly delighted in 1848 at the prospect of the apparently imminent triumph of the liberal republican nationalism associated with Mazzini, and for the rest of her life she continued to hold Mazzini in high regard. Nationalism lost ground in the 1850s, however, and became less unambiguously a progressive cause. In the 1860s it again emerged as a major force in European politics, but was not regarded in England with any great enthusiasm. The position of the British government was one of strict neutrality and non-involvement. Disraeli, who was more attracted by great causes than most of his compatriots, sarcastically compared the conference which followed Bismarck's seizure of Schleswig-Holstein in 1863 to a Carnival which the British representatives attended 'as men in distressed circumstances go to a place of amusement – to while away the time with a consciousness of impending failure'.[7] Britain also avoided involvement in Bismarck's next adventure, the Seven Weeks' War against Austria, which secured both German and Italian reunification. (Incidentally it is against the background of this world-changing campaign that Daniel, Gwendolen and Grandcourt come together in Genoa.) Again in 1867 Britain characteristically agreed to guarantee Luxembourg's security and then announced that she would not do so against any of the other guaranteeing powers. None of these developments seem to have much interested George Eliot at the time. Her feelings towards Mazzini did not prevent her from reverencing Cavour, who had had Mazzini sentenced *in absentia* to death, and she was even respectful towards Bismarck. The 1860s was a time of political disenchantment for her, especially in the matter of progressive causes. She preferred to think of politics in remote and abstract terms. The ideal of national identity is celebrated in *The Spanish Gypsy*, but it remains an intensely subjective, almost a private experience.

All this changed with the Franco-Prussian war of 1870. Belated British efforts to prevent war breaking out carried, according to Lord Acton, 'neither authority nor conviction' because they were 'tainted with ignorance of the central transactions of the [previous] five months'.[8] George Eliot, too, was to be rudely awakened to her own ignorance by the progress of the war. At first she almost automatically supported the Germans, presumably because of her deep respect for German culture and an understandable dislike of Napoleon III. The contrast was a simple one. On the one side there was the 'selfish pride' of the 'iniquitous' French, on the other those 'German energies' to which the world was so indebted.[9] Soon, however, the hideousness of the war became apparent to her, and she began to feel dismay about the 'moral condition' of the German people.[10] Frederic Harrison's eloquent attack on Bismarckism moved her to tears. As French suffering intensified, so did her gratitude for what France had 'contributed to the mind of Europe'.[11] For the first time in her life she became addicted to newspaper reading. The experience was in fact very like her celebrated description in *Daniel Deronda* of that 'terrible moment' which comes

> to many souls when the great movements of the world, the larger destinies of mankind, which have lain aloof in the newspapers and other neglected reading, enter like an earthquake into their own lives – when the slow urgency of growing generations turns into the tread of an invading army or the dire clash of civil war (ch.69).

Bismarck had proclaimed his contempt for 'the vague and change-

able concept of humanity' and his conviction that 'the great questions of our time will . . . be decided . . . by Blood and Iron'.[12]
George Eliot now knew what he meant, that he was literally willing
to pit Blood and Iron against the concept of humanity to which she
had devoted her life. It followed that that concept, together with the
idea of nationhood in the name of which Bismarck claimed to be
fighting, had both to be thought out anew.

She was no longer able to tolerate the negative character of British
public life, or the mannered detachment characteristic of the British
ruling class which she associated with it. Her feelings on this subject
are evident even in the more sympathetic portraits of public men in
Daniel Deronda: those of Mr Gascoigne and Sir Hugo Mallinger are
both masterly studies, subtler and sharper than those of the
Debarrys and Mr Brooke. Mr Gascoigne, obscure, naive and
likeable, exhibits all the worldly wisdom and concealed vulgarity of
the gentleman. His sexual double-standards do not make him a
hypocrite, his snobbery does not make him stupid, and there is
nothing contradictory in our being pleased when he finds a patron in
Sir Hugo as the novel closes. But this does not justify his subservience to mercenary and snobbish complacencies, any more than Sir
Hugo's honest heart justifies the intellectual shallowness and assured
insularity of his political attitudes. Not that Sir Hugo thinks of
himself as unintellectual or chauvinistic – on the contrary. 'Dons', he
assures Daniel, 'make a capital figure in society; and occasionally he
can shoot you down a cartload of learning in the right place, which
will tell in politics' (ch.16), and he professes to have no objection to
Daniel's doffing 'some of our national prejudices' (ch.33). Nevertheless he thinks Daniel should 'keep an English cut' and avoid carrying
unselfishness and generosity 'too far'; the business of the country
could never be done, he points out, 'if everybody looked at politics
as if they were prophecy'. In itself none of this is particularly
shocking. What it sanctions, however, without, of course, anyone
being so ill-bred as to remark on it, as a social order in which
Mallinger Grandcourt can appear as a great man, his movements
from house to house having an importance equal to 'the results of the
American War' (ch. 9), and his name carrying its ominous suggestion of almost royal splendour. He completely embodies the a-
political character of British public life and he and not Mr Bult
therefore is the true political man in the novel. To be a-political,
however, is not quite the same as being truly neutral. It can hardly
be an accident, for example, that in the account of Grandcourt's
negations in the 28th chapter, which we have already analysed, we
are reminded that 'a cottony milkiness' such as his 'may be preparing

one knows not what biting or explosive material'. Dynamite had been invented in 1867. The allusion makes Grandcourt the locus of a brutality no less real and active than 'the tread of an invading army'. In other words, just as the most exquisite aestheticism in 'A College Breakfast Party' aligns itself ultimately with selfish, pipe-smoking materialism, so in *Daniel Deronda* perfect gentlemanly detachment is in secret alliance with 'Blood and Iron'.

The attribution of such broad political significance to the figure of Grandcourt must affect our view of his relations with Gwendolen. There is evidence that George Eliot thought of Gwendolen as something more than the ignorant, vivacious middle-class girl she appears to be. According to the Notebooks the name Gwendolen was that of an Ancient British moon-goddess, and was associated with Gweno, the Venus of British astrology. More significantly it was also the name of the wife of Locrine, son of Brutus, mythical progenitor of the British people.[13] In the novel, therefore, Gwendolen probably represents the soul of Britain, so that her 'terrible moment' in the penultimate chapter may point allusively to the possibility of British society, free at last from the Grandcourtian incubus, awakening to a new intensity of political awareness and seriousness of political will.

It is certainly the case that in the course of the 1870s George Eliot successfully identified a new and virulent threat to the humanism on which she had based her life. A new spirit of brutal faithlessness was abroad, based on the urbanities of aestheticism and political agnosticism and the will to violence in men and nations. The threat came jointly, as it were, from Pater and Bismarck, nor was it less dangerous for being capable of concealment behind the impeccable manners of an English gentleman. It may even be that like Freud later she was facing the possibility that 'under the influence of cultural urges, some civilizations, or some epochs of civilization – possible the whole of mankind – have become "neurotic".'[14] In any case, desperate defensive strategies seem to have been called for. Eagleton has argued that '*Daniel Deronda* marks one major terminus of nineteenth century realism – a realism buckling under ideological pressures it is unable to withstand',[15] and both Robert Preyer and U. C. Knoepflmacher[16] have maintained that in *Daniel Deronda* George Eliot abandons the deterministic premises on which the whole of Victorian rationalism was based. She is protecting humanism, in other words, by abandoning the logic on which it depends. The novel's air of desperation certainly struck her contemporaries. It was not just that it tendentiously defends highly specific interpretations of the basic teachings of Judaism, the Law and the Prophets, the Unity of God, Divine Election, and the Messianic Kingdom; it does so in Edward Dowden's words by rejecting 'the exactitude of Science' for the inexactitudes of mysticism[17] in a way that seems to call scientific humanism itself into question.

The matter is not as simple, however, as Dowden appears to have thought. *Daniel Deronda* does not in any comprehensive way jettison scientific norms. On the contrary, in important respects it firmly reiterates commonly held views on the subject, views which had already been expressed in earlier works by George Eliot. The scientist, for example, is offered in the commentary as the archetypal previsionary: his 'forecasting ardour . . . feels the agitations of discovery beforehand, and has a faith in its preconception that surmounts many failures of experiment' (ch.41).[18] The artist too enjoys previsionary powers of a strictly naturalistic kind. Klesmer and men like him, we are told, experience a 'fervour of creative work and theoretic belief which pierces the whole future of a life with the light of congruous, devoted purpose' (ch.22). There are also a number of particular instances of prevision in the novel which are either carefully explained or are so casual as not to require explanation, Klesmer's lightning recognition of Mab Meyrick's musical powers, or Lush's feeling that Grandcourt is 'fey – led on by an ominous fatality' (ch.28) are key examples. Incidents and comparisons of this kind, however, are contextual only. They provide points of reference by means of which the experiences of Gwendolen, Deronda and Mordecai, the major previsionaries in the novel, can be located. On these the novel's meaning depends.

Gwendolen's intuitions would seem to be quite as explicable as Dino's in *Romola*. In a certain sense she really does see the future. Her reactions to the dead face, for example, are direct intimations of Grandcourt's death. More impressive, perhaps, are her casual prophecies like her prediction that 'Lord Grandcourt' – rejected by Gwendolen herself – will ride across to Quetcham to propose to Miss Arrowpoint only to find her 'just married to a needy musician' (ch.9). As if in a dream, this subtly combines and distorts two future events. Grandcourt (who is not destined for a peerage) will indeed propose marriage to Gwendolen, but she will not laugh at him for failing to bring her the ring she asked for, nor will he fall at her feet. Miss Arrowpoint, meanwhile, will engage herself to a musician, though not exactly a 'needy' one. Obliquity such as this makes Gwendolen's prognostications towards the end of the novel particularly convincing. Immediately before their last sea-trip she sobs to Grandcourt, 'Perhaps we shall be drowned' (ch.54) – a fate in fact reserved for him alone. As in the earlier novels, prophecy is deceptive but not magical. Barbara Hardy is exactly right in attributing Gwendolen's powers, like Mordecai's, to 'an appropriate mind and nervous system'.[19] As it was in *Romola*, prevision is really the indirect self-knowledge of 'quiveringly-poised natures' (ch. 37). Gwendolen's prophecies are censored wishes which she tends to act out impulsively when opportunities to do so arise.

The integration of this organicist conception of an unfolding personal destiny with Lamarckian notions of race is no less compatible with current scientific opinion, and George Eliot manages it with considerable success. Just as a murderous impulse can be secretly incorporated in the life of a young girl, so the 'heritage of Israel' can beat 'in the pulses of millions' and live 'in their veins as a power without understanding, like the morning exaltation of the herds; it is the inborn half of memory, moving as in a dream among writings on the walls' (ch. 42). Modern critics have resented the introduction of these 'rather dated speculations'[20] into the novel, but granted their premises they are handled to some effect. The image of the morning herd, for example, is remarkably vivid, and the allusion to the writing on the wall in the Book of Daniel the more effective for its remoteness. Again, when Deronda speaks of the 'ancestral life' lying in those disinherited like himself 'as a dim longing for unknown objects and sensations', and compares 'their inherited frames' to 'a cunningly-wrought musical instrument, never played on, but quivering throughout in uneasy mysterious moanings of its intricate structure' (ch. 63), the imaginative possibilities in Lamarckian theories of inheritance are subtly developed. In this area at least George Eliot deploys musical analogies well, considerably enriching, for example, the Princess's desperate assertion that her body gave her the right to sing, though the representation of Daniel's affinity with Jewish ritual on similar grounds is less successful.

The real importance of organicist and Lamarckian conceptions, however, is that, as in earlier novels, they explain prophecy, in this case the prophetic principle at the heart of Judaism. For just as, to quote 'A College Breakfast Party',

> God, duty, love, submission, fellowship,
> Must first be framed in man, as music is,
> Before they live outside him as a law (p. 246)

so Judaism must first be framed in Jews. But if Mordecai's religion and personality are thus literally identical, and if, as the case of Gwendolen shows, it is possible intuitively to grasp the future tendencies of one's own personality, then Mordecai's vision of his people's future is simply a valid insight into his own essence which, in his case as in Gwendolen's, is identical with the desires of the heart. It is consequently legitimate on strictly scientific grounds for him to believe that the 'thoughts of his heart . . . [are] too precious, too closely inwoven with the growth of things, not to have a further destiny' (ch.38). Prophetic consciousness is accordingly inseparable from Law in a strictly scientific sense (as indeed Sephardo implicitly argued in *The Spanish Gypsy*). But scientific and divine Law, Positivism and the Torah, are also fundamentally connected. Feuerbach indeed called Judaism 'the most complete presentation of Positivism in religion'[21] because in subjecting secular intercourse as well as morals to the prescriptions of a religious Law it implicitly symbolized that universal and morally significant regularity on which both the scientific and ethical philosophies of necessity were based: among Jews, Mordecai declares, 'religion and law and moral life . . . made one growth' (ch.42). Prophecy, then, is a term implicit in Law in both its senses, and therefore in the Jewish conception of the Divine as well, for as Kalonymos asserts, 'duty is the love of law; and law is the nature of the Eternal' (60). The Divine Unity, the Law and the Prophets are thus consecrated and organic manifestations of each other and of Positivism itself.

It is clear, then, that unlike the priest's religion in 'A College Breakfast Party', the Judaism of *Daniel Deronda* does not involve an invisible or supernatural order. Mordecai and Daniel are not in fact orthodox Jews at all, and the Torah seems hardly to differ in status from the Cabbala in George Eliot's thought. Moreover, throughout the novel she uses Jewish respect for the Divine Name in the interests of distinctly humanistic periphrases. More specifically, Feuerbach's conception of the 'Thou' and Comte's conception of immortality naturalize the apparently mystical friendship between Daniel and Mordecai. 'Friends', Feuerbach writes, 'compensate for each other; friendship . . . requires diversity, for [it] rests on a desire for self-completion'.[22] Mordecai and Daniel complete each other in just this way. Their relationship is in no sense mystical. For Mordecai, Daniel is explicitly said to be 'something more ample than the second soul bestowed, according to the Cabbalists to help out the insufficient first' (ch.38), and their union after Mordecai dies is simply a Positivist form of immortality, what Comte called a second life 'in the heart and intellect of others'.[23]

Judaism, then, far from undermining humanist or scientific principles in *Daniel Deronda* expresses and endorses them – hence, indeed, the special status accorded to it over all other nationalisms. 'Every people has its special mission', Mazzini wrote, 'which will co-operate towards the general mission of Humanity. That mission

is Nationality'.[24] Mordecai makes a comparable declaration when he
says: 'Each nation has its own work, and is a member of the world,
enriched by the work of each' (ch.42). But whereas for Mazzini all
Nationalisms were in principle equal, for Mordecai the fact that the
Jewish 'confession of the divine Unity' embraces as its consequence
the ultimate unity of mankind, makes 'Israel . . . the heart of
mankind'. Judaism, therefore, is more than a paradigm of nationhood. Jews are the bearers of a uniquely redemptive vision of human
possibilities from which all other peoples can and must learn. In this
sense they really are a people set apart.

The Judaism of *Daniel Deronda* embodies and consecrates in
human history the ideals of nationality and the premises of the
scientific method. Both, however, are subordinate to the highly
specific political thesis which is at the heart of the novel's teaching. It
is a thesis which was carefully developed by George Eliot in order to
counter her growing political disillusionment with public life
throughout the 1860s and 1870s. As Eagleton rightly indicates, she
could not see a solution to the problems of her time in the normal
processes of history. Graham Martin complains that 'history is
located wholly outside England' in *Daniel Deronda*,[25] but in fact the
novel locates it outside Europe and America as well. There is
nothing to hope for in continental wars any more than in British
inertia. This sense of historical impotence, moreover, is applied as
uncompromisingly to Jewish as to Gentile culture. The gambling
drunken Lapidoth is as representative of nineteenth-century Jewishness as Grandcourt is of nineteenth-century Englishness. His
wanderings, as William Baker has shown, not only reflect the
specific experiences of Salomon Maimon but more generally the
'widespread and gradual breakup of traditional settlements and
occupations'[26] throughout the post-Napoleonic period. No less
typical, though in a different way, are the Cohen family (the Poysers
and Dodsons of the post-ghetto Diaspora) and, on a more exalted
level, the Princess Halm-Eberstein and Herr Klesmer himself. The
Princess acts her way out of the narrow lot of Jewish womanhood
just as Rahel Levin had done,[27] only to find herself trapped in
Gentile roles yet denied Gentile liberties. Her weakness, however,
is infidelity to her art as much as to her Jewish heritage. Klesmer's
Jewishness in contrast (his name is Polish-Yiddish for a wandering
musician)[28] is subsumed into an authentic artistic greatness which
accurately embodies the impact of Jewish genius on German culture
in the nineteenth century. At the same time, however, for all the
passion with which he asserts the political relevance of his art to an
astonished Mr Bult, Klesmer has something of the air of Leviathan

stranded. The Jewish world in *Daniel Deronda* is historically authentic and representative – the novel amazed Freud by its knowledge of Jewish intimate ways that 'we speak of only among ourselves'[29] – but it is also just as historically and politically impotent as the world of the Gentile characters. It is certainly not to Jewish culture as it then existed that George Eliot looks in her pursuit of a purified nationalist ideal. She ignores, for example, the *Alliance Israelite Universelle*, just as she rejects the assumptions and policies of both Chancellor Bismarck and Foreign Secretary Stanley. Nor does she place any more confidence in the common life of the Jews than in the common life of the Gentiles. Instead she turns to sheer chance, overtly placing all her hopes in those improbabilities which are a part of probability, but which are nevertheless generally regarded as unrepresentative, exceptional and therefore insignificant. A modern equivalent of such a conception of progress, however, is to be found in the evolutionist's reliance on rare but crucial genetic changes which by chance match some feature of an organism's environment. What we witness in *Daniel Deronda* is, in effect, the accidental but entirely possible formation of a new field of force in history, a force which operates not within any existing culture – that, George Eliot had attempted to describe without success in *Felix Holt* – but rather between two cultures, the Jewish and the Gentile, at the edges or interstices of social life and consciousness. The eccentricity and loneliness of the central characters in *Daniel Deronda*, and the hazardous nature of their meetings, are thus intrinsic to the conception of history on which the novel is deliberately and consciously based.

But while this reading may account for the improbabilities of plot and characterization in the novel, Mordecai's precise predictions concerning them have still to be explained. Mordecai himself, however, is not unaware of the hazardous nature of these predictions. He admits, for example, that the Deliverer he is waiting for might turn 'his back towards him' (ch. 38); 'the history of our people's trust', he tells Daniel, 'has been full of illusion'; yet in a curiously phrased reversal of this conclusion he adds, '*So it might be with my trust of you, if you would make it an illusion. But you will not*' (ch.40 – George Eliot's emphasis). This effect is repeated later when he admits that if Daniel were to reject him and say he was not a Jew, then he – Mordecai – would know he had been deluded; yet he insists, that 'hour will never come'. This undoubtedly is the point where in a sense Dowden is proved correct, and the premises underlying the scientific method are indeed defied in the novel. According to all the distinguished contemporaries who influenced

George Eliot, and especially according to Comte, science abandons 'the vain search after . . . the causes of phenomena, and applies itself to the study of their laws, – that is, their invariable relations of succession and resemblance'.[30] Of course it belongs to the nature of probability that improbable things will happen, but the prognosticating powers of the investigating scientist are limited to predictions about whether possible relations of succession and resemblance will prove in the event to be invariable. It is an absolute repudiation of the scientific method, therefore, and so, astonishingly, of that notion of Law consecrated by Judaism, for Mordecai to claim as he does the power of making predictions about coincidences and choices in the future which of their nature could never be part of a sequence. In the light of such claims it is not surprising that George Eliot has to assure us, on no less than five occasions, that Mordecai is sane according to the standard Associationist criteria.

This apparent repudiation of the notion of Law is nevertheless fundamental to Mordecai's intuitions into the nature of Judaism. Defending his own rationality during the debate at the 'Hand and Banner', he asks; 'what is it to be rational?' (ch.42), and proceeds to argue that whatever the answer to that question may be it must be consistent with 'the prophetic consciousness of our nationality'. He then identifies authentic rationality with choice. Only by so doing can he bring into play the two remaining principles of the Jewish religion. The 'strongest principle of growth', he insists,

> lies in human choice. The sons of Judah have to choose that God
> may again choose them. The Messianic time is the time when
> Israel shall will the planting of the national ensign . . . Shall man,
> whose soul is set in the royalty of discernment and resolve . . .
> say . . . ask no choice or purpose of me? That is the blasphemy of
> this time. The divine principle of our race is action, choice,
> resolved memory . . . the vision is there; it will be fulfilled.

This is an emphatically Feuerbachian reading of Jewish exclusiveness. The people chosen by God become the people who choose divine values, and in doing so they enter the Messianic Kingdom. The Judaism of *Daniel Deronda* is thus none other than the Nietzschean religion of the 'independent, long-range will, which dares to make promises' in its fullest most historically potent form. And this is why Mordecai's certitude *must* have the appearance of irrationality. Unlike the premonitions of Gwendolen and Daniel, his vision of the future is set in the royalty of *resolve* as well as of *discernment*. It is not simply seen but chosen; it is a judgment as well as an intuition, a divine wager with history. George Eliot has clearly moved a very long way since she constructed an entire novel, *Romola*, in order to dissolve choice in mere process.

This emphasis on choice, however, raises the question once again of whether *Daniel Deronda* is anti-determinist or not. The issue was very much a live one for George Eliot because while the novel was being written George Henry Lewes was putting his own rigorously determinist and 'Spinozan' views on the question of free will into final form; 'actions, sensations, emotions and thoughts', he argues in *The Study of Psychology*, 'are subject to casual determination no less rigorously than the movements of the planets'.[31] There is thus no such faculty as the will; voluntary acts are simply felt as distinct manifestations of a variously unfolding self, the experience of selfhood and of having a will being indistinguishable. Lewes does, however, distinguish between physical and moral or subjective causation. In the former, fixed conditions yield unvarying results, while the latter, though equally necessitated, is subject to the infinite variability of experience. Moral causation may properly be called free, therefore, only as opinion may be called free, insofar, that is, as we are conscious of the possibility of both being varied. This variability allows both opinion and behaviour to be more or less consistent with the moral law, just as architecture can be more or less consistent with mechanical laws. Habit, or the basic animal ability to accept training, makes possible something like a pro-grammatic control of this human variability, though considerable differences between one volition and the next inevitably persist. What seem to be similar acts, for example, can be 'an immediate outleap of heroic generosity' on the one hand or the outcome of 'a dire struggle between discerned duty and . . . egoistic desire' on the other.[32]

On two important occasions in *Daniel Deronda*, Gwendolen Har-leth uses this metaphor of the sudden leap to describe an act of the will. On one occasion she tells Daniel that when her 'blood is fired' she can 'do daring things – take any leap' (ch.36) but that doing so frightens her. Clearly one problem with such impulses is that they are unpremeditated, indistinguishable from laying a stake, more like 'a brief remembered madness' (ch.6) than fully human acts. Two such moments of madness in particular are crucial in Gwendolen's experience, her acceptance of Grandcourt and her response to his cry from the water. Is she free and responsible at these moments, or maddened and afraid? The entire Gwendolen narrative is in a sense devoted to this question; it attempts 'to thread the hidden pathways of feeling and thought which lead up to every moment of action' (ch.16 – epigraph), and it does so with considerable subtlety and circumspection. It is thus impossible to say exactly what happens either when Gwendolen is manoeuvred into accepting Grandcourt, or when she momentarily holds her hand as her heart says 'Die' and he struggles in the water. It is of the latter moment that Gwendolen uses the image of the leap for a second time. 'I was leaping away from myself', she tells Daniel, '. . . I was leaping from my crime' (ch.56). Is a reflex action of repentance more or less responsible than a reflex of greed, fear or revenge? We have been assured by the author that 'drifting depends on something besides currents, when the sails have been set in advance' (ch.27), and by Daniel that 'when we are calm we can use our memories and gradually change the bias of our fear, as we do our tastes' (ch.36). Clearly, then, the main direction of the Gwendolen narrative is towards Lewes's concepts of necessity, habit and variability. The result, however, is a fiction which is aesthetically deeply satisfying and which ironically meets Pater's requirements that 'modern art' should react to the 'magic web' of necessity 'woven through and through us' by representing 'men and women in these bewildering toils so as to give the spirit at least an equivalent for the sense of freedom'. The Gwendolen narrative may thus be precisely characterized as both determinist and Paterian.

George Levine, however, has argued that there is a kind of heroism in the Deronda narrative which works in the opposite direction and by envisaging a 'significant and conscious tampering with the course of history'[33] is basically in conflict with the kind of determinism we have seen Lewes defend. The possibility of such a tampering is undoubtedly raised during the 'Hand and Banner' debate, though not quite in the form suggested by Levine. Thus Daniel makes a notably cautious reply to Lilly's confident assertion that 'changes taking place according to [the laws of development] are necessarily progressive' (ch.42). He distinguishes between 'degrees of inevitableness' in human choices and actions, and 'degrees of wisdom in hastening or retarding', and insists that it is always possible to mistake 'a tendency which should be resisted for an inevitable law'. (Some of Guildenstern's anxieties about historical degeneration seem to be at work here.) Clearly Daniel is working from determinist premises, but his phrase 'degrees of inevitableness' slightly but significantly varies Lewes's concept of variability, and prepares the ground for Mordecai's assertion that 'the strongest principle of growth lies in human choice'. Not that this resolves the problem either: the question remains – what degree of inevitableness attaches to a particular volition – the placing of a stake, for example, or the acceptance of a husband, or a friend, or a vocation?

Levine further develops his case for an anti-determinist motif in *Daniel Deronda* by quoting from one of George Eliot's letters which, he suggests, anticipates the solution of modern linguistic analysis to the problem of free will: 'every fresh morning', George Eliot writes,

> is an opportunity that one can look forward to for exerting one's will. I shall not be satisfied with your philosophy till you have conciliated necessitarianism – I hate the ugly word – with the practice of willing strongly, of willing to will strongly, and so on, that being what you certainly can do.[34]

The insight which this letter anticipates is to be found in Gilbert Ryle's attack on the very notion of voluntary action: 'If I cannot help willing to pull the trigger', Ryle argues, 'it would be absurd to describe my pulling it as "voluntary". But if my volition to pull the trigger is voluntary . . . then it must come from a prior volition and that from another *ad infinitum*'.[35] In other words, to talk of willing strongly, of willing to will strongly and so on is to involve oneself in a logically vicious regress. However, the consequences of accepting Ryle's negative attitude to this logical *impasse* are well exemplified by his pupil, A. J. Ayer, when in *The Central Questions of Philosophy* he demonstrates his respect for his own overriding criteria of positivist consistency by calling in question 'our ordinary notion of responsibility'.[36] The importance of George Eliot's letter on necessity, therefore, is that it shows she had anticipated both the logical difficulty advanced by Ryle and the moral dilemma exposed by Ayer. Her solution to these difficulties is not that of modern philosophers, however. She accepts that willing in any sense adequate to a serious conception of responsibility is logically impossible, but she will not abandon it since it remains morally necessary. (One is reminded of Mordecai's refusal to accept any rationality which precludes the prophetic consciousness of nationality.) This reaction effectively aligns George Eliot with Nietzsche rather than with Ryle or Ayer. For her, as for Nietzsche, the will has, and can only have, the status of a premise, unsupported by scientific or analytical argument. For George Eliot, however, unlike Nietzsche, the will has itself to be willed in violation of a determinist logic which in other respects supports and applies the purely humanistic conceptions of religion and law to which she is also committed. It has to be willed in the interests of that religion and that law, the logic of which precludes it. That is why there is indeed a willed element in the text of *Daniel Deronda*, though not as F.R. Leavis maintained, as a consequence of some 'inner connivance'. Far from there being 'an element of the tacitly *voulu*'[37] in the novel,

Daniel Deronda makes its own deliberateness a matter of carefully if painfully emphasized thematic concern.

Hence the novel's notorious aesthetic inconsistency. Half of the text perfectly exemplifies, in the subtle unfolding of its own inherent possibilities, the organicist and determinist principles to which the author is committed; half wilfully abandons process for choice. The following passage is an excellent example of how in the Gwendolen narrative both text and character participate in each other's organic movement:

> even without her potent charm and peculiar filial position Gwen-dolen might . . . still have played the queen in exile, if only she had kept her inborn energy of egoistic desire, and her power of inspiring fear as to what she might say or do. However, she had the charm, and those who feared her were also fond of her; the fear and the fondness being perhaps both heightened by what may be called the iridescence of her character – the play of various, nay, contradictory tendencies. For Macbeth's rhetoric about the impossibility of being many opposite things in the same moment, referred to the clumsy necessities of action and not the subtler possibilities of feeling. We cannot speak a loyal word and be meanly silent, we cannot kill and not kill in the same moment; but a moment is room wide enough for the loyal and mean desire, for the outlash of a murderous thought and the sharp backward stroke of repentance (ch.4).

On the basis of passages such as this one could apply to George Eliot Eagleton's description of Conrad as a 'fastidious *worker* of his text' bent on achieving a 'scrupulous refinement of recalcitrant language into concrete image and expressive nuance',[38] except, of course, that unlike Conrad – or Pater, or James – George Eliot refuses to regard 'human communication as no more than a transiently consoling illusion', or human freedom as something for which art can provide a soothing equivalent. Committed to the 'royalty of discernment and resolve', she is compelled to jettison the purely literary values and notions of decorum that are at the heart of the Paterian, Jamesian and Conradian aesthetic, and at the heart also of her own rendering of Gwendolen's history.

Accordingly the Deronda narrative is about its own literary awkwardness. This can be demonstrated with some precision by comparing the standing of fantasy in the two narratives. The grounds on which Gwendolen's virginal fantasies are condemned significantly combine literary and moral criteria. Her daydreaming, we are told, is like a 'genteel romance . . . full of vague power, originality and general rebellion' (ch.6), in which she goes 'to the North Pole, or [rides] steeplechases or [goes] to be a queen in the East' (ch.7). In this and other respects Anna Gascoigne is Gwendolen's foil and opposite. It is true that Anna has her own absurd fantasies also – she plans to retire to Canada with Rex – but they are not egoistically self-dramatizing, and in general she and Rex act as norms of conventional, lucid and formed feeling against which Gwendolen's hectic fantasies can be condemned. (The mildly Trollopian novel in which they might have been central characters is not developed in the text because it does not need to be.) In the Deronda narrative, on the other hand, the terms of the comparison are strikingly reversed. The Meyricks are a cosmopolitan and metropolitan equivalent of the young Gascoignes, but it is they, not the formless daydreamers, who are put in their place. The grand pictures on their walls, for example, reduce the great aesthetic tradition of Europe to 'the medium of a little black and white' (ch.20), so that it makes a feeble impression when compared with the Hebrew hymns which Mirah's mother sang to her, and which significantly she heard without understanding. This is entirely typical of the way in which the Deronda narrative repeatedly sanctions that emotion-in-ignorance which the Gwendolen narrative repudiates. Mordecai actually dissolves material realities, such as the buildings and ships on the river – 'the signs of world-commerce' – into a 'half-hazy, half-luminous' dream, 'as a fine symphony to which we can hardly be said to listen makes a medium that bears up our spiritual wings' (ch.38). This is familiar territory: music is once again acting as a solvent in which tensions are drowned and out of which, through a specious, heavily metaphorical rhetoric, solutions and resolutions triumphantly emerge. What is striking about *Daniel Deronda*, however, is its condemnation of just such formlessness as unliterary and immoral in one case and its sanctioning of it as humanly necessary in another. This is particularly noticeable when Mordecai's longings are compared with appropriate reverence to 'the boy's and girl's picturing of the future beloved' and when his shared experience with Daniel is said to be 'as intense a consciousness as if they had been two undeclared lovers' (ch.40). Comparisons of this kind draw the reader's attention not only to the similarities between Mordecai's fantasies and Gwendolen's but also to the different criteria by which George Eliot judges them.

   That the text takes cognizance of such contradictions and so incorporates them into its teaching is made explicit in the case of Daniel himself. A comparison of Daniel and Grandcourt is illuminating in this connexion. Technically, each presents George Eliot with a similar problem. Morally polarized, they carry between them a great weight of significance, yet the formation of their remarkable adult personalities is not susceptible to explanation according to ordinary process or experience. We are told nothing, therefore, about Grandcourt's personal development, which gives the evil he embodies the character of a visitation. He is nonetheless represented with great literary tact and blends beautifully with his English country-house world. Daniel, on the other hand, is related to that same world only by way of gratuitous contrast. With his Titian-like hands, his love of history and the innate balance of his political views he is, like Grandcourt, the product of himself, but unlike Grandcourt, the awkwardness and arbitrariness of the characterization are not dealt with at all tactfully. In itself, his aloofness, like Felix Holt's self-centredness, is not unconvincing. (Only his hunting, boating and cricketing seem absurd since he is unimaginable in the company of huntsmen and cricketers.) However, although we see something of his lonely boyhood, and his anxiety about his origins, we are not meant to think of such experiences as in any adequate way explaining him. This would have been to concede too much to quotidian circumstances. But George Eliot is also acutely conscious of the aesthetic consequences of making Daniel a pyschic mystery in this way. Daniel himself, for example, is made to feel the dangers of 'turning himself into a sort of diagram instead of a growth' (ch.42), which interestingly recalls the famous phrase which George Eliot used about the dangers of 'aesthetic teaching' lapsing 'from the picture to the diagram',[39] and makes explicit the connexion between his unconvincing social relations and his uncertain status as a hero of a novel of the 'Jamesian' kind.

Daniel and Mordecai are thus deliberately offered to the reader on non-Paterian, non-necessitarian terms. Just as they themselves make acts of will, so they are actively and arbitrarily willed by George Eliot not just passively and subtly discerned. It is clear, however, that George Eliot is embarrassed by the awkward unliterariness of this procedure rather as she had been in the case of Felix Holt. She therefore makes compromisingly appeasing gestures towards existing literary and social norms, especially in Daniel's case. Daniel's love-story is particularly clumsy in this respect. Seen always from a distance, Mirah could have been an impressive minor figure – a symbol of artistic and Jewish purity in the Gentile world of cheap theatres and fashionable drawing-rooms, absorbing as a seed 'the chance confusion of its surroundings into its own definite mould of beauty' (ch.20). But Mordecai describes the 'life of a people' as similarly absorbing the thought of other nations into its own forms (ch.42), and this clearly indicates that just as Gwendolen represents the soul of Britain, so Mirah represents the soul of Israel. She has therefore to be thrust into a narrative prominence comparable with Gwendolen's, and is accordingly given a personal history which weakly imitates David Copperfield's, then an entirely uninteresting, and equally conventional story of misunderstanding involving Gwendolen and Hans, leading to a climactic *éclaircissement* and a wedding in the final chapter. This is not just feeble, however; it offends against the basic structure and the deepest meaning of the entire novel. All the other histories in the narrative remain significantly incomplete. Gwendolen is left with an entirely open future in the penultimate chapter while Daniel in his political role literally disappears into a future even more opaque than Fidalma's. This is entirely appropriate. It gives the novel a structure identical in form with the most significant acts of its major characters. It ensures that *Daniel Deronda* must always be read, at least to some extent, as a prophecy, a hypothesis, a wager – as a work, in other words, awaiting completion; and it is against this fundamental characteristic of its aesthetic structure that the love-story of Mirah and Daniel offends.

On the other hand, *Daniel Deronda* can never be judged by purely aesthetic standards because it dares to make such promises. The twentieth-century reader is constantly and inevitably drawn into passing judgments on George Eliot's guesses, prophecies and hypotheses in this novel, and there can be no doubt that she anticipated his doing so. In one respect, moreover, the novel has been overwhelmed by events. The history of the Jews in Germany and in Palestine in the past hundred years is too terrible to be discussed in this context. It is only necessary to insist that the central prophetic commitment in *Daniel Deronda* – that in choosing to make their own history, the Jews will justify and reconcile *all* other nationalisms – has been tragically obscured but not refuted by the passage of time. More precise judgments, however, on relatively minor but still important issues can be made. Specifically, one can ask how well the assumptions and hypotheses on which George Eliot based her Zionist-Nationalist vision have survived in the intellectual climate of the twentieth century.

George Eliot was probably more aware than many of her contemporaries how tentative these assumptions were, how little 'profound research' had been done 'into psychological functions and the mysteries of inheritance'.[40] She was not to know that with regard to the latter Mendel had already conducted the decisive experiments which disproved both the Lamarckian hypothesis and her own speculations about 'the in-born half of memory'. The novel's main hypothesis has thus been partially overthrown before it was written. And an even greater threat to its future intellectual viability, that is to the success of George Eliot's wager with history, was present in her treatment of the psychological functions. The failure of Positivism to identify the problem of the non-egoistical instincts, of compassion, self-denial and self-sacrifice, as we saw in an earlier chapter, had a sustained and damaging effect on all George Eliot's writing, and there can be no doubt about its continuing influence on *Daniel Deronda*. But as we also noted, *Daniel Deronda* is at the same time the one novel in which intimate and disturbing connexions between altruism and sadism (that is, between Daniel and Grand-court) are at last recognized and exposed. George Eliot's fidelity to traditional humanist values, in other words, may be sentimental in parts of the novel, and even disingenuous, but it is certainly not maintained in bland ignorance of the radical ambiguity in an altruistic morality. And, as her handling of the political themes discussed in this chapter also shows, she was painfully aware of what that ambiguity had meant in recent European history. It was in the context of this knowledge, however, that she made her wager. The very fact of her making it means that the specific views which she proposes and defends in the novel are subordinate to the manner in which she seeks to sustain them or rather that they are constituted and expressed precisely in that effort. Choice itself is finally and quite explicitly recognized as the supreme value in *Daniel Deronda* to which all other values, real or potential, are subordinated.

It is important to register the explicitness of this recognition, and its radical character. The kind of willing which George Eliot endorses makes *resolve* a condition of *discernment;* aesthetic, assimilative, organic and even scientific values yield thematically and structurally in *Daniel Deronda* to conscious choice. The will is not to be absorbed into a system or an orthodoxy, no matter how subtle or scientific it may be, any more than the Jews, whose religion consists in choosing and being chosen, are to be assimilated into a uniformly liberal and rational Western collectivity. This religion of the will does not seek or need justification in scientific analysis, not even in those imaginative leaps which enable the scientific intellect to penetrate the ordered sequences of nature. It is rather the condition and basis of all rational acts of the mind whatsoever they may be. There is no satisfactory 'scientific' or 'literary' way, for example, of demonstrating that Emmanuel Deutsch, the Jewish scholar and 'dear Rabbi' on whom the characterization of Mordecai is largely based, and who died on a fruitless journey to Jerusalem in 1873, was historically a more significant figure than the great German Chancellor, who had established the Second Reich in the Palace of Versailles two years earlier: insights of that order can only be willed – they are the condition, not the consequence, of historical analysis. Thus the arbitrament which the Priest calls Faith in 'A College Breakfast Party', and the defiance of God in favour of his own conscience of which Laertes boasts, and the autonomous realm of art proclaimed by Hamlet, are all one. The final lesson George Eliot has to teach us is that men and women need not be passively determined in faith or doctrine or art. Believers, teachers and artists can on the contrary exercise that royalty of discernment and resolve which she believed she had discovered in Judaism; even the novel is a creature of the will, and for that very reason it can contend with principalities and powers.

Conclusion

George Eliot's self-consciousness

A BASIC assumption of this study has been that George Eliot was continually making specific judgments about morality, history, psychology, art and science, the full complexity of which she attempted to communicate to the readers of her novels. Her starting point was the philosophy of necessity which in its ethical form demands intense and sustained self-scrutiny. From the beginning therefore we are confronted in her works with the problem of conscious intention. In accordance with this principle she developed clear and explicit opinions on a wide variety of matters. Her view of history and society was Positivist, her view of religion Feuerbachian and her view of mind Associationist. There were, however, questions about which she had to make judgments on her own account, specifically on the relativity of truth, the origin, nature and extent of evil, the legitimacy or otherwise of extreme subjective endeavour, and the nature of freedom and choice. This she did with great difficulty, but with no less deliberation, coming in some cases to striking and even disturbing conclusions. Among the most important of these were her decision in *Middlemarch* to develop an absolute notion of sanctity, and her commitment in *Daniel Deronda* to the 'royalty of discernment and resolve'. Thus the starting point and the conclusion of George Eliot's didacticism are the same: she begins with a conviction that it is morally necessary to make clear and coherent judgments about values and she ends heroically, one might almost say wilfully, putting them into effect.

One implication of this entire endeavour, as was noted earlier, is the emphasis it places on the individual consciousness, the intensity of its focus on the human subject. The important human occasions are not events but acts, manifestations of selfhood and expressions of choice. Nor was there any way George Eliot could avoid the logic of such a teaching being applied to her own performances as a novelist. To the extent that she satisfied her own criteria of responsibility, she had herself to inform the whole corpus of thought and intuition suggested by her novels with an intimately personal sense of their consequences. Like the historian in her review of Mackay's *The*

Progress of the Intellect she had to make manifest in her own person and in their noblest form those processes of evolution, heredity, survival and fixed inexorable law which John Morley suggested the readers of her novels find themselves immersed in. Conditioned by a recognition of the self-expressive nature of art, her work could never be unconsciously self-revelatory like the preaching of Dinah Morris: *Romola*, by her own acount, could only be written out of her own 'varying unfolding self'.[1] This she found painfully embarrassing, but resisting that embarrassment was itself the kind of moral necessity which made the artistic endeavour exemplary. The alternative to the kind of exposure experienced by the artist was a dehumanizing isolation which could lead finally to madness. This is one of the major themes of *Impressions of Theophrastus Such*.

Apart from 'The Modern Hep! Hep! Hep!', which is seemingly written in George Eliot's own voice, among the best of these curiously fussy little essays and sketches, purportedly written by an eccentric but wise observer of the human scene, is 'How We Encourage Research', a piece about an amateur philologist and man of letters who has a strikingly original idea, the soundness of which is uncertain, but which is in any case very much at odds with the views of a prominent and influential professional scholar. In the ensuing controversy, the philologist is very shabbily treated by the press and the intellectual community, and unfortunately this arouses his combative and egoistical instincts, so that the controversy itself comes to absorb all his attention, and so destroys his life. The philologist's situation is thus comparable with that of the artist or the teacher: his effectiveness as a scholar and as a man depends on his own capacity to withstand the humiliations of public exposure, and on society's willingness to react sensitively to his susceptibilities. His problem is like Amos Barton's and Silas Marner's.

In the next piece, we are invited to examine weaknesses exactly the reverse of the philologist's. 'One Surprised at his Originality' is about a man altogether without ideas but entirely unaware of his own lack of originality or depth, who sustains his own good opinion of himself by never reading or talking at any length, 'the total privacy with which he [enjoys] his consciousness [being] the very condition of its undisturbed placid nourishment and gigantic growth' (p.78). Comparable cases are those of a young dissenter who marries into a fashionable, sceptical world in which he is inhibited from communicating the idealistic enthusiasms of his youth, and a writer who continues to think of himself as a remarkable young man even when he is 40. The ex-dissenter's problem is uncertainty in the presence of others about his own selfhood:

in his most unreserved moments of friendly intercourse, even when speaking to listeners whom he thinks likely to sympathise with the earlier part of his career, he presents himself in all his various aspects and feels himself in turn what he has been, what he is, and what others take him to be (for this last is what we must all more or less accept) (p. 139).

The moral of the piece is in this last point. The perennially youthful writer, on the other hand, trapped in a self-image originally created by other people's judgments, not his own, is the reverse of the ex-dissenter: 'being strongly mirrored for himself in the remark of others, he [comes] to see his real characteristics as a dramatic part, a type to which his doings [are] always in correspondence' (pp. 179–80), and so he never accepts adult status. In all these cases subtly different kinds of exposure to the scrutiny of others and subtly different reactions to such exposure are at one and the same time the basis of moral health and a threat to it.

The logic of this situation, of course, applies to Theophrastus Such himself as much as it applies to his characters. The soundness of a writer's personality is measured by his reaction to the opinions of other people, among whom must be included his readers. The writer can never be superior to society. What he has to impart is continually qualified by his self-consciousness before those to whom he wishes to impart it. This Theophrastus Such explicitly acknowledges. 'I am . . . offering some slight confessions in an apologetic light', he declares, 'to indicate that if in my absence you dealt as freely with my unconscious weaknesses as I have dealt with the unconsious weaknesses of others, I should not feel . . . your freedom . . . an exceptional case of evil speaking . . . Let me', he continues, 'at least try to feel myself in the ranks with my fellow-men' (p. 7). Publication of his *Impressions* is Theophrastus Such's way of dealing with his own eccentricity, of escaping, even at the cost of self-exposure, the dangers of solipsism about which he writes so obsessively. It is surely appropriate to recognize the author behind the author in this case, at least to the extent of taking *Impressions of Theophrastus Such* as an indirect but explicit acknowledgment by George Eliot of the reader's right to 'deal with' the unconscious weaknesses revealed in her own performances as a writer.

The importance of being able to make an acknowledgment of this kind is suggested by the first of her two short stories, 'The Lifted Veil'. Significantly it was written between *Adam Bede* and *The Mill on the Floss*, when George Eliot's true identity was becoming publicly known. Haight has indeed suggested that its title may reflect 'the unsuccessful attempts to preserve her incognito'.[2] For Thale it is 'a parable of the artist, whose unusual sensibility and awareness of the thoughts of others alienate him from his kind'.[3] Knoepflmacher sees it as demonstrating George Eliot's 'self-division'.[4] Gillian Beer argues that it reflects George Eliot's 'intermittent doubts about her role as a maker of fictions',[5] and that Latimer's mind-reading and previsionary powers 'express the determinism and solipsism latent in the act of writing fiction. The single self of the writer can see within and beyond the characters . . . who exist only within his own creativity unless a relation can be engendered between writer and reader'.[6] This last point is clearly important in the present discussion. 'A Poet', the unhappy Latimer declares, 'pours forth his song and *believes* in the listening ear and answering soul' (ch.1). This suggests, however, that Latimer's condition is in fact the opposite of the artist's, since his degrading timidity prevents him from discussing his problems even with his friend Charles Meunier. The real barrier between him and humanity is not his visionary experience, but his inability to endure the exposure of talking about it. Indeed he may not have any preternatural powers at all. His childhood was hardly conducive to mental good health, and his special experiences, particularly his capacity to listen to other people's thoughts, are clinically suggestive of paranoia. The exposure and shame from which he shrinks, therefore, would appear to be essential components of a healthy life. George Eliot's *'jeu de melancolie'*[7] may read oddly and even unpleasantly, but 12 years after publishing it she still cared 'for the idea which it embodies and which justifies its painfulness'.[8] That idea, I suggest, is her conviction that exposure to the scrutiny of others is a necessary and humanizing experience. It would follow that for all its strangeness 'The Lifted Veil' is a fitting prelude to her public assumption of the role of novelist and teacher.

But if the relations between artist or teacher and the public are indeed an intense and exemplary form of the personal intercourse by which human nature achieves and sustains humanity, then it follows that lack of trust – trust of self and trust of others – must be judged a defect in art as well as life, a principle which George Eliot's own performance as an artist would seem to confirm. In the early fiction an implicit distrust of herself and her readers leads to her notoriously disingenuous interventions as male author, who in 'Janet's Repentance' recalls his feelings as a tail-coated youth convinced that Confirmation should be restricted to girls, and in *Adam Bede* actually prays that he may never seduce a girl like Hetty Sorrel. Such distrust of herself and the reader has specifiable literary effects such as the heavy rhetoric of *Adam Bede*, or something very like its opposite (in George Eliot's other short story, 'Brother Jacob'). The major difficulty with 'Brother Jacob' is the sardonic shallowness of its tone, which is clearly an index of George Eliot's unease with her plot and her characters: it acts as a continual reminder that we are not meant to take either all that seriously. Henry James preferred 'Brother Jacob' to 'The Lifted Veil',[9] and it has been defended recently as an allegory on the grounds that its 'realistic details support the symbolic narrative'.[10] But it is in realistic detail that the story is weak. How, for example, does the idiot brother manage to make his way, on his own, to David's shop? 'Brother Jacob', in short, is intolerably clumsy. It is also cold, trivial, and spiritually mean. In trying to ease the tension between naturalism and fable by diluting both, George Eliot makes her characters shallow and her plot a farce. She clearly lacks a working confidence in the reader's ability to react to material such as this with appropriate sophistication. She expects us to carp and to patronize.

This makes all the more remarkable the detachment and implicit confidence in the reader's powers which characterize the style of her next attempt to fuse naturalism and fable, *Silas Marner*. It will be recalled how automatically George Eliot's early reviewers adopted a patronizing, even contemptuous tone towards many of her characters, the provincial middle classes in *The Mill on the Floss*, or the rustics and servants in 'Mr Gilfil's Love-story' and *Silas Marner* itself. But George Eliot herself had a clearer sense of the reader's ability to respond to Raveloe and its people with a proper regard for complexities. The following description of Dolly Winthrop is representative:

> Mrs Winthrop was . . . in all respects a woman of scrupulous conscience, so eager for duties that life seemed to offer them too scantily unless she rose at half-past four, though this threw a scarcity of work over the more advanced hours of the morning, which it was a constant problem with her to remove. Yet she had not the vixenish temper which is sometimes supposed to be a necessary condition of such habits: she was a very mild, patient woman, whose nature it was to seek out all the sadder and more serious elements of life, and pasture her mind upon them (ch. 10).

In some respects the tone of this passage is reminiscent of 'The Lifted Veil', yet the values Dolly represents are the opposite of contemptible and the ironic placing of her goodness ultimately legitimizes what she and Silas have to say about Luck. It does so by showing us George Eliot herself trusting her readers to press beyond the kind of trivial response to humble characters which the reviewers assumed to be normal. In leaving us free to react in our own way to

Dolly's goodness, Mr Macey's intelligence and Priscilla's harsh good-heartedness, George Eliot exemplifies in her own procedures as a writer precisely that kind of open-ended 'trustening' which the fable as a whole seeks to enforce.

The kind of trust thus informing *Silas Marner* is essentially 'literary'. It is constituted in the sheer skill with which George Eliot avoids sacrificing her own urbanity or ours in celebrating Dolly's lack of it. Throughout her fiction, however, there is another and more burdensome kind of trust which she imposes on us and which is altogether more difficult to adjust to, if only because it is associated in our minds with her most serious deficiencies as a writer, that is with the mean-heartedness of 'Brother Jacob' or parts of *Felix Holt* on the one hand, and the overblown rhetoric of *Adam Bede* or *Romola* on the other. It is one thing, after all, to seek acceptance of one's characters while leaving the reader responsible for his own reactions to them; it is another to impose one's own personality upon him. This is a problem, it seems to me, which not even the eclectic and liberal flexibility of the best post-war English critical practice has been able adequately to cope with. An example of such flexibility is W. W. Robson's essay on 'Purely literary values', in which he argues for the relevance of an author's personality to a critical judgment of his work. Though 'we need not go outside [a novel] to infer it', Robson writes, '. . . it would be critical purism to maintain that our sense of [that personality] is not increased by our knowledge of the biographical facts; or that we ought, as critics, to try to keep this knowledge out of our minds'.[11] Even this apparently undoctrinaire approach, however, is inadequate to George Eliot's situation, and for reasons which Robson, himself advances for going as far as he does. He suggests that much 'theoretical system-building' (and he might now wish to include Marxist and structuralist criticism in this condemnation) '. . . springs from fear – fear of the greatness of literature, fear of ourselves or of our pupils, fear of sincerity whether in ourselves or others'.[12] But this kind of sincerity he is talking about is not 'that of "committed" (or propaganda) literature, which cannot of its very nature reflect the inward and intimate movements of the human will'. For him the 'relevant kind of sincerity is something that has to be *achieved* by inner discipline'.[13] And this is just the kind of sincerity which, so frequently, George Eliot lacks in her more self-revelatory moments, yet at just such moments, according to her own principles, she expects us to attend to her and judge her.

A painful example of such a moment occurs in *Adam Bede*, when she admits to feeling 'ready to crush' Hetty's beauty, 'for inability to comprehend the state of mind into which it throws' her (ch.7). However, the exact nature of the feeling confessed to here is obscured by the sexually ambiguous authorial persona, and our embarrassment is correspondingly difficult to place. With *The Mill on the Floss*, on the other hand, the presence (in the text) of George Eliot's varying unfolding self becomes more specifically meaningful. The story of Maggie's childhood, adolescence and young woman-hood was bound to seem self-revelatory to a public newly apprised of the author's identity, and George Eliot knew it. The little girl in the first chapter is obviously if only tentatively the narrator. Throughout the subsequent narrative Maggie's personal emotions and public notoriety continually verge on George Eliot's and veer away from it. The descriptions of Maggie's religious enthusiasms, her feeling for music, her reactions to the men who kiss her, were certain to be scrutinized for what they revealed of the author's own sensuousness and sensuality. The first chapter, moreover, not only shows us George Eliot observing her past self; in its direct address to the reader it registers her readiness to be observed as well. There is obviously an element of self-indulgence in the subsequent narrative, but at least to the extent that human physiology and the minutiae of domestic and local circumstance constitute the basis for George Eliot's awakened sense of the historical process in *The Mill on the Floss*, autobiographical reminiscences and intensities drawn from a provincial, pre-industrial past and deliberately exposed to the scrutiny of a Victorian metropolitan present must also be seen and judged as a serious attempt at historical self-location. Both ideologi-cally and personally, the attempt was insufficiently open. Neverthe-less, as we move through the novel's shifting perspectives we are permitted to glimpse George Eliot herself earnestly attempting to enact in her performance as a narrator the values she is committed to expressing.

Just such an authorial presence becomes an increasingly im-portant, and also an increasingly embarrassing, presence in her subsequent fictions. The difficulty this poses for the critic operating within Robson's frame of reference is that the acuteness of the embarrassment is often a measure of the courage, that is the self-consciousness, that went into writing them. This courage can be especially difficult to value adequately when it is associated with the weakest part of a fiction. The story of Tessa in *Romola* is an example. The redundancy of this part of the novel makes its inclusion particularly remarkable. Neither Romola's spiritual formation, nor either of the two plots is significantly advanced by it. Infidelity is not the cause of the breakdown of Romola's marriage, and in any case a far more appropriate kind of sexual misconduct is suggested by Tito's manner of greeting the young woman who admits him to Dolfo Spini's. But if Tessa is unnecessary, it follows that her inclusion in the novel represents a more or less deliberate choice, made at whatever level, and it suggests that in spite of the inconvenience and embarrassment that would result, George Eliot felt the need to include in her work one way or another the basic experiences of sex and birth. A related gratuitousness and a related courage can be detected in the presentation of Romola herself. George Eliot could have kept Romola's spiritual development at a discreet distance, as she does with such success in alluding to her physical relations with Tito. But this would have been inconsistent with her determination to register 'that intensity of life which seems to transcend both grief and joy – in which the mind seems to itself akin to elder forces that wrought out our existence before the birth of pleasure and pain' (ch.60). Such an effort necessarily involved her in an attempt to understand the bodies of her major characters as intimately as possible. Romola's second flight and semi-suicide are presented in strikingly physical terms. We are told that she 'longed for that repose in mere sensation which she had sometimes dreamed of in the sultry afternoons of her early girlhood, when she had fancied herself floating naiad-like on the waters' (ch.61). In the light of Tito's wish that she should enjoy the 'happiness of the nymphs', the sexual component of this longing is undisguised. Again, when she puts to sea in conscious imitation of Boccaccio's Gostanza, the fact that the *Decamerone* had been burned as salacious in the Pyramid of Vanities cannot have been entirely absent from George Eliot's mind. Finally, in the description of the 'soft warmth' of the sun penetrating 'Romola's young limbs' as she lies asleep in the boat, there is a further implicit suggestion that her experiences *in extremis* are in a broad and restorative sense erotic.

It would seem, then, that behind the evasiveness of the plotting and psychology of *Romola* there is a concealed openness, a secretive impulse to tell the truth. The novel suggests, if only implicitly, that the great spiritual endeavours of mankind cannot after all be considered separately from the commonplaces of sex, birth and extreme physical endeavour. This in no way excuses what must be called the great vice of the novel, its elaborate transformation of Romola's will into mere process, a transformation which brings George Eliot's own will most tangibly and uncomfortably into play, especially at the climax of the novel. From the point of view of orthodox liberal criticism this element of deliberation in *Romola* is what is wrong with the novel, since it fails to reflect those 'inward and intimate movements of the . . . will' which Robson defends as a central literary value. George Eliot's indifference to logic and decorum in *Romola*, her refusal to accept the composure and caution required by a rationalist, determinist, post-Christian world-view, are thus on several counts indefensible. Nevertheless there is a lot of evidence that her obstinate determination to stress the importance of heroic spiritual endeavour in a world that was coming to distrust it gave her the imaginative energy to break out of the rich but limited completeness of *Silas Marner* into the radical and generous comprehensiveness of *Middlemarch* and *Daniel Deronda*.

Middlemarch is in some respects George Eliot's most important confessional work, and the extent and significance of its revelations are closely connected with the comparison of Dorothea to Teresa of Avila, that is to a Catholic saint who had been notoriously depicted by Crashaw and Bernini in the throes of sexually compromising ecstasy. The introduction of such a figure into the ambience of Mrs Cadwallader is particularly remarkable. Teresa herself, after all, could write of her soul being

> pierced to the depths of its entrails, or sometimes to the heart, by an arrow, so that it does not know what is wrong or what it desires. It knows quite well that it desires God, and that the arrow seems to have been tipped with some poison which makes it so hate itself out of love of the Lord that it is willing to give up its life for Him.[14]

Even more relevant to Dorothea and Will is the angel whose coming forms the subject of Bernini's sculpture:

> He was not tall but short, and very beautiful; and his face was so aflame that he appeared to be one of the highest rank of angels, who seem to be all on fire . . . In his hands I saw a great golden spear, and at the iron tip there appeared to be a point of fire. This he plunged into my heart several times so that it penetrated to my entrails. When he pulled it out, I felt that he took them with it, and left me utterly consumed by the great love of God. The pain was so severe that it made me utter several moans. The sweetness caused by this intense pain is so extreme that one cannot possibly wish it to cease, nor is one's soul then content with anything but God.[15]

We can be certain that the mistress of the implicit sexual imagery in Lydgate's proposal scene and Dorothea's experiences in Rome would have seen the implications of such symbolism even if Teresa herself, St John of the Cross, and later commentators on their life and work had not made it explicitly, even notoriously well known. Thus the rationalizations about sexuality in *Middlemarch* shape themselves in the context of a clearly seen appreciation of possible connexions between sexuality and supreme spiritual endeavour. George Eliot did not, of course, think of the latter as an inhibited or deflected manifestation of the former – for her that would not have been to think scientifically but cynically, in the fashion of Mrs Cadwallader. But she undoubtedly realized when she invoked the Teresan tradition in Dorothea's case that the judgment would be made by others. She had therefore to trust in their capacity to reach beyond their first thoughts towards nobler conclusions.

She must also have known that Dorothea would be identified with herself. In seeing Dorothea as 'a product of George Eliot's own "soul-hunger"', F. R. Leavis was mistaken only in assuming that the 'alteration between . . . poised impersonal insight'[16] in the novel and embarrassing identifications with her central character was invisible to George Eliot. But she can hardly have been ignorant of what she was about when she gave Dorothea her own most impressive physical quality, that voice which F.W.H. Myers was to describe as having a 'subdued intensity and tremulous richness [which] seemed to environ her uttered words with . . . mystery'.[17] *Middlemarch*, in short, is an intense act of authorial self-consciousness, the cynical misinterpretations of which by her more sophisticated readers George Eliot must have been able clearly and painfully to anticipate. (Her discriminating young acquaintance, Henry James, suggested that after marrying Casaubon, Dorothea would probably have chosen a hussar for her second husband.[18]) But as she had done with increasing intensity in nearly all her fiction, George Eliot covered her face with the embarrassment inherent in writing as she did, and defiantly insisted on the supreme importancce of the spiritual life, however common minds might interpret it. One cannot claim poise, wisdom or aesthetic success for this defiance. F.R. Leavis's strictures on the artistic deficiencies of *Middlemarch* stand. Personal and ideological dishonesties damage the novel's coherence, and the resulting confusions are not treated with impersonal wisdom or honest doubt, but are clumsily circumvented by tedious explanation and over-plotting. In standing by embarrassing opinions and in making the strongest possible claims for the inner lives of women like Dorothea, or Teresa, or herself, George Eliot effectively betrays the shared, impersonal urbanity which we find in the most appreciated parts of her fiction, from the description of Amos Barton preaching in the workhouse to the carefully reticent and supremely subtle study of Mrs Bulstrode in *Middlemarch*. Yet it is when she offends against taste, sense and honesty in this way, when her writing is ugly, her analysis slack and her sentiments possibly corrupt, that she demands, according to her own principles, a special kind of critical attention. Such moments are the testing ground of a trust between her readers and herself which is far more significant than is possible in a successful exchange of literary pleasure, however rich and humane. Reading the novels should, therefore, exact from us, as writing them plainly exacted from her, a real, unliterary testing of the will – of our capacity to accept, respect, and even *submit to* the fatality of her inner life.

The word 'fatality' is crucial. George Eliot undoubtedly saw herself as an intricate synthesis of personal determinations in a world physically, psychologically and socially no less intricately determined; for her all human performances are characterized by process as well as by choice. Much of our sense of Rousseau's character, Theophrastus Such observes, comes 'not from what he means to convey, but from what he unconsciously enables us to discern' (p.7). Thus at the heart of the writer's performances there is a willingness to surrender to the 'elder forces' of his being. George Eliot accepts loss of control as an essential if paradoxical component of keeping it in art and in life, she also knows that the kind of indiscipline thus revealed in her work may be personally compromising. And it is. There is a haphazard quality about some of the images of cruelty in *Daniel Deronda*, for example, which prevents their being justified in terms of any clear didactic or aesthetic purpose. Thus Mirah is so distressed at the suggestion of a possible intimacy between Daniel and Gwendolen that she is compared to creatures who 'in intense pain bite and make their teeth meet even through their own flesh, by way of making their agony bearable' (ch.61). Mordecai is savage in a comparable way when he says to Lapidoth –

> That such a man [as you] is our father is a brand on our flesh, which will not cease smarting. But . . . though human justice were to flog you for crimes, and your body fell helpless before public scorn we would still say, 'This is our father . . .' (ch.66).

The three principal Jewish characters in *Daniel Deronda* are thus permitted to think, feel and act with implicit but intense violence towards themselves and towards others, and this is taken unthinkingly as a sign of the ferocity of their virtue rather than the ultimate complication in their moral lives. Similar judgments could be made about Janet Dempster, Dinah Morris, Maggie Tulliver, Romola, Felix Holt and Dorothea Brooke. Cruelty and retribution take extreme forms in all George Eliot's work. Even the mild Theophrastus Such writes approvingly of 'the horsewhip when applied to the back of Cruelty' and of his belief 'that he who applies it is a more perfect human being because his outleap of indignation is not checked by a too curious reflection on the nature of guilt' (p.189) – a sentiment calculated to produce an infinitely extended line of flagellation. Even in the essays and reviews there are passages which focus on such images with ill-judged intensity,[19] while in the novels images of flesh being flogged, cut, burnt or bitten are almost commonplace. In all her writing George Eliot unwittingly displays an intimate acquaintance with Thanatos.

What is important about such moments in her work, however, is not what they might suggest to the analyst, but the lack of caution they reveal in George Eliot's procedures as an author. She writes without blandness, discretion, or self-protective irony – and she does so deliberately. Her work is thereby constituted in Neccessity or Submission to process on the one hand, and choice or discernment in resolve on the other. In their own formation the novels intimately and honestly exemplify the basic dilemma which is their main concern didactically – discernment of the laws of necessity and resolution in spite of them to conduct one's life in their light. It is George Eliot's consciousness of this tension in her relationship with her vast readership which I believe constitutes the essence of her teaching.

This brings me to a final point. The emphasis on the explicitness of that teaching and the deliberation of her performance as an artist and a teacher which has characterized this study is clearly at variance with the current practice of liberal literary criticism. It is no less inconsistent with the assumptions of Althusser, Macherey, Eagleton and other Marxist critics about the nature of literary production. The weakness of such criticism, however, from a precisely Marxist point of view, is that it turns the text-as-ideological-product into a kind of fetish. The result, as far as George Eliot is concerned, is an entirely unjustified reduction of her teaching to a mere message, a trivially organicist moral. To argue, as Eagleton does, that the 'ideological matrix of George Eliot's fiction is set by the *increasingly* corporate character of Victorian capitalism and its political apparatus'[20] (my italics) is to make a degrading conclusion to her career virtually inevitable. It is no surprise to find that Eagleton ends his analysis with a quotation from *Impressions of Theophrastus Such* which purports to demonstrate that the 'corporate society which in *Daniel Deronda* remained a goal to be realized, and so an idealist critique of contemporary England, has now become an effusive celebration of the *status quo*. The voice of liberal humanism has become the voice of jingoist reaction'.[21] Such rigorously exclusive attention to the ideological matrix, however, renders invisible how George Eliot herself acts in her own writing, as against what, at a relatively superficial level, she may be thought to be saying. It ignores the extent to which she is both the signifier and the signified in her own work. And as long as the literary text is thus seen primarily as a product rather than as a practice, critics like Kettle will continue to think of her as a writer who failed to see herself as a character in history.[22]

In this connexion I find a certain relevance in Althusser's comments on Lenin's writings on the 1917 Revolution. 'Lenin', Althusser wrote, 'meets Imperialism in his political practice in the modality of a *current* existence: in a concrete present. The Theoretician of history or the historian meet in another modality, the modality of non-currency and abstraction'.[23] George Eliot's literary practice may be seen as approximating more to the former than to the latter. As a practice in the modality of a *current* existence her specifically literary didacticism differs from the teaching of a theoretician. She is a character in that real history in which her books were not only produced but read, and this relationship is as much part of her meaning as her implied relations with the 'history' of which she writes in those books. She knew perfectly well that she was acting on a social present, and this gives relevance to her intentions. Her novels will and specify a relationship, at once intimate and uncompromisingly didactic, with a real and current mass audience. She and they are similarly trapped by circumstances and opinion – that is by history and ideology – but the modality of current existence, the historically specific confusion, anxiety, folly and vice in which she and her readers find themselves – is transcended by a literary practice through which her attitude towards them acquires fundamental importance. For in choosing to regard them as being capable of responding to her work with a freedom comparable to her own, in thinking of them as well as of herself in terms of freedom as well as necessity, she creates the essential conditions for the true didacticism which she describes in her famous letter to Frederic Harrison. She thereby makes reading her work an act of incalculable historical as well as personal importance.

The most sympathetic portrait we have of her, in my opinion, is the sketch done at a charity concert by the Princess Louise. It suggests the dilemma her felt personality poses to the readers of her fiction. It is unique among her portraits in suggesting a mind at once vacant and at work. Her back is very straight, her chin thrust slightly forward giving a look of graceful strength to her heavy jaw and nose. Her mouth, sealed and unsmiling, is nevertheless relaxed, and her eyes, suggesting assurance and concentration, make a perfect image of eminent Victorian womanhood in full public view. For that very reason, the intelligent sensitivity evident in it is disturbing as well as vulnerable, suggesting repressions, at times quite brutal repressions, of herself and others, which would make the appearance of passionate openness to the music especially doubtful. It is by no means obvious that we should accept such a personality as that of a great moralist. It will be George Eliot's vindication as a teacher if she can finally persuade her readers to reach beyond prevailing notions of both art and criticism in order to attempt just such an acceptance.

Notes

NOTE

Places of publication are given only for works published in the United Kingdom.

All references to George Eliot's letters are to *The George Eliot Letters*, ed. G.S. Haight (7 vols., 1954–6), cited throughout as *Letters:* references to her essays are to *Essays of George Eliot*, ed. T. Pinney (1963), cited as *Essays*, unless otherwise indicated. Quotations from George Eliot's fiction and verse, and from *Impressions of Theophrastus Such*, are from the Cabinet Edition (1878–80). Chapter references to the fiction and page references to the poems and sketches are given parenthetically in the text; chapter references follow the usual modern enumeration.

INTRODUCTION

1. *Letters*, IV, 300.
2. J. Morley, *Critical Miscellanies* (3 vols., 1886), III, 127.
3. *'George Eliot Moralist and Thinker', Round Table Series II* (1884), 3.
4. *Ibid.*, 3–5.
5. *Ibid.*, 6.
6. W. Baker, 'A new George Eliot manuscript', in *George Eliot: Centenary Essays and an Unpublished Fragment*, ed. A. Smith (1980), 10–11.
7. See H. Spencer, *The Principles of Psychology* (1855), 437.
8. See *Ibid.*, 339–487.
9. See *Ibid.*, 491–620.
10. J. Mill, *Analysis of the Phenomena of the Human Mind* (2 vols., 1869 edn), I, ix.
11. A. Bain, *The Senses and the Intellect* (1855), 1.
12. See *ibid.*, 6.
13. A. Bain, *The Emotions and the Will* (1859), 10.
14. *The Senses and the Intellect*, 331.
15. Detailed references to Comte's thought are given in later chapters.
16. L. Feuerbach, *The Essence of Christianity*, trans. George Eliot (Harper Books edn, 1957), 20.
17. *Ibid.*, 179.
18. *Ibid.*, 12.
19. See *Ibid.*, 66.
20. *George Eliot. The Critical Heritage*, ed. D. Carrol (1971), 498.
21. Republished in F.R. Leavis, *The Great Tradition* (1948).
22. I am thinking of the treatment of George Eliot's ideas in, for example, D. Daiches, *George Eliot. Middlemarch* (Studies in English Literature No. 11, 1963); Q.D. Leavis, 'Introduction' to George Eliot, *Silas Marner. The Weaver of Raveloe* (Penguin Books edn, 1967); and M. Green, *Yeats's Blessings on Von Hügel. Essays on Literature and Religion* (1967).
23. Throughout this book I rely particularly on the following: B. Hardy, *The Novels of George Eliot* (1959); J. Thale, *The Novels of George Eliot* (1959); W.J.

Harvey, *The Art of George Eliot* (1961); J. Bennett, *George Eliot. Her Mind and Her Art* (1962); and contributors to the following collections of essays; *Middlemarch. Critical Approaches to the Novel*, ed. B. Hardy (1967); *Critical Essays on George Eliot*, ed. B. Hardy (1970); *This Particular Web. Essays on Middlemarch*, ed. I. Adam (1975); and *George Eliot: Centenary Essays*, ed. A. Smith (1980).

24. In *Critical Essays on George Eliot*, 151–98.
25. *Ibid.*, 153.
26. *Ibid.*, 158.
27. The most important studies in this connexion are B. Willey, *Nineteenth Century Studies. Coleridge to Matthew Arnold* (1950); B.J. Paris, *Experiments in Life: George Eliot's Quest for Values* (Detroit, 1965); and F. Bonaparte, *Will and Destiny. Morality and Tragedy in George Eliot's Novels* (New York, 1975). The latter, however, is a book with which I find myself in constant disagreement, mainly because its concentration on a few leading ideas in George Eliot's world-view leads to conclusions which detailed study appears to contradict.
28. Some of the most interesting work of this kind has been published in the collections of essays listed in n.23 above. In addition the following are of special interest: J. Weisenforth, 'Demythologizing *Silas Marner*', *English Literary History*, XXXVII (1970), 226–44; B. Swann, '*Middlemarch*: realism and symbolic form', *ELH*, XXXIX (1972), 279–308; W. Baker, *George Eliot and Judaism* (Salzburg, 1975); J. Hillis Miller, 'Optic and semiotic in *Middlemarch*', in *The World of Victorian Fiction* (Harvard English Studies 6), ed. J.H. Buckley (1975); B. Swann, '"Silas Marner" and the new myths', *Criticism*, XVIII (1976), 102–21; K.K. Collins, 'G.H. Lewes revised. George Eliot and the moral sense', *Victorian Studies*, XXI (1977–78) 463–83; A. Minz, *George Eliot and the Novel of Vocation* (1978); H. Witemeyer, *George Eliot and the Visual Arts* (1979), F. Bonaparte, *The Triptych and the Cross. The Central Myths of George Eliot's Poetic Imagination* (1979) – an excellent study – and M.P. Ginsburg, 'Pseudonym, epigraphs and narrative voice: *Middlemarch* and the problem of authorship', *ELH*, XLVII (1980), 542–58.
29. I have found the following works of most interest in this field: U.C. Knoepflmacher, *Religious Humanism in the Victorian Novel, George Eliot, Walter Pater, and Samuel Butler* (1965); L. Lerner, *The Truthtellers. Jane Austen, George Eliot, D.H. Lawrence* (1967); W.H. Marshall, *The World of the Victorian Novel* (1967); B. Smale, *George Eliot and Flaubert. Pioneers of the Modern Novel* (Athens, Ohio, 1974); J. King, *Tragedy in the Victorian Novel. Theory and Practice in the Novels of George Eliot, Thomas Hardy and Henry James* (1978); J. Wilt, *Ghosts of the Gothic, Austen, Eliot, and Lawrence* (Princeton, N.J., 1980); G. Levine, *The Realistic Imagination. English Fiction from Frankenstein to Lady Chatterley* (1981).
30. See G.S. Haight, *George Eliot, A Biography* (1969), 460 *et passim*.
31. See A. Kitchell, *Quarry for Middlemarch* (1950); J. Beaty, '*Middlemarch' from Notebook to Novel* (1960); W. Baker (ed.), *Some George Eliot Notebooks: An Edition of the Carl H. Pforzheimer Library's George Eliot Holograph Notebooks, MSS 707, 708, 710, 711* (Salzburg, 1976—); *The George Eliot-George Henry Lewes Library: An Annotated Catalogue of the books at Dr Williams's Library*, London (1977); *The Libraries of George Eliot* (*English Literary Studies* Monograph Series No. 24, 1981); J.C. Pratt and V.A. Neufeldt, *George Eliot's Middlemarch Notebooks. A Transcription* (1979).
32. See in particular U.C. Knoepflmacher, *Religious Humanism and the Victorian Novel*; G. Levine, *The Realistic Imagination*; and various essays in the collections cited in n.23 above.
33. See, for example, U.C. Knoepflmacher, *George Eliot's Early Novels. The Limits of Realism* (Berkeley and Los Angeles, 1968); B. Paris, *A Psychological Approach to Fiction. Studies in Thackeray, Stendhal, George Eliot, Dostoevsky, and Conrad* (1974),

R. Rediger, *George Eliot: The Emergent Self* (New York, 1975); Wilt, *op.cit.*; L. Comer Emery, *George Eliot's Creative Conflict. The Other Side of Silence* (1976).

34.   J. Derrida, *Writing and Difference*, trans. with an Introduction and Additional Notes by A. Bass (1978), 226–7.

35.   K. Wojtyła (Pope John Paul II), *The Acting Person* (1979), 8.

1. MORALITY AND RELIGION

1.   'The creed of Christendom', *Leader*, III *(1851)*, *899*.
2.   *Essays*, 413.
3.   *The Essence of Christianity*, trans. George Eliot (Harper Books edn, 1957) 114.
4.   A. Comte, *System of Positive Polity, or Treatise on Sociology, Instituting the Religion of Humanity* (4 vols., 1875–7), IV, 44.
5,   *Ibid.*, II, 17.
6.   *Ibid.*, IV, 44.
7.   *Essays*, 400.
8.   *Ibid.*, 402.
9.   *Ibid.*, 407.
10.   *Ibid.*, 409.
11.   *Ibid.*, 218.
12.   H. Spencer, *Autobiography* (2 vols., 1904), II, 469.
13.   *Letters*, III, 227.
14.   *System of Positive Polity*, IV, 34–5.
15.   A. Comte, *Appeal to Conservatives*, joint trans. D.C. Donkin and R. Congreve (1889), 48–9.
16.   *Essays*, 160.
17.   *Ibid.*, 172.
18.   See D. and S. Oldfield, 'Scenes of Clerical Life', and J. Goode, 'Adam Bede', in *Critical Essays on George Eliot*, ed. B. Hardy (1970).
19.   *The Essence of Christianity*, 60.
20.   In *Critical Essays on George Eliot*, 34.
21.   *Ibid.*, 37.
22.   J. Wesley, *Letter on Preaching Christ*, quoted in V. Cunningham, *Everywhere Spoken Against. Dissent in the Victorian Novel* (1975), 151.
23.   See *ibid.*, 8–18.
24.   *The Essence of Christianity*, 21.
25.   G.H. Lewes, *The Study of Psychology* (Problems of Life and Mind, Third Series, Problem the First) (1879), 146.
26.   *The Essence of Christianity*, 12.
27.   H. Crabb Robinson, *On Books and their Writers*, ed. E.J. Morley (3 vols., 1938), II, 787.
28.   See H. Spencer, 'The Origins and Function of Music', *Essays Scientific, Political and Speculative* (3 vols., 1858, 1863, 1875), I; *The Essence of Christianity*, 3–5.
29.   *Letters*, II, 504.
30.   *The Essence of Christianity*, 313.
31.   A. Comte, *The Catechism of Positivism; or Summary Exposition of the Universal Religion* (1858), 21.
32.   See G.S. Haight, *George Eliot, A Biography* (1969), 250–1.
33.   *The Essence of Christianity*, 60.
34.   *Ibid.*, 278.

2. HEREDITY AND PSYCHOLOGY

1.   *Essays*, 53.

2. *Ibid.*, 55.
3. 'Belles Lettres and Art', *Westminster Rev.*, LXVI, 269.
4. *System of Positive Polity, or Treatise on Sociology, Instituting the Religion of Humanity* (4 vols., 1875–7), I, 335.
5. *The Emotions and the Will* (1859), 287.
6. *Ibid.*, 313.
7. *The Essence of Christianity*, trans. George Eliot (Harper Books edn, 1957) 46.
8. *System of Positive Polity*, I, 431.
9. *The Emotions and the Will* (1859), 130–1.
10. *System of Positive Polity*, II, 311; see also *ibid.*, II, 373 and III, 17–19.
11. *The Senses and the Intellect* (1855), 338.
12. See 'Dickens in relation to criticism', *Fortnightly Rev.*, XVII (1872), 141–54.
13. *The Senses and the Intellect*, 78–9.
14. *The Senses and the Intellect* (3rd rev. edn, 1868), 342–3.
15. *The Emotions and the Will*, 35.
16. *Ibid.*, 437.
17. *The Essence of Christianity*, 186.
18. *Letters*, III, 382.
19. *The Senses and the Intellecct*, 234.
20. *A Century of George Eliot Criticism*, ed. G.S. Haight (1966 edn), 52.
21. *Essays Scientific, Political and Speculative*, (3 vols., 1858, 1863, 1875) II, 355.
22. *System of Positive Polity*, II, 179.
23. *Ibid.*, I, 104.
24. *Essays on Education and Kindred Subjects* (Everyman's Library edn), 1911, 108.
25. See *Essays*, 274.
26. See *Essays Scientific, Political and Speculative*, I, 10.
27. See *The Positive Philosophy of Auguste Comte*, freely trans. and condensed by H. Martineau (2 vols., 1853), II, 7.
28. See 'Uncivilised man', *Blackwood's Mag.* (Jan. 1861), 32.
29. *The Emotions and the Will*, 157.
30. *Ibid.*, 346.
31. See *ibid.*, 128–9.
32. *The Senses and the Intellect*, 398.
33. *Ibid.*, 397.
34. *The Positive Philosophy*, II, 151.
35. *Ibid.*, II, 135.
36. *Ibid.*, II, 138.
37. *The Essence of Christianity*, 72.
38. *Essays*, 213.
39. *Essays on Education and Kindred Subjects*, 46.
40. *Ibid.*, 81.
41. *Ibid.*, 51.
42. *System of Positive Polity*, IV, 20.
43. *Ibid.*, II, 26.
44. *The Emotions and the Will*, 130.
45. *Ibid.*, 95.

3. HISTORY AND EVOLUTION

1. *Essays*, 336.
2. Quoted in J.W. Burrow, *Evolution and Society: A Study in Victorian Social Theory* (1966), 128.
3. *The Principles of Psychology*, 465.
4. *Essays*, 274.

5. *Ibid.*, 278.
6. *System of Positive Polity, or Treatise on Sociology, Instituting the Religion of Humanity* (4 vols., 1875–7), III, 37.
7. *Ibid.*, III, 20.
8. See *The Positive Philosophy of Auguste Comte*, freely trans. and condensed by H. Martineau (2 vols., 1853), I, 4.
9. *The Essence of Christianity*, trans. George Eliot (Harper Books edn, 1957), 186.
10. *System of Positive Polity*, III, 19–20.
11. *Essays*, 403.
12. *The Positive Philosophy*, II, 369.
13. *The Essence of Christianity*, 131–2.
14. *The Positive Philosophy*, II, 217.
15. *System of Positive Polity*, II, 142.
16. *Ibid.*, II, 184.
17. *Ibid.*, II, 191.
18. *Ibid.*, II, 199.
19. *The Senses and the Intellect* (3rd edn, 1858), 358–9.
20. *System of Positive Polity*, III, 462.
21. *The Positive Philosophy*, II, 343.
22. *Ibid.*, II, 261.
23. *Ibid.*, II, 262.
24. *Ibid.*, IV, 263.
25. *Ibid.*, II, 264.
26. *Ibid.*, II, 295.
27. *System of Positive Polity*, II, 262.
28. *Ibid.*, II, 339.
29. *The Positive Philosophy*, II, 47.
30. *The Essence of Christianity*, 194.
31. *Ibid.*, 209.
32. J. Bennett, *George Eliot. Her Mind and Her Art* (1962), 119.
33. B. Hardy, 'The Mill on the Floss', in *Critial Essays on George Elitot*, ed. B. Hardy (1970), 46.
34. *Essays*, 29.
35. *Critical Essays on George Eliot*, 48.
36. T. Eagleton, *Criticism and Ideology. A Study in Marxist Literary Theory* (1976), 116.

4. POLITICS AND CLASS

1. *A Century of George Eliot Criticism*, ed. G.S. Haight (1966 edn), 159.
2. *Essays*, 421-2.
3. *Ibid.*, 424.
4. A. Comte, *Subjective Synthesis, or Universal System of Conceptions adapted to the Normal State of Humanity* (First Volume, 1891), 4.
5. *System of Positive Polity, or Treastise on Sociology, Instituting the Religion of Humanity* (4 vols., 1875–7), III, 523.
6. *Essays*, 425.
7. See *The Positive Philosophy of Auguste Comte*, freely trans. and condensed by H. Martineau (2 vols., 1853), II, 12–20.
8. *Ibid.*, I, 27.
9. See *ibid.*, II, 30.
10. *Ibid.*, II, 454.
11. *The Catechism of Positivism; or Summary Exposition of the Universal Religion* (1858), 2.

12. *Appeal to Conservatives*, joint trans. D.C. Donkin and R. Congreve (1889), 5.
13. *The Positive Philosophy*, I, 463.
14. *Ibid.*, II, 467.
15. See *Essays*, 282–3.
16. P. Coveney, 'Introduction', *Felix Holt, the Radical* (Penguin Books edn, 1972), 63.
17. *System of Positive Polity*, III, 147.
18. *Felix Holt*, ed. cit., 32.
19. *Letters*, IV, 215.
20. *The Positive Philosophy*, II, 325.
21. See V. Cunningham, *Everywhere Spoken Against. Dissent in the Victorian Novel* (1975), 172–3.
22. *Ibid.*, 188.
23. *System of Positive Polity*, I, 71.
24. B. Hardy, *The Novels of George Eliot* (1959), 62.
25. R. Liddell, *The Novels of George Eliot* (1977), 41.
26. *Felix Holt*, ed. cit., 35.
27. *Essays*, 426.
28. *George Eliot, The Critical Heritage*, ed. D. Carrol (1971), 275.
29. A. Kettle, 'Felix Holt the Radical', in *Critical Essays on George Eliot*, ed. B. Hardy (1970), 109.
30. *George Eliot, The Critical Heritage*, 427.

5. ART AND VISION

1. *George Eliot, The Critical Heritage*, ed. D. Carrol (1971), 179.
2. *A Century of George Eliot Criticism*, ed. G.S. Haight (1966 edn), 46.
3. *George Eliot, The Critical Heritage*, 214.
4. *Ibid.*, 208.
5. *Essays*, 268–9.
6. *Ibid.*, 270.
7. 'Art and Belles Lettres', *Westminster Rev.*, LXX (1856), 626.
8. *The Positive Philosophy of Auguste Comte*, freely trans. and condensed by H. Martineau (2 vols., 1853), II, 247.
9. *Fortnightly Rev.*, I (1865), 24.
10. *System of Positive Polity, or Treatise on Sociology, Instituting the Religion of Humanity* (4 vols., 1875–7), I, 253.
11. *Ibid.*, I, 228.
12. *Appeal to Conservatives*, joint trans. D.C. Donkin and R. Congreve (1889), 59.
13. *Letters*, IV, 300.
14. See G. Levine, '"Romola" as fable', in *Critical Essays on George Eliot*, ed. B. Hardy (1970), 78–98.
15. *System of Positive Polity*, III, 408.
16. *The Essence of Christianity*, trans. George Eliot (Harper Books edn, 1957), 208.

6. THEORY AND PRACTICE

1. K. Marx, 'Theses on Feuerbach', K. Marx and F. Engels, *On Religion* (Moscow, [n.d.]), 69–72.
2. *Essays*, 272.
3. See, for instance, *The Positive Philosophy of Auguste Comte*, freely trans. and condensed by H. Martineau (2 vols., 1853) I, 11 and II, 463.
4. *Essays*, 329.
5. 'Belles Lettres', *Westminster Rev.* LXVI (1856), 307.

6. *Essays*, 283.
7. *Ibid.*, 285.
8. *Ibid.*, 384.
9. *Ibid.*, 398.
10. *Ibid.*, 416.
11. *Ibid.*, 420.
12. *Ibid.*, 423.
13. *Ibid.*, 425.
14. G.S. Haight, *George Eliot, A Biography* (1969), 395.
15. *Ibid.*, 382.
16. 'Adam Bede', in *Critical Essays on George Eliot*, ed. B. Hardy (1970), 36.
17. *Ibid.*, 25.
18. *Ibid.*, 26.
19. *Ibid.*, 29.
20. *Ibid.*, 34.
21. See I. Gregor and B. Nicholas, *The Moral and the Story* (1962), 17.
22. See 'Looking Backward', *Impressions of Theophrastus Such*, 42.
23. D. Craig, *The Real Foundations. Literature and Social Change* (1974), 134.
24. *Ibid.*, 136.
25. W. Allen, *George Eliot* (1965), 159.
26. Q. Anderson, 'George Eliot in Middlemarch', in *From Dickens to Hardy* (Pelican Guide to English Literature 6), ed. B. Ford (1958), 285.
27. G. Martin, '"Daniel Deronda": George Eliot and political change', in *Critical Essays on George Eliot*, 140.
28. Quoted by W.J. Harvey, 'Criticism of the novel. Contemporary reception', in *Middlemarch. Critical Approaches to the Novel*, ed. B. Hardy (1970), 47.
29. D. Daiches, *George Eliot. Middlemarch* (Studies in English Literature No. 11, 1963), 47.
30. *Letters*, V, 168.

7. MALADY OF CONSCIENCE

1. F. Nietzsche, *Twilight of the Idols*, *The Portable Nietzsche*, sel. and trans. with an Introduction, Preface, and Notes by W. Kaufmann, (New York, 1968), 515.
2. F. Nietzsche, *The Birth of Tragedy* and *The Genealogy of Morals*, trans. F. Golffing (New York, 1956), 167.
3. *Ibid.*, 257.
4. *Ibid.*, 265.
5. *Ibid.*, 294.
6. *Ibid.*, 285–6.
7. *Ibid.*, 287.
8. *Ibid.*, 299.
9. *Ibid.*, 190–1.
10. *Ibid.*, 158.
11. *Ibid.*, 273.
12. *Ibid.*, 292.
13. *Ibid.*, 272.
14. *Ibid.*, 221.
15. *Ibid.*, 217.
16. *Ibid.*, 219.
17. *Ibid.*, 226.
18. *Ibid.*, 153.
19. *Ibid.*, 254.
20. *The Essence of Christianity*, trans. George Eliot (Harper Books edn, 1957), 13.

21. *The Senses and the Intellect* (3rd edn, 1858), 1.
22. *The Essence of Christianity*, 59.
23. *Essays*, 264.
24. B. Hardy, *The Appropriate Form. An Essay on the Novel* (1964), 106.
25. *The Genealogy of Morals*, 299.

8. LUST AND ANGER

1. S. Freud, *Civilization and Its Discontents*, trans. and ed. J. Strachey (1962 edn), 74.
2. *Ibid.*, 44.
3. *Ibid.*, 87.
4. *Ibid.*, 68.
5. *The Emotions and the Will* (1859), 150.
6. *Ibid.*, 159.
7. *Ibid.*, 167.
8. J. Lacan, *Écrits. A Selection*, trans. from the French by A. Sheridan (1977), 25–6.
9. *Ibid.*, 6.
10. *Ibid.*, 19.
11. *Civilization and Its Discontents*, 12.
12. *George Eliot. The Critical Heritage*, ed. D. Carrol (1971), 474.
13. *The Emotions and the Will*, 96.
14. *Ibid.*, 95.
15. *George Eliot. The Critical Heritage*, 214.
16. *Essays*, 21.
17. Lacan, *Écrits*, 5.
18. *Ibid.*, 2.
19. *Ibid.*, 28.
20. *Ibid.*, 27.
21. *Ibid.*, 4.
22. *Ibid.*, 137.
23. *Ibid.*, 5.
24. *Ibid.*, 6.
25. *Ibid.*, 24.
26. *Ibid.*, 104.
27. *Ibid.*, 105.
28. *Ibid.*, 10.
29. *Ibid.*, 16.
30. *Ibid.*, 25.

9. CONTEXTS OF UNCERTAINTY

1. F. Nietzsche, *The Genealogy of Morals*, trans. F. Golffing (New York, 1956), 255.
2. *Ibid.*, 236.
3. *Ibid.*, 235.
4. 'Belles Lettres', *Westminster Rev.*, LXVI (1856), 307.
5. *Essays*, 263.
6. *Ibid.*, 264.
7. 'Heine's poems', *Leader*, VI (1855), 843.
8. *Essays*, 220.
9. *Ibid.*, 224.
10. *Ibid.*, 245.

11. *Ibid.*, 230.
12. *Ibid.*, 245.
13. *Ibid.*, 287–8.
14. *The Complete Prose Works of Matthew Arnold*, ed. R.H. Super (11 vols., 1960–77), III, 119.
15. *Ibid.*, III, 122.
16. V. Woolf, *The Common Reader* (1925), 210.
17. *Silas Marner, ed. cit.*, 31.
18. J. Bennett, *George Eliot. Her Mind and Her Art* (1962), 136.
19. L. Haddakin, 'Silas Marner', in *Critical Essays on George Eliot*, ed. B. Hardy (1970), 74.
20. *George Eliot* (1965), 119.
21. Quoted in G.S. Haight, *George Eliot, A Biography* (1969), 367.
22. *George Eliot. The Critical Heritage*, ed. D. Carrol (1971), 200.

10. THE PROBLEM OF EVIL

1. R. Williams, *Culture and Society 1780–1950* (Penguin Books edn, 1961), 117.
2. *George Eliot. The Critical Heritage*, ed. D. Carrol (1971), 255.
3. *Ibid.*, 275.
4. See *The Positive Philosophy of Auguste Comte*, freely trans. and condensed by H. Martineau (2 vols., 1853), II, 292.
5. *The Genealogy of Morals*, trans. F. Golffing (New York, 1956), 226.
6. *Letters*, IV, 496.
7. *Ibid.*, IV, 485.
8. *George Eliot's Life as Related in her Letters and Journals*, ed. J.W Cross (3 vols., 1885), III, 42.
9. *A Century of George Eliot Criticism*, ed. G.S. Haight (1966 edn), 58.
10. *Civilization and Its Discontents*, trans. and ed. J. Strachey (1962 edn), 68.
11. *Ibid.*, 69.
12. See J. Thale, *The Novels of George Eliot* (1959), 127.
13. *Civilization and Its Discontents*, 80.
14. *Ibid.*, 72.
15. *Ibid.*, 84.
16. *The Emotions and the Will* (1859), 37.
17. A. Comte, *Subjective Synthesis, or Universal System of the Conceptions adapted to the Normal State of Humanity* (1891), 13. George Eliot read the original French version in 1866. See *Letters*, IV, 227, where, however, the work is incorrectly identified.
18. See G.H. Lewes, *The Study of Psychology* (Problems of Life and Mind, Third Series, Problem the First) (1879), 147.

11. JUDGMENT AND RAPTURE

1. *The Genealogy of Morals*, trans. F. Golffing (New York, 1956), 160.
2. M. Green, *Yeats's Blessings on von Hügel. Essays on Literature and Religion* (1967), 10.
3. *Ibid.*, 93.
4. I am indebted to Simon Dentith for information on this point.
5. *The Genealogy of Morals*, 160.
6. *The Essence of Christianity*, trans. George Eliot (Harper Books edn, 1957), 97.
7. *Ibid.*, 89.
8. *Ibid.*, 92.
9. *Ibid.*, 89.

10. *Ibid.*, 98.
11. *Ibid.*, 151.
12. *George Eliot. Her Mind and Her Art* (1962), 123.
13. *Criticism and Ideology. A Study in Marxist Literary Theory* (1976) 115.
14. *The Essence of Christianity*, 64.
15. *Ibid.*, 34.
16. *Ibid.*, 5.
17. *George Eliot. The Critical Heritage*, ed. D. Carrol (1971), 356.
18. *The Emotions and the Will* (1859), 16.
19. *The Senses and the Intellect* (3rd edn, 1858), 537.
20. *Essays on Education* and Kindred Subjects (Everyman's Library edn, 1911), 3.
21. *George Eliot. The Critical Heritage*, 359.
22. *Ibid.*, 359.
23. See U.C. Knoepflmacher, 'Fusing fact and myth: the new reality of *Middlemarch*', in *This Particular Web*. Essays on Middlemarch, ed. I. Adam (1955), 43–72; and G. Beer, 'Myth and the single consciousness: *Middlemarch* and *The Lifted Veil*', *ibid.*, 91–115.
24. Q. Anderson, 'George Eliot in *Middlemarch*', in *From Dickens to Hardy* (Pelican Guide to English Literature 6), ed. B. Ford, 291.
25. See W.J. Harvey, *The Art of George Eliot* (1961), 147–8, and D. Daiches, *George Eliot. Middlemarch* (Studies in English Literature No. 11, 1963), 21.
26. See D. Carrol, 'Middlemarch and the externality of fact', *This Particular Web*, 80.
27. *Ibid.*, 81.
28. J. Bennett, *George Eliot. Her Mind and Her Art* (1962), 171–2.
29. A.E.S. Viner, *George Eliot (Writers and Critics)* (1971), 87.
30. *George Eliot. The Critical Heritage*, 327.
31. Quoted in *George Eliot and her Readers. A Selection of Contemporary Reviews*, ed. J. Holstrom and L. Lerner (1966), 92.
32. See *ibid.*, 80.
33. See D. Daiches, *George Eliot. Middlemarch*; W.J. Harvey, *The Art of George Eliot*; J. Thale, *The Novels of George Eliot*; D. Oldfield, 'The language of the novel. The character of Dorothea', in *Middlemarch. Critical Approaches to the Novel*, ed. B. Hardy (1967), 63–86.
34. G. Beer, 'Myth and the single consciousness', *This Particular Web*, 94.
35. D. Daiches, *George Eliot. Middlemarch*, 11.
36. D. Carrol, 'Middlemarch and the externality of fact', *This Particular Web*, 78.
37. *George Eliot. The Critical Heritage*, 355.
38. See B. Hardy, *The Appropriate Form. An Essay on the Novel* (1964), 109 and D. Daiches, *George Eliot. Middlemarch*, 21.
39. *George Eliot. The Critical Heritage*, 319.
40. 'Middlemarch and the passions', *This Particular Web*, 19.
41. See *The Emotions and the Will*, 310.
42. *The Senses and the Intellect*, 552; see also *The Emotions and the Will*, 416.
43. *George Eliot. The Critical Heritage*, 355.
44. J. Beaty, 'The text of the novel. A study of the proof', *Middlemarch. Critical Approaches to the Novel*, 61–2.
45. D. Daiches, *George Eliot. Middlemarch*, 57.
46. See L. Lerner, *The Truthtellers. Jane Austen, George Eliot, D.H. Lawrence* (1967), 249–69.
47. *The Life of Saint Teresa of Avila By Herself*, trans. J.M. Cohen (1957), 144.
48. *Ibid.*, 140.
49. *Ibid.*, 145.
50. *Ibid.*, 35.

51. *Ibid.*, 148.
52. *Ibid.*, 151.
53. *Ibid.*, 179–80.
54. *Ibid.*, 214.
55. *Ibid.*, 328.
56. *The Genealogy of Morals*, 160.

12. DISCERNMENT AND RESOLVE

1. W. Pater, *The Renaissance. Studies in Art and Poetry to which is added the essay on Raphael from 'Miscellaneous Studies'.* With an Introduction and Notes by K. Clark (Fontana Library edn, 1961), 218.
2. *Ibid.*, 223.
3. See *The Study of Psychology* (Problems of Life and Mind, Third Series, Problem the First) (1879), 71–80.
4. *The Essence of Christianity*, trans. George Eliot (Harper Books edn, 1957), 112.
5. *Ibid.*, 216.
6. *Ibid.*, 113.
7. Quoted by G. Craig, 'The system of alliances and the balance of power', in *The Zenith of European Power 1830–70 (The New Cambridge Modern History*, X), ed. J.P.T. Bury (1960), 272.
8. Quoted by M. Foot, 'The origins of the Franco-Prussian War and the remaking of Germany', *ibid.*, 599.
9. *Letters*, V, 142.
10. *Ibid.*, V, 118.
11. *Ibid.*, V, 142.
12. Quoted by J. Joll, 'Prussia and the German Problem, 1830–66', *The Zenith of European Power*, 511–12.
13. See W. Baker (ed.), *Some George Eliot Notebooks: An Edition of the Carl H. Pforzheimer Library's George Eliot Holograph Notebooks*, MSS 707, 708, 710, 711 (Salzburg, 1976—), 101–2.
14. *Civilization and Its Discontents*, trans. and ed. J. Strachey (1962 edn), 91.
15. *Criticism and Ideology, A Study in Marxist Literary Theory* (1976) 123.
16. See R. Preyer, 'Beyond the liberal imagination: vision and unreality in *Daniel Deronda*', *Victorian Studies*, IV (1960–1), 33–54 and U.C. Knoepflmacher, *Religious Humanism and the Victorian Novel, George Eliot, Walter Pater, and Samuel Butler* (1965), 116–48.
17. *George Eliot. The Critical Heritage*, ed. D. Carrol (1971), 445.
18. See G. Levine, *The Realistic Imagination. English Fiction from Frankenstein to Lady Chatterley* (1981), 291–316.
19. B. Hardy, Introduction, *Daniel Deronda* (Penguin Books edn, 1967), 27.
20. R. Preyer, 'Beyond the liberal imagination', 36.
21. *The Essence of Christianity*, 32.
22. *Ibid.*, 167.
23. A. Comte, *The Catechism of Positivism; or Summary Exposition of the Universal Religion* (1858) 77.
24. Quoted by J.P.T. Bury, 'Nationalities and nationalism', *The Zenith of European Power*, 225.
25. G. Martin, '"Daniel Deronda": George Eliot and political change', *Critical Essays on George Eliot*, ed. B. Hardy (1970), 149.
26. W. Baker, *George Eliot and Judaism* (Salzburg, 1975), 111.
27. See *ibid.*, 35–6.
28. See *ibid.*, 234.
29. E. Jones, *The Life and Work of Sigmund Freud*, ed. and abridged in one volume

by L. Trilling and S. Marcus (Pelican Books edn, 1964), 166.
30. *The Positive Philosophy of Auguste Comte*, freely trans. and condensed by H. Martineau (2 vols., 1853), I, 2.
31. *The Study of Psychology*, 102.
32. *Ibid.*, 147.
33. G. Levine, 'Determinism and responsibility', in *A Century of George Eliot Criticism*, ed. G.S. Haight (1966 edn), 353.
34. *Letters*, VI, 166.
35. G. Ryle, *The Concept of Mind* (Peregrine Books edn, 1963), 65–66.
36. A.J. Ayer, *The Central Questions of Philosophy* (Pelican Books edn, 1976), 43; see also 227–33.
37. *The Great Tradition* (1948), 96.
38. *Criticism and Ideology*, 135.
39. *Letters*, IV, 300.
40. *Essays*, 409.

CONCLUSION

1. *Letters*, IV, 49.
2. *George Eliot, A Biography* (1969) 295.
3. *The Novels of George Eliot* (1959), 13.
4. U.C. Knoepflmacher, *George Eliot's Early Novels. The Limits of Realism* (Berkeley and Los Angeles, 1968), 160.
5. G. Beer, 'Myth and the single consciousness: *Middlemarch* and *The Lifted Veil*', *This Particular Web, Essays on Middlemarch*, ed. I. Adam (1975), 96.
6. *Ibid.*, 96–7.
7. *Letters*, III, 41.
8. *Ibid.*, III, 380.
9. See *A Century of George Eliot Criticism*, ed. G.S. Haight (1966 edn), 130–1.
10. R.V. Rediger, *George Eliot: The Emergent Self* (New York, 1975), 435.
11. W.W. Robson, *Critical Essays* (1966), 7.
12. *Ibid.*, 10.
13. *Ibid.*, 12.
14. *The Life of Saint Teresa of Avila By Herself*, trans. J.M. Cohen (1957), 209.
15. *Ibid.*, 210.
16. *The Great Tradition* (1948), 89.
17. 'George Eliot', *Century Magazine*, XXXIII, 62.
18. *George Eliot, The Critical Heritage*, ed. D. Carrol (1971), 426.
19. See, in particular, George Eliot's remarkable reactions to a German legend in which an old woman, hoping to recover her youth, is laid alive on a fire and after being 'terribly burnt' is beaten with a hammer 'so that . . . great pieces flew from her.' 'German Mythology and Legend', *Leader*, VI (1855), 917–18.
20. *Criticism and Ideology. A Study in Marxist Literary Theory* (1976), 111.
21. *Ibid.*, 125.
22. See 'Felix Holt the Radical', *Critical Essays on George Eliot*, ed. B. Hardy (1970), 114.
23. L. Althusser, *For Marx*, trans. B. Brewster (1977), 178.

Index

Acton, John, Lord, 71, 74, 75, 212
Allen, W., 164
Althusser, L., 104, 241–2
altruism,
  and art, 106
  and emotions, 9
  and family life, 48
  Freud on, 134, 136
  growing preponderance of, 2, 7, 23, 56, 115
  and industry, 19
  Lacan on, 147
  Nietzsche on, 121–2, 131–2, 183
  and submission, 24, 181
  and violence, 147–9, 228
  (see also Eliot, George)
Anglicanism, 24–5, 75–6, 79, 208
animals, and human psychology, 5, 30–1, 43, 145, 221
architecture, 90, 93–4
Arnold, M., 156
art,
  and class, 87–90
  idealism in, 87–8
  intellect and performing arts, 189–90
  and Judaism, 221
  and mind-body states, 91
  and morality, 32, 60, 88, 93, 153–4
  Nietzsche on, 153
  Pater on, 207
  and Positivism, 94, 98–9
  and prophecy, 94
  and real world, 86, 87
  and science, 60, 94
  and self-expression, 231
  (see also Eliot, George)
asceticism, 119, 120, 124, 131–2, 133, 175, 183
Associationism,
  and Bain, 4, 119
  history of, 5, 38
  and Lewes, 38
  and love of power, 47
  and mental disorder, 39, 220
  and mind-body states, 43, 53, 141, 193
  and Nietzsche, 121
  and Positivism, 11
  and psychoanalysis, 133–4

  rhetoric of, 54, 131
  and sexuality, 140–1
  and tenderness, 43, 131
  (see also Bain, A.; psychology)
atheism, 30, 31, 36, 43, 119–20, 134, 145, 153, 165, 182
Ayer, A.J., 223

Bain, A.,
  on art and science, 60
  and Associationism, 4, 38, 119
  on conscience, 39, 200
  and George Eliot, 5, 10, 46
  and Lewes, 12
  on love of power, 47, 133, 147, 173, 181
  on madness, 40–3
  and Marx, 103
  and Nietzsche, 119
  on performing artists, 189–90
  and primitive experience, 8
  and psychoanalysis, 133
  on scholars and misers, 40
  on self-love, 47
  on sexuality, 133, 173
  on tenderness, 43, 47, 53–4, 140–1
  on unconscious, 129
  on unity of mind, 5–6
  on willing, 201
  on women, 53, 96–7
  (see also Associationism; psychology)
Baker, W., 218
Balzac, H. de, 156
Barrett Browning, E., 106, 154
Beaty, J., 203
Bedient, C., 12
Beer, G., 233
Bennett, J., 65, 163, 186
Bichat, M., 192
Bismarck, O. von, 211–13, 214, 219, 229
Blackwood's Magazine, 195
Boccaccio, G., 237
Boehme, J., 186
Bray, C., 10, 17, 24, 122, 209
Brown, T., 5
Browning, R., 165, 167
Buckle, H., T. 17
Bunyan, J., 25
Butler, S., 85